POLITICS AND ECONOMICS OF THE MIDDLE EAST

IRAQ

FINAL ASSESSMENTS OF THE SPECIAL INSPECTOR GENERAL AND POST-U.S. WITHDRAWAL DEVELOPMENTS

POLITICS AND ECONOMICS OF THE MIDDLE EAST

Additional books in this series can be found on Nova's website under the Series tab.

Additional E-books in this series can be found on Nova's website under the E-book tab.

IRAQ

FINAL ASSESSMENTS OF THE SPECIAL INSPECTOR GENERAL AND POST-U.S. WITHDRAWAL DEVELOPMENTS

GUSTAVO D. RYDER
EDITOR

publishers
New York

Library of Congress Cataloging-in-Publication Data

ISBN: 978-1-62948-478-5

Published by Nova Science Publishers, Inc. † New York

CONTENTS

PREFACE

This book provides a review of SIGIR's history, delving into the perennial challenges and various successes in Iraq and examines events in Iraq this last quarter marked by a sharp rise in violence. Final assessments of the Special Inspector General and post-U.S. withdrawal developments are discussed.

Chapter 1 – Regarding U.S. relief and reconstruction plans, programs, and operations in Iraq, the Special Inspector General for Iraq Reconstruction provides independent and objective:

- oversight and review through comprehensive audits, inspections, and investigations
- advice and recommendations on policies to promote economy, efficiency, and effectiveness
- prevention, detection, and deterrence of fraud, waste, and abuse
- information and analysis to the Congress, the Secretary of State, the Secretary of Defense, and the American people

The jurisdiction of the Office extends to amounts appropriated or otherwise made available for any fiscal year to the Iraq Relief and Reconstruction Fund, the Iraq Security Forces Fund, the Commander's Emergency Response Program; or for assistance for the reconstruction of Iraq under the Economic Support Fund, the International Narcotics Control and Law Enforcement account, or any other provision of law.

Chapter 2 – Nearly two years after the 2011 U.S. withdrawal from Iraq, increasingly violent sectarian divisions are undermining the fragile stability left in place. Sunni Arab Muslims, who resent Shiite political domination and perceived discrimination, have escalated their political opposition to the government of Prime Minister Nuri al-Maliki through demonstrations and violence. Iraq's Kurds are embroiled in separate political disputes with the Baghdad government over territorial, political, and economic issues. The rifts impinged on provincial elections during April—June 2013 and could affect the viability of national elections for a new parliament and government expected in March 2014. Maliki is expected to seek to retain his post in that vote.

The violent component of Sunni unrest is spearheaded by the Sunni insurgent group Al Qaeda in Iraq (AQ-I) as well as groups linked to the former regime of Saddam Hussein. These groups, emboldened by the Sunni-led uprising in Syria as well as perceived discrimination against Sunni Iraqis, are conducting attacks against Shiite neighborhoods, Iraqi Security Force (ISF) members, and Sunni supporters of Maliki with increasing frequency and lethality.

The attacks appear intended to reignite all-out sectarian conflict and provoke the fall of the government. To date, the 800,000 person ISF has countered the escalating violence without outside assistance and Iraqi forces have not substantially fractured along sectarian lines. However, a July 2013 major prison break near Baghdad cast doubt on the ISF ability to counter the violence longer term.

U.S. forces left in December 2011 in line with a November 2008 bilateral U.S.-Iraq Security Agreement. Iraq refused to extend the presence of U.S. troops in Iraq, seeking to put behind it the period of U.S. political and military control. Some outside experts and some in Congress have asserted that U.S. influence over Iraq has ebbed significantly since, tarnishing the legacy of U.S. combat deaths and funds spent on the intervention. Program components of what were to be enduring, close security relations—extensive U.S. training for Iraq's security forces through an Office of Security Cooperation—Iraq (OSC-I) and a State Department police development program—have languished or are ending in part because Iraqi officials perceive the programs as indicators of residual U.S. tutelage. The U.S. civilian presence in Iraq has declined from about 17,000 to about 10,500 and is expected to fall to 5,500 by the end of 2013. Still, Iraqi efforts to acquire sophisticated U.S. equipment such as F-16 combat aircraft, air defense equipment, and attack helicopters gives the Administration some leverage over Baghdad.

Although recognizing that Iraq wants to rebuild its relations in its immediate neighborhood, the Administration and Congress seek to prevent Iraq from falling under the sway of Iran, with which the Maliki government has built close relations. However, the legacy of the 1908-88 Iran-Iraq war, Arab and Persian differences, Iraq's efforts to reestablish its place in the Arab world, and Maliki's need to work with senior Iraqi Sunnis limit, Iranian influence over the Baghdad government. Still, fearing that a change of regime in Syria will further embolden the Iraqi Sunni opposition, Maliki has not joined U.S. and other Arab state calls for Syrian President Bashar Al Assad to leave office and Iraq has not consistently sought to prevent Iranian overflights of arms deliveries to Syria.

Iraq took a large step toward returning to the Arab fold by hosting an Arab League summit on March 27-29, 2012, and has substantially repaired relations with Kuwait, the state that Saddam Hussein invaded and occupied in 1990. In June 2013, the relationship with Kuwait helped Iraq emerge from some Saddam-era restrictions under Chapter VII of the U.N. Charter.

In: Iraq
Editor: Gustavo D. Ryder

ISBN: 978-1-62948-478-5
© 2013 Nova Science Publishers, Inc.

Chapter 1

SPECIAL INSPECTOR GENERAL FOR IRAQ RECONSTRUCTION: FINAL REPORT TO THE UNITED STATES CONGRESS[*]

SIGIR MISSION STATEMENT

Regarding U.S. relief and reconstruction plans, programs, and operations in Iraq, the Special Inspector General for Iraq Reconstruction provides independent and objective:

- oversight and review through comprehensive audits, inspections, and investigations
- advice and recommendations on policies to promote economy, efficiency, and effectiveness
- prevention, detection, and deterrence of fraud, waste, and abuse
- information and analysis to the Congress, the Secretary of State, the Secretary of Defense, and the American people

The jurisdiction of the Office extends to amounts appropriated or otherwise made available for any fiscal year to the Iraq Relief and Reconstruction Fund, the Iraq Security Forces Fund, the Commander's Emergency Response Program; or for assistance for the reconstruction of Iraq

---

[*] This is an edited, reformatted and augmented version of Final Report to the United States Congress, Public Laws 108-106 and 95-452, as amended, dated September 9, 2013.

under the Economic Support Fund, the International Narcotics Control and Law Enforcement account, or any other provision of law.

(Section 3001 of Public Law 108-106, as amended)

MESSAGE FROM THE SPECIAL INSPECTOR GENERAL FOR IRAQ RECONSTRUCTION

I am pleased to submit to the Congress and the Secretaries of State and Defense the Final Report from the Special Inspector General for Iraq Reconstruction.

This Final Report culminates almost a decade of oversight work and was preceded by 220 audits, 170 inspections, 36 Quarterly Reports, 9 lessons-learned studies, 3 special reports, and 1 evaluation. Together, they comprise over 20,000 pages of reporting on the use of $60 billion in U.S. taxpayer dollars for Iraq's reconstruction. SIGIR's work made a difference for the good. It imposed accountability and transparency upon a challenging rebuilding program, producing 90 convictions and nearly $2 billion in financial benefits. And SIGIR operated efficiently, with annual costs averaging about $25 million.

Our success stemmed from our values and our people. SIGIR's values were straightforward and posted in our vestibule for all to see: professionalism, productivity, and perseverance. Professionalism meant ensuring fairness, integrity, and respect in every engagement. Productivity meant executing as much work as possible in tight time frames so as to aid reconstruction managers in implementing course corrections. Perseverance meant meeting our mission by pushing through the inevitable adversities that accompany war-zone work. The most devastating adversity occurred on March 24, 2008, when a rocket launched by terrorists hit the Embassy compound, killing one of my auditors, Paul Converse. Paul was one of hundreds of SIGIR personnel— auditors, investigators, and inspectors—who willingly braved the threats in Iraq to accomplish our mission. I thank all of them for their heroic service.

The first section of this Final Report provides a review of SIGIR's history, delving into the perennial challenges we faced and various successes we achieved along the way. Section 2 updates the work of my investigative team, outlining indictments, convictions, and sentencings of those who criminally violated the sacred trust placed in them in Iraq. The Congress extended the life of our organization to achieve more investigative results; as Section 2 documents, we did. The last section provides an overview of events in Iraq this quarter, one marked by a sharp rise in violence.

It has been my great honor to lead SIGIR from inception to conclusion. I close by expressing my sincere gratitude to the Congress and the Departments of State and Defense for their support during our organizational life. We could not have succeeded without it. I will always be grateful for it.

Respectfully submitted,
Stuart W. Bowen, Jr.

Q&A With U.S. Ambassador to Iraq Robert Stephen Beecroft

In late August, the Ambassador commented on the future of U.S. support for Iraq, the rise of violence over the summer, and Iraq's economic development.

How can the United States best continue to support Iraq?

The United States will continue to support the development of Iraqi democracy, strengthen transparency and the private sector to spread prosperity more broadly across Iraqi society, and help improve Iraq's relations with its neighbors. We will continue to advance these goals through implementation of the U.S.-Iraq Strategic Framework Agreement, which strengthens our partnership through cooperation in a variety of areas, including political and diplomatic coordination; defense and security cooperation; education and cultural development; energy; law enforcement and judicial development; expansion of trade and finance; and improving services, technology usage, the environment, and transportation resources. Implementation of many of these programs will rely increasingly on Iraqi financial resources. As challenges to Iraqi security persist, helping the Government of Iraq (GOI) confront al-Qaeda and other terrorist groups and militias will also remain critical.

What signs of foreign commercial investment in Iraq are you seeing in 2013?

Iraq is on track to be one of the fastest-growing economies in 2013, as it was in 2012, despite a difficult security environment and a less-than-consistent business climate. American companies have taken advantage of numerous opportunities.

General Electric is now employing 150 professionals in 5 offices to service its existing base of 130 power-generating turbines and to develop new business in the energy and healthcare sectors. General Motors has built showrooms in Baghdad, Erbil, and Sulaymaniyah. Ford, John Deere, and Caterpillar have representation in Iraq as well. Coca-Cola and PepsiCo continue to have strong sales. Coke has bottling plants in Erbil, Kerbala, and Hilla; and the PepsiCo plant in Erbil employs 300 to supply the Kurdistan Region. Citigroup opened an office in Baghdad this year, and several U.S. hotel chains, including Sheraton, Marriott, Hilton Doubletree, Wyndham, and Best Western, continue to develop properties in the Kurdistan Region. Iraqi Airways received the first of 30 Boeing 737-800s in August.

U.S. energy companies, including ExxonMobil, Occidental, Chevron, Hess, Hunt, HKN, Marathon, and Murphy, play major roles in Iraqi hydrocarbon development. Oil services companies, including Baker Hughes, Cameron, Halliburton, Schlumberger, and Weatherford, support oil-pipeline refurbishing and development. Emerson, CH2M Hill, and KBR are also key U.S. contributors to Iraq's expanding energy sector.

Many European and Asian companies also continue to win new contracts in Iraq's fast-growing market.

What is your view of the current security situation in Iraq?

April through August was a very violent period in Iraq, with casualties from terrorist attacks reaching a level not seen since 2008. Terrorist networks, specifically al-Qaeda and its affiliates, continue to execute attacks against the Iraqi population, military, police forces, and Iraq's energy infrastructure. Political and sectarian divisions have given al-Qaeda and its affiliates greater freedom of movement in the largely Sunni north and west of the country.

The security environment is further complicated by external factors, including the deteriorating situation in and porous border with Syria. The United States is cooperating with the GOI to help dismantle the terrorist networks responsible for these attacks. Among other steps, we are encouraging the government's efforts to better undercut al-Qaeda by taking concrete steps to address the legitimate grievances of the Sunni community and further incorporate members of this community into security operations.

How are the U.S. Embassy and OSC-I working to support the Iraqi Security Forces (ISF)?

We are working with the ISF to improve the training, equipment, and opportunities for regional engagement that will permit Iraq to integrate productively into the region and defend its territory and airspace. The United States is committed to a strategic security relationship with Iraq, in accordance with the Strategic Framework Agreement. We have delivered over $14 billion in Foreign Military Sales equipment maintenance, logistical support, and on-site training at Iraqi military bases, and we will continue to work with Iraq to identify its future defense needs. Our focus is long-term, with the goal of supporting Iraq in professionalizing and modernizing its military.

How will the U.S. diplomatic footprint evolve over the next year?

The U.S. Mission in Iraq has approximately 10,900 direct-hire and contract employees as of September 1, 2013—the vast majority of whom provide support to mission functions and sites. As we close or transition to Iraqi control several more sites, we expect our population to drop below 6,000 by January 1, 2014.

SECTION 1. SIGIR IN REVIEW

Oversight under Fire

On April 16, 2003, less than a month after Coalition forces entered Iraq, General Tommy Franks, Commander, U.S. Central Command (CENTCOM), issued an order titled "Freedom Message to the Iraqi People." In it, he announced the creation of "the Coalition Provisional Authority [CPA] to exercise powers of government temporarily, and as necessary, especially to provide security, to allow the delivery of humanitarian aid, and to eliminate weapons of mass destruction."

Shortly thereafter, President George W. Bush appointed retired Ambassador L. Paul "Jerry" Bremer III both as the CPA's Administrator and as his envoy to Iraq. From May 2003 to June 2004, the CPA ruled Iraq, overseeing a massive expansion in relief and rebuilding efforts.

Although the military continued to follow the original plan to "liberate and leave," with a complete departure from Iraq ostensibly to occur by the end of September 2003, the civilian side shifted to a substantially different agenda, one of "occupy and rebuild," for which there had been very limited pre-war planning.

On the same day that General Franks announced the CPA's creation, the President signed into law a supplemental appropriations act establishing the Iraq Relief and Reconstruction Fund (IRRF). The amount appropriated to the IRRF in April 2003—$2.48 billion—reflected the pre-war strategy of limited post-conflict relief and reconstruction, which did not anticipate the extensive expenditure of U.S. funds. The United States assumed that Iraq would soon support its own relief and reconstruction.

Almost three-fourths of the initial IRRF monies went to the U.S. Agency for International Development (USAID); consequently, the CPA had little control over it. To pay for programs and projects, the CPA chiefly used Iraqi resources: seized cash, vested assets, and oil revenues funneled into a new account called the Development Fund for Iraq (DFI).

In May 2003, United Nations Security Council Resolution (UNSCR) 1483 had established the DFI. The funds were housed at the Federal Reserve Bank of New York. During its 14-month tenure as the sovereign power in Iraq, the CPA controlled the use of billions of dollars in oil revenues that flowed into the DFI.

As it rapidly stood up, the CPA faced a damaged, dilapidated, and increasingly unstable country. Virtually all financial transactions in Iraq occurred in cash. This raised risks of fraud, waste, and abuse. Oversight was needed. Yet, in the early months of the reconstruction program, the CPA had no independent "watchdog."

During the summer of 2003, Ambassador Bremer and his team crafted an ambitious plan to rebuild the country, one that sought to touch every aspect of Iraqi life. Pursuant to that plan, in September 2003, the President asked the Congress for $20.3 billion for Iraq's reconstruction. The Congress responded in November 2003, passing the Emergency Supplemental Appropriations Act for Defense and for the Reconstruction of Iraq and Afghanistan, 2004 (P.L. 108-106), which appropriated $18.4 billion to the IRRF. The legislation also closed the oversight gap by establishing the Coalition Provisional Authority Inspector General (CPAIG) "to provide for the independent and objective conduct and supervision of audits and investigations relating to the programs and operations of the Coalition Provisional Authority."

During the next nine years, the rebuilding effort grew into the largest overseas aid program since the Marshall Plan—a massive campaign supported by more than $60 billion in U.S. taxpayer dollars and more than $20 billion in Iraqi funds controlled by the United States.

Inspector General Bowen (center) and Assistant Inspector General for Inspections Brian Flynn (left) visit a project site in Iraq.

On November 15, 2003, nine days after signing the law establishing the CPA-IG, the President announced that sovereignty would return to Iraq at the end of June 2004. The CPA's impending closure triggered the termination provision in P.L. 108-106 for the CPA-IG, meaning that it would shut down at the end of December 2004. But this was not to be.

In October 2004, the Congress, recognizing the need for continued oversight, transformed the CPA-IG into the Special Inspector General for Iraq Reconstruction (SIGIR). By this act, it extended the life of this novel oversight entity well beyond the end of 2004. In a series of subsequent actions, the

Congress repeatedly added to SIGIR's mandate, extending its tenure in each instance.

SIGIR's successive congressional expansions and extensions proved profitable. Over nine-plus years of existence, the organization cost about $245 million to operate, while providing more than $1.8 billion in financial benefits, including nearly $645 million in direct savings from SIGIR's audits and more than $192 million in seizures and court-ordered monetary penalties from SIGIR's investigations. SIGIR's professional staff completed 390 audits and inspections and executed investigations that led to 90 convictions. This string of productivity included 37 Quarterly Reports to the Congress and 37 testimonies on Capitol Hill. Importantly, the organization generated nine lessons-learned reports, the last of which, *Learning From Iraq,* suggested reforms that could strengthen the U.S. national security architecture and avert the kind of fraud, waste, and abuse that occurred too often during the Iraq stabilization and reconstruction operation (SRO).

What follows is a brief chronological history of SIGIR.

FY 2004: Closing the Oversight Gap

On November 6, 2003, the President signed P.L. 108-106 into law, creating the CPA-IG and charging it to oversee the activities of the CPA. The law provided the new office with the kinds of duties and responsibilities borne by other U.S. government inspectors general.

On January 20, 2004, after White House review and selection of a candidate, Secretary of Defense Donald Rumsfeld, in consultation with Secretary of State Colin Powell, appointed Stuart W. Bowen, Jr., to serve as the CPA-IG. When Inspector General Bowen made his first trip to Baghdad in early February 2004, the CPA had less than five months left in its tenure.

At that time, the CPA was overseeing numerous programs and projects, funded chiefly by the DFI. USAID controlled most of the $2.48 billion in U.S. money appropriated for the Iraq Relief and Reconstruction Fund 1 (IRRF 1). The $18.4 billion approved by the Congress in November 2003 (IRRF 2) would not be under contract until early May 2004, shortly before the CPA shuttered. Thus, the CPA-IG's early reviews focused on the CPA's management of the DFI.

Setting up Shop

After his appointment, Inspector General Bowen immediately opened a new office in Arlington, Virginia, staffing it with detailees from other U.S. agencies. He quickly began recruiting auditors and investigators willing to serve in Iraq. Ten days into his new job, the Inspector General flew to Baghdad to open an office at the Republican Palace, where the CPA operated.

During that first trip, the Inspector General saw large amounts of cash being carted out of the Republican Palace and loaded into SUVs with little apparent oversight or controls in place. Moreover, the CPA comptroller's staff repeatedly complained to him about poor controls over the DFI. This signaled a troubling lack of accountability, later confirmed by SIGIR's audits.

After surveying operations and meeting with senior CPA officials, the Inspector General returned to Washington and contracted for the services of a major U.S. audit firm to support the new office's operations. The agency had imminent reporting requirements, with its first Quarterly Report due to the Congress at the end of March. Existing Pentagon contracting vehicles permitted the rapid engagement of experienced personnel, including those needed to meet human-resource and administrative functions. Eventually, SIGIR in-sourced most of the functions performed by contractors in the early years.

The complexities of working in a war zone complicated the operational challenges inevitable in a "start-up." An increasingly dangerous environment in Iraq, difficult access to work sites, and poor IT systems burdened early efforts. Providing direction and support from seven time zones away, the CPA-IG's headquarters staff in Virginia drafted policies, established operational processes, and obtained security clearances for incoming personnel. These new staff members brought with them a broad range of technical, administrative, and professional competencies.

OCTOBER 2003–
MARCH 2004

NOVEMBER
• P.L. 108-106 establishes CPA-IG to oversee CPA programs

JANUARY
• Secretary of Defense in consultation with Secretary of State appoints Inspector General Stuart Bowen

FEBRUARY
• Inspector General travels to Baghdad on his first trip

MARCH
• IIGC: CPA-IG establishes monthly DC meetings of the Iraq Inspectors General Council to coordinate efforts of all IGs performing oversight in Iraq
• CPA-IG Hotline and website established

Many of those who joined the CPA-IG soon found themselves working in one of the most dangerous places in the world. Other U.S. oversight agencies could not compel their auditors and investigators to deploy to the war zone.

But the CPA-IG made such service a condition of employment.

By the end of July 2004, the CPA-IG had issued 11 audits and 2 Quarterly Reports to the Congress and had 104 people on board: 75 serving in the United States and 29 deployed to Baghdad. The Baghdad staff comprised auditors and investigators on six-month details from agencies like the Department of Defense IG, Defense Criminal Investigative Service (DCIS), and Air Force Audit Agency, as well as "3161" temporary government employees (named after Title 5, Section 3161, of the U.S. Code, which provides a streamlined method for temporary government organizations to hire personnel).

Coordinating Early Oversight

The first audits focused on the CPA's compliance with its own rules, which were largely derived from existing federal regulations. These reports shed light on needless excesses (such as paying for contractor food and laundry at the Federal Deployment Center located at a luxury resort in Kuwait) and laid the groundwork for future studies that would expose fraud, waste, and abuse.

In March 2004, the CPA-IG opened its Hotline, established with the support of the Defense IG. It immediately began receiving tips about alleged fraud. A team of 5 (including 1 in Baghdad) processed Hotline submissions, providing leads to the 12 auditors and 10 investigators then working in country. U.S., Iraqi, and third-countrynational whistle-blowers paved the way to the CPA-IG's first investigations. In the early fall of 2004, a Hotline tip resulted in a case that led to the recovery and return to Iraq of $500,000 in DFI money embezzled by an Iraqi official.

Other oversight entities soon began to review Iraq reconstruction programs and projects in 2004, creating the potential for overlapping efforts. To obviate this, the Inspector General established the Iraq Inspectors General Council (IIGC), which facilitated coordination of all oversight work in Iraq. Its members included:

- Department of Defense Inspector General (Co-Vice Chairperson)
- Department of State Inspector General (Co-Vice Chairperson)
- U.S. Agency for International Development Inspector General
- Defense Contract Audit Agency
- Department of the Army Inspector General

- U.S. Army Audit Agency
- Department of the Treasury Inspector General
- Department of Commerce Inspector General
- Department of Health and Human Services Inspector General
- Government Accountability Office (observer member)
- International Advisory and Monitoring Board (observer member)

Audit Highlight
Coalition Provisional Authority Comptroller Cash Management
Controls Over the Development Fund for Iraq
(SIGIR 04-009, 7/28/2004)

At $20.7 billion in 2004, the DFI was the largest pot of money controlled by the CPA and became the focus of the CPA-IG's earliest audits. During the course of this spring 2004 review, auditors found very weak controls over the DFI and immediately issued an alert to the CPA Administrator that the funds were susceptible to fraud, waste, and abuse.

Despite this early warning, little changed. Several further DFI audits accomplished over the next year found similar problems. One led to the opening of a formal criminal investigation that uncovered a wide-ranging criminal conspiracy involving several senior CPA officials. Ultimately, from July 2004 to October 2012, SIGIR produced 23 audit reports related to the U.S. government's management of the DFI. Inadequate or missing documentation was a recurring theme.

The CPA-IG's Audits Directorate instituted the Iraq Accountability Working Group (IAWG) in Baghdad, integrating the work of varying oversight staffs deployed to Iraq. Most audit agencies conducted operations in the United States or elsewhere in the Middle East region, but the CPA-IG and USAID IG established oversight presence early and maintained consistent staffing in Baghdad throughout the entire program.

CPA-IG investigators coordinated with other law-enforcement agencies, including DCIS, State IG, U.S. Army Criminal Investigation Command (CID), and Federal Bureau of Investigation (FBI). This produced real progress on early cases, some of which required cooperation from the Iraqi government.

Closing Averted

The CPA closed on June 28, 2004, triggering the CPA-IG's statutory shutdown date, ostensibly December 28, 2004. The approaching organizational sunset prompted many CPA-IG detailees to return to their home agencies. During the summer of 2004, the office began a process of closure and transition. By fall, the Audits Directorate had lost over half of its staff, with the overall organization dropping to less than two-dozen personnel.

As the CPA-IG ramped down, the Iraq reconstruction program ramped up: Hundreds of new large-scale programs and projects funded by the IRRF 2 were underway. The Congress recognized the importance of continuing oversight. Thus, on October 28, 2004, it transformed the CPA-IG into SIGIR, giving it a broad mandate over the IRRF.

FY 2005: Expanding Oversight

The October 2004 authorizing legislation for SIGIR implemented several major changes:

- It provided the agency with the authority to oversee the IRRF, making it the first IG office with the power to delve into spending without regard to departmental jurisdiction.
- It set the organization's termination date at 10 months after the date upon which 80% of the IRRF had been obligated. Based on that formula, SIGIR would operate for at least two more years.
- It directed the Inspector General to report to the Secretaries of State and Defense, an unprecedented executive-branch reporting chain, but one that reflected the civil-military nature of SROs.

APRIL 2004– SEPTEMBER 2004

JULY
· Early shutdown of CPA triggers ramp down of CPA-IG staffing; Audit personnel decreases 42%

SIGIR Personnel
75 U.S.

29 Baghdad

AUGUST
· IAWG: CPA-IG establishes monthly Iraq Accountability Working Group in Baghdad to coordinate IIGC members working in Iraq

SEPTEMBER
· Lessons Learned/Risk Factors Initiative kicks off——over 9 years, results in multiday forums on human capital, program management, and contracting; 9 lessons-learned reports; 3 special reports; 1 evaluation

SIGIR promptly established new memorandums of agreement and understanding with State and Defense to clarify roles and responsibilities and to provide adequate support for a staff in Baghdad. By January 2005, the agency had a staff of 39, including 9 in Iraq. The Inspector General developed a new strategic plan calling for almost three-quarters of its auditors and investigators to be deployed forward in Iraq. In the summer of 2005, State authorized 45 staffing billets for SIGIR at the Embassy in Iraq.

Timely Reporting

SIGIR soon began issuing reports on the use and misuse of the DFI. A January 2005 audit revealed that the CPA failed to implement sufficient managerial, financial, and contractual controls to guarantee that $8.8 billion of these Iraqi funds was used in a transparent manner. The audit concluded that there was no assurance the CPA used these funds for the bene_t of the Iraqi people as mandated by UNSCR 1483.

As the IRRF's obligation and expenditure rates increased, oversight output quickly ratcheted up.

The law authorizing SIGIR prompted a major shift in audit planning for FY 2005 and FY 2006. The new strategy prioritized performance audits to assess the economy, efficiency, and effectiveness of projects funded by the IRRF.

Auditors scoped their work to ensure quick reporting, with most audits completed in about four months. This reflected a philosophy oriented toward greater transparency, seeking to provide management with information on programs and projects in time to implement programmatic course corrections. To that end, SIGIR kept reconstruction managers informed about findings by issuing interim reports on audit progress. In Iraq, time lost on a wayward program caused waste. Transparency in the oversight process helped limit these losses.

A new group of SIGIR auditors accompanied the shift in strategy. Many new hires came from the Government Accountability Office (GAO), where performance audits are the stock in trade. This influx of talent bolstered audit productivity and infused a new level of professionalism into the organization. To ensure continuity and alacrity in conveying results to reconstruction managers, SIGIR required extended deployment periods for auditors, ensuring that they remained in country until completing the audits assigned to them. This pushed up productivity.

SIGIR's auditors derived promising leads for future audits from Hotline allegations, investigative referrals, and other information gathered while operating in Iraq. The sharing of best-practice insights with other oversight agencies through the IIGC in Virginia and the IAWG in Baghdad improved the efficiency and effectiveness of the audit work.

SIGIR received 884 Hotline contacts in its 10 years of operation: 156 contributed to investigations, 80 to inspections, and 29 to audits.

A June 2005 SIGIR audit raised what would become a central theme in the organization's next phase of oversight reporting: the lack of sufficient information on the cost to complete ongoing projects. Many reconstruction projects exceeded the time for completion defined in the contract. SIGIR found that project managers could not accurately estimate costs to complete, opening the possibility of budget exhaustion before a project was finished. This proved to be a valid concern; many projects ultimately transferred to Iraqi control were only partially complete because implementing agencies ran out of money.

Another SIGIR audit reviewed the processes for paying award fees on IRRF contracts. It revealed that contracting officers sometimes paid companies fees despite very poor performance. By mid-2005, U.S. Ambassador to Iraq Zalmay Khalilzad heeded SIGIR's cautionary findings and pushed for a shift to more manageable and efficient fixed-cost contracting vehicles. This led to the termination of most of the IRRF's expensive cost-plus contracts.

SIGIR's audits provided a detailed picture of the management and expenditure of IRRF money. That tableau revealed a "reconstruction gap," which amounted to the difference between the number of projects that the United States proposed to build and the number of projects that it actually could complete. Because of increased spending on, security, rising costs of materials, project delays and overruns, and multiple reprogrammings of funds, reconstruction managers left numerous projects on the drawing board or incomplete.

Assessing the Quality of Construction

With the new performance-audit strategy fully in place, SIGIR's work exposed inadequately designed, poorly constructed, or unsustainable projects. Moreover, U.S. personnel and Iraqis complained that projects reported by reconstruction managers as successfully completed were in fact unfinished. To address this problem, in June 2005 the Inspector General established an Inspections Directorate, whose members would travel all over Iraq to provide on-site reporting about the status of reconstruction projects.

The new Assistant Inspector General for Inspections rapidly developed an innovative set of best practices for the program that quickly produced highly effective results. Multi disciplinary inspection teams—combining auditing and engineering experience—visited reconstruction project sites throughout Iraq, assessing the quality of work against contract specifications and promptly issuing reports. The inspections sought to determine whether:

- project results would be consistent with original objectives
- project components were adequately designed before construction or installation
- construction or rehabilitation work met the standards of the design
- the contractor's quality-control plan and the U.S. government's quality-assurance program were adequate

By July 2005, Inspections Directorate personnel had visited a wide variety of project sites and reported the results in assessments to the relevant agencies. The team completed 16 assessments before the end of the year and then formed two more teams to increase productivity in 2006. SIGIR's on-site inspections commonly revealed poor workmanship. The report on al-Sumelat Water Network, which covered a project located in a dangerous area west of Baghdad, exemplified how the paperwork on a project misrepresented actual conditions. The project had been reported as completed; it was not.

**Inspection Highlight Al-Sumelat Water Network
(PA-2005-004, 3/15/2006)**

Early in the Iraq reconstruction program, it became clear that there would be gaps between expected and actual results. A case in point was al-Sumelat Water Supply Project, a $743,650 IRRF project awarded in February 2005, to design and construct a pipeline that would carry potable water from an existing main to several communities.

In preparation for a July visit to the project site, SIGIR's inspection team reviewed documents and interviewed U.S. government and contractor personnel. A June contractor report and a Project and Contracting Office (PCO) study indicated that the project was 100% complete. The USACE project engineer told SIGIR that all work was done, though he had never observed the pipeline and had relied on an Iraqi employed by USACE to inform him of progress. The Iraqi employee reported that the pipeline had been pressure tested and had all the components required by the contract. But when told that SIGIR would be visiting the site, the Iraqi employee admitted that much of the pipeline work was not done.

When SIGIR's inspection team arrived, it found that the "completed" project was merely a long ditch, containing mostly unconnected pipes. SIGIR quickly provided its report to USACE and PCO officials. The government stopped payments to the contractor. USACE subsequently began requiring photographs of the various phases of construction work when its personnel could not perform site visits.

Because of the worsening security situation in the late summer of 2005, SIGIR launched a ground-survey initiative, employing local contractors to visit sites in areas to which SIGIR personnel could not travel. Iraqi nationals could safely get to health facilities, schools, and other projects built by the United States located in areas too dangerous for Americans to visit. This innovation led to rapid reporting that flagged project concerns. Another novel SIGIR initiative implemented the review of satellite imagery of project sites in areas too dangerous for ground visits, whether by U.S. or Iraqi staff. The aerial assessment program put everyone on notice that SIGIR oversight could reach all of Iraq, regardless of security conditions.

Investigative Task Force Takes Shape

As the office's investigators ramped up operations, they recognized the need for greater collaboration and coordination. In mid-2005, SIGIR's investigative chief formed the Special Investigative Task Force for Iraq Reconstruction (SPITFIRE), which included the Department of Homeland Security's Bureau of Immigration and Customs Enforcement (ICE), the Criminal Investigation Division of the Internal Revenue Service, and State IG.

SPITFIRE enabled law-enforcement agencies to share information, deconflict work, and provide support to one another on the plethora of cases arising in Iraq. Shortly after its formation, SPITFIRE coordinated with the Department of Justice's Asset Forfeiture and Money Laundering Section, with four full-time prosecutors working on Iraq cases. This became the first of several task forces that SIGIR formed, all of which added to productivity and led to more convictions.

Investigative efforts bore fruit. In November 2005, SIGIR agents arrested Philip Bloom and Robert Stein for fraud. Both were eventually convicted and imprisoned for committing one of the most egregious crimes uncovered during the program. The case arose from an April 2005 whistle-blower complaint alleging irregularities at the CPA-South Central Region that prompted an audit of the operation in Hilla, Iraq. SIGIR auditors traveled to Hilla and found significant suspicious activity related to contract awards by comptroller Stein to Bloom, the contractor.

Investigators quickly opened a criminal case, eventually discovering that Stein rigged bids affecting 20 construction contracts. In total, Bloom received more than $8.6 million in fraudulent contract awards. In return, he provided multiple co-conspirators—including an Army colonel and two lieutenant colonels— payments of more than $1 million in cash, expensive vehicles, airline tickets, computers, and jewelry.

OCTOBER 2004– MARCH 2005

▶ **OCTOBER**
• P.L. 108-375 re-designates CPA-IG as SIGIR, extending the life of the organization until at least 2006.

▶ **JANUARY**
• Following redesignation, SIGIR builds back from loss of detailees who had returned to agencies in anticipation of closure

SIGIR Personnel

30 U.S.
●●●●●●●●●●
●●●●●●●●●●
●●●●●●●●●●

9 Baghdad
●●●●●●●●●

Better Data, Better Insight

Early audits of the IRRF revealed that each of the agencies carrying out reconstruction activities in Iraq used different IT systems for tracking contractual, financial, and project management information. Seeking to identify what data systems were in use, SIGIR asked for direct access and issued periodic data calls. These actions revealed severe information-management weaknesses, leading to audits of the entire IT system. SIGIR then developed its own repository of project data, publishing a running list each quarter of the thousands of reconstruction contracts awarded.

The Defense Department's centralized database for Iraq, called the Iraq Reconstruction Management System (IRMS), became operational in late 2005. SIGIR audits of the system revealed that the IRMS lacked consistency, accuracy, and completeness because the executing agencies failed to regularly enter required data into the system. SIGIR's in-house data-collection initiative proved critical, providing the most complete accounting of U.S. reconstruction projects available.

Audit Highlight
Award Fee Process for Contractors Involved in Iraq
Reconstruction (SIGIR 05-017, 10/25/2005)

Government contracts sometimes include provisions for an award fee to reward contractors who perform well. What needs to be accomplished to earn the fee is usually specified in the contract. Given that billions of dollars would be spent reconstructing Iraq, an effectively overseen award-fee process was critical to incentivizing good work.

In 2005, SIGIR examined the award-fee process for 18 contracts funded by the Iraq Relief and Reconstruction Fund. Together, the contracts were worth approximately $7 billion, with potentially more than $300 million in award fees at stake.

The audit found significant deficiencies in the award-fee process for all 18 contracts, including the failure to document the appointment of key individuals to monitor and evaluate the contractors' performance, to prepare monthly performance reports, to hold monthly Award Fee Evaluation Board meetings, and to document self-assessments from the contractors. As a result of SIGIR's audit, the contracting offices quickly reformed their award-fee processes to comply with federal requirements.

Reporting Expands

While virtually all other U.S. inspectors general report semiannually to the Congress, SIGIR reported quarterly. This ensured that the Congress received information about Iraq in a timely fashion. It also served as a forcing function, incentivizing agencies to cooperate with SIGIR.

In July 2005, SIGIR began presenting comprehensive overviews of the overall status of the reconstruction program, communicating the various challenges confronting U.S. program managers. A new Quarterly Report section— based on SIGIR's observations, agency responses to questions from SIGIR, and SIGIR's analysis— answered the important question of how the United States was doing in Iraq. It became the most reliable record of the Iraq reconstruction program's history and progress.

The Lessons Learned Initiative

Early reporting on weaknesses within program management systems led the Inspector General to initiate a lessons-learned program that sought to convert audit findings into advice and best practices. There is no standard lessons-learned approach within the U.S. inspector-general community. The efficacy of the SIGIR program indicates that perhaps departmental IGs might consider implementing such an approach.

The SIGIR initiative shifted into high gear in September 2005, with the gathering of U.S. government and industry leaders at an all-day forum to explore the human-resource challenges experienced in the reconstruction program and to identify potential solutions.

**APRIL 2005–
SEPTEMBER 2005**

APRIL
• SIGIR begins work to assemble consolidated database of U.S. reconstruction funding and project information

JUNE
• Inspections Directorate begins engineering reviews of reconstruction project sites/contracts
• Testimony on DFI audits (House Committee on Government Reform)

JULY
• SPITFIRE: Special Investigative Task Force on Iraq Reconstruction, now coordinating resources of the IRS, ICE, DoS IG, and DoJ's Criminal Division

SEPTEMBER
• SIGIR hosts Human Capital Management Lessons Learned Forum at Johns Hopkins University
• Testimony on sustainability and the cost to complete projects (House Appropriations Committee)

This was the first of five forums hosted by SIGIR, with two others on procurement and contracting occurring in December 2005, another in the spring of 2006 on program management, and one on applying Iraq's hard lessons (to improve the overall structure for managing SROs) in the fall of 2009.

These various events brought together operators and overseers to evaluate findings and provide recommendations that could increase the efficiency and effectiveness of SROs in Iraq. Subsequent interviews with senior Defense, State, and USAID officials strengthened the forums' recommendations. SIGIR then circulated draft reports to stakeholders for review, including Defense, State, USAID, the U.S. Army Corps of Engineers (USACE), the Office of Management and Budget, and key Iraq reconstruction leaders. The process ensured the most thoroughly vetted conclusions and fostered active discussion about the complex problems arising from the rebuilding program.

FY 2006: Rising Influence

In November 2005, the Congress extended SIGIR's mandate again. Under the new legislation, SIGIR would continue operating until 180 days after 80% of IRRF funds were *expended*. This new formula added at least another year to SIGIR's tenure, extending it into FY 2008.

SIGIR's staff grew to over 100 (including 64 auditors, investigators, and inspectors), a 40% increase from the previous year. About half the staff worked from the Baghdad office. Ambassador Khalilzad authorized 10 additional billets for SIGIR in Baghdad, allowing the expansion of in-country staff to 55.

OCTOBER 2005– MARCH 2006

▶ **OCTOBER**
- Testimony on the Reconstruction Gap (House Committee on Government Reform)

▶ **NOVEMBER**
- P.L. 109-102 changes SIGIR closure date from 180 days following obligation of 80% or more of the IRRF to 80% or more "expended."

▶ **DECEMBER**
- SIGIR hosts two Lessons Learned Forums on contracting and procurement at the George Washington University Law School

▶ **JANUARY**
- Lessons in Human Capital Management

▶ **FEBRUARY**
- Two testimonies on contracting issues (Senate Armed Services Committee) and on Iraq stabilization and reconstruction (Senate Foreign Relations Committee)

With the extension of its mandate and the experiential maturation of its staff, SIGIR earned greater influence with Iraqi and U.S. officials. As the year progressed, the Inspector General testified to Congress that the cooperation SIGIR began to experience was "refreshing."

Throughout the continual personnel turnover in the reconstruction program, SIGIR remained a source of stability and continuity, championing issues critical to the potential success of U.S.-funded projects and programs.

The Departments of State and Defense struggled to achieve a shared vision for the rebuilding effort. In response, the Inspector General prepared an October 2005 legal opinion calling for the Chief of Mission to assert his statutory leadership of the program through the State-led Iraq Reconstruction Management Office, the temporary entity charged with formulating reconstruction policy.

Interagency discontinuities would commonly burden the rebuilding effort and lead to SIGIR's most important recommendation—the creation of an integrated office to plan, manage, and oversee SROs.

The Iraq Reconstruction Management Office began including SIGIR staff in key reconstruction planning meetings. With SIGIR's in-country knowledge base and capabilities now well known, senior leaders across the U.S. reconstruction program began to request specific reviews of projects and programs:

- The Commander of the Multi-National Force-Iraq, General George Casey, asked SIGIR in the summer of 2005 to study how the Federal Acquisition Regulation might be amended to provide more efficient contracting in a war zone.
- Deputy Secretary of Defense Paul Wolfowitz asked SIGIR to examine the Commander's Emergency Response Program.
- The State Department endorsed SIGIR's broader reporting approach, asking for more analyses of the growing repository of information SIGIR had collected.
- Ambassador Khalilzad supported SIGIR's outreach to Iraqi judicial and law-enforcement entities, viewing them as vital to establishing anticorruption institutions in Iraq. In addition to its work to help set up and train Iraq's ministry inspectors general, SIGIR provided support to the Commission on Public Integrity, forging agreements to share information on cases.

Oversight Expands

Virtually all of the IRRF was obligated by the end of 2005, with many U.S.-funded projects transferring to Iraqi control. SIGIR's auditors and inspectors continued to raise important questions about whether U.S. implementing agencies had plans in place for the successful transition and sustainment of these projects. Auditors also reported on the shift to direct contracting with Iraqi firms and on the rising costs to complete the final tranche of IRRF projects.

Audit Highlight
Management of the Primary Healthcare Centers Construction Projects (SIGIR 06-011, 4/29/2006)

In March 2004, the CPA awarded a $243 million IRRF-funded task order to Parsons Delaware, Inc., to construct and equip 150 primary healthcare centers across Iraq by December 2005. A 2006 SIGIR audit found that just 6 of the centers were complete by that time, even though $186 million had been spent. Of the remaining 144 centers, 8 were eliminated from the contract, 1 was placed under another contract, and 135 remained partially constructed (with contracts for 121 subsequently terminated for convenience, some of which were later awarded to other contractors for completion).

SIGIR's auditors determined that substandard contractor performance and weak U.S. government management oversight contributed to the program's failure. The contractor lacked qualified engineering staff to supervise its design work, failed to check the capacity of its subcontractors to perform the required work, failed to properly supervise the subcontractors' work, and failed to enforce quality-control activities. The government was unresponsive to contractor requests for equitable adjustments and schedule delays based on unplanned or changed conditions, it suffered from high personnel turnover and organizational turbulence, and it failed to follow proper contracting procedures.

Eventually, 133 centers were completed at a cost of about $345 million or about $102 million more than originally estimated.

With the assistance of Iraqi contractors, the Inspections Directorate completed 96 ground surveys during the first three quarters of 2006, providing quick reports on projects in every reconstruction sector. These surveys yielded crucial visibility in areas to which U.S. inspectors were unable to travel, revealing problems requiring further assessment.

By the end of the year, inspection teams had produced inspections on 49 projects. Further, SIGIR had completed 66 aerial assessments of projects located all over Iraq. In June 2006, SIGIR began performing sustainment assessments to determine if completed projects were operating at capacity when accepted from the contractor by the U.S. government.

Thanks to the work of the SPITFIRE task force, SIGIR's Investigations Directorate saw the first prosecutions of procurement fraud cases. Former CPA comptroller Robert Stein pled guilty in February 2006 to charges stemming from his role in the scheme to defraud the U.S. government, including conspiracy, bribery, money laundering, possession of machine guns, and being a felon in possession of a firearm. His co-conspirator, Philip Bloom, pled guilty in April 2006 to charges of conspiracy, bribery, and money laundering.

SIGIR investigators successfully executed their first undercover sting operation in March 2006, catching a U.S. government translator soliciting bribes. Investigators began to coordinate with the U.S. Army Procurement Fraud Branch on the suspension and debarment of contractors found guilty of misconduct through SIGIR investigations of Iraq reconstruction, a path for action that would yield excellent results.

APRIL 2006–
SEPTEMBER 2006

APRIL
• SIGIR hosts Lessons Learned Forum on program and project management at the National Defense University

JUNE
• **Testimony** on infrastructure security and closing the Reconstruction Gap (House Committee on International Relations)

JULY
• *Lessons in Contracting and Procurement*

AUGUST
• **Testimony** on contracting and procurement lessons learned (Senate Homeland Security and Governmental Affairs Committee)

SEPTEMBER
• **Testimony** on contracting and procurement lessons learned (House Committee on Government Reform)

In 2006, SIGIR joined DCIS, the Major Procurement Fraud Unit of Army CID (CIDMPFU), FBI, State IG, and USAID IG to establish the International Contract Corruption Task Force (ICCTF), which coordinated and deconflicted criminal investigations emanating from Iraq and Kuwait. The ICCTF ensured information sharing and maximized the effectiveness of the investigative resources in Iraq.

Revealing Lessons Learned

In January 2006, SIGIR released the first report in its Lessons Learned Initiative—*Iraq Reconstruction: Lessons in Human Capital Management*. The second installment, *Iraq Reconstruction: Lessons in Contracting and Procurement*, followed in July 2006. Both took a longer view of the Iraq reconstruction experience, seeking to identify the causes of shortfalls, derive apropos lessons, and provide guidance to operators. In June 2006, the Inspector General testified before the Congress on the recommendations from both SIGIR reports, many of which would again be raised by the Commission on Wartime Contracting in Iraq and Afghanistan (CWC) in its final report in 2011.

Outreach to the Iraqi Government

The fight against corruption is central to lasting progress in Iraq. The issue became so serious in 2006 that Prime Minister al-Maliki referred to his country's corruption problem as a "second insurgency."

SIGIR became a strong voice in the anticorruption movement, championing efforts to:

- build Iraq's first inspector-general system
- establish a strong Commission on Public Integrity (CPI, later called the Commission of Integrity, or COI), Iraq's equivalent of the U.S. Federal Bureau of Investigation
- support Iraq's oldest anticorruption institution, the Board of Supreme Audit (BSA), the equivalent to the U.S. Government Accountability Office

The Inspector General met regularly with the CPI Commissioner, with the BSA President, and with many of Iraq's IGs.

SIGIR supported Iraq's efforts to stand up the 26 original offices of Iraq's ministry inspectors general, including:

- pressing for the initial $11 million allocated by the CPA for the IG system
- facilitating the establishment of an Iraqi IG association
- providing training for select Iraqi audit personnel
- funding an effort to translate the U.S. *Government Auditing Standards* into Arabic to serve as a model instructional guide
- facilitating training through one- and two-week tailored programs at the Sadat Academy in Cairo and London for 640 Iraqi IG auditors, inspectors, and investigators

The Inspector General met regularly with the Chief Justice of Iraq's Supreme Court to keep abreast of the needs of the judiciary as they faced deadly attacks and daily intimidation. SIGIR tracked the plight of Iraq's judges and the U.S. efforts to help secure them, their families, and the witnesses who were essential to prosecuting wrongdoing.

To ensure full access in Iraq to its reporting, SIGIR translated into Arabic (and posted online) many of its audits and all of its Quarterly Reports. This proved particularly valuable to the Iraqi anticorruption institutions. Many of these audits reviewed the progress of U.S. programs to build the capacity of these institutions, finding that very little reconstruction money was devoted to this critical concern.

At the Inspector General's urging, the U.S. ambassador led an anticorruption summit in November 2005, which resulted in a proposal to form a joint U.S.- Iraqi Anticorruption Working Group and an agreement to provide more training for officials from the BSA, CPI, and IGs. The working group identified several major priorities, including promotion of market reforms and reduction of subsidies, reinforcement of the weak law-enforcement structure, and creation of a public education campaign on corruption issues.

Despite these and other U.S. efforts, corruption continues to be a major impediment to progress in Iraq.

Iraqi leadership demonstrated particular interest in SIGIR's oversight of the Development Fund for Iraq. The CPA used the DFI to finance most of the early reconstruction program. The Inspector General regularly briefed Iraqi officials on the results of DFI audits.

He also led conversations about issues such as asset transfer, Government of Iraq (GOI) cost sharing, and sustainment with U.S. and Iraqi officials alike.

As the Iraq Security Forces Fund became a primary reconstruction source, these conversations widened to embrace how these funds could enable the Iraqi Security Forces to reach necessary capability levels.

By developing good contacts with Iraqi offices, SIGIR's Quarterly Report team began to obtain a fuller picture of the rebuilding program's effects.

Moreover, the Inspector General and Deputy Inspector General met regularly with Iraqi leaders and those in the Kurdistan Regional Government to better understand the issues affecting the country. Thus, the Quarterly Report became as much a resource for the Iraqi government and Iraqi citizens as it was for the U.S. government and U.S. taxpayers.

Inspection Highlight
Pipeline River Crossing, Al Fatah, Iraq
(SA-05-001, 1/27/2006)

After ignoring a geologist's warning, the CPA wasted almost $76 million in DFI funds when it attempted to repair a set of damaged oil and gas pipelines by rerouting the pipelines under the Tigris River. Drilling through the loose, sandy soil beneath the river proved to be impossible, and the project was abandoned in August 2004, when it was only 28% complete.

When SIGIR assessed the project in late 2005, its inspection team noted several factors that contributed to the project's failure: a flawed construction design, a subcontract without performance requirements, a compartmentalized project-management structure, and inadequate oversight by the U.S. government (USACE) and the prime contractor (KBR).

The pipelines were subsequently repaired under a separate $29.7 million IRRF-funded contract awarded to Parsons Iraq Joint Venture.

FY 2007: Expanding Mandate

In October 2006, SIGIR received the Gaston L. Gianni, Jr., Better Government Award from the President's Council on Integrity and Efficiency, just as the Congress passed two pieces of legislation expanding its jurisdiction to include funds other than the IRRF. The John Warner National Defense Authorization Act for Fiscal Year 2007 (P.L. 109-364), deemed "any United

States funds appropriated or otherwise made available for fiscal year 2006 for the reconstruction of Iraq, irrespective of the designation of such funds" to be amounts appropriated or otherwise made available to the IRRF (and thus subject to SIGIR's jurisdiction). This act also mandated that SIGIR would terminate on October 1, 2007, allowing for a transition of operations through December 31.

Two months later, the Iraq Reconstruction Accountability Act of 2006 changed SIGIR's end date yet again. It changed the end date to 10 months after 80% of the total "IRRF" (which now included the FY 2006 funds) had been expended. The new estimated closing time now extended deep into FY 2008. The new law also required SIGIR to prepare a final forensic audit report on all funds deemed to be the IRRF.

Just five months afterward, the Congress *again* changed SIGIR's mandate and estimated end date, adding all FY 2007 reconstruction funding to SIGIR's authority and effectively extending SIGIR's lifespan into FY 2009. The legislation provided $35 million to SIGIR for its operating budget, to remain available until January 31, 2008.

Audit Highlight
Review of DynCorp International, LLC,
Contract Number S-LMAQM-04-C-0300,
Task Order 0338, for the Iraqi Police Training Program Support
(SIGIR 06-029, DoS-OIG-AUD/IQO-07-20), 1/30/2007)

Under a $1.8 billion IRRF-funded contract with DynCorp, the Department of State (DoS) Bureau of International Narcotics and Law Enforcement Affairs (INL) issued a $152 million task order in June 2004 to support 500 police trainers for an initial 3-month period and to construct 6 camps for the training program.

SIGIR's 2007 audit of the task order uncovered numerous problems, finding that DoS did not have the capacity to manage so large a program. The audit revealed poor contract administration by INL and the DoS Office of Acquisition

Management that resulted in property not accounted for and millions of dollars put at unnecessary risk. Specifically, DoS paid about $43.8 million (including $4.2 million for unauthorized work) for the manufacture and temporary storage of residential camp trailers that were never used.

> In addition, DoS spent another $36.4 million for weapons and equipment, including armored vehicles, body armor, and communications equipment that could not be accounted for.
>
> In an October 2007 report (SIGIR 07-016), SIGIR identified major problems with the DynCorp contract.
>
> The most disturbing finding was that INL had not validated the accuracy of invoices it had received from DynCorp and, as a result, did not know what it received for approximately $1.2 billion in expenditures. SIGIR's report resulted in a full audit of all DynCorp invoices on the contract and the recovery of $600 million in unsupported charges.
>
> SIGIR returned to review this contract again in FY 2010 and found weak INL oversight of DynCorp task orders. As a result, $2.5 billion in U.S. funds was deemed vulnerable to waste and fraud. (See SIGIR 10-008, 1/25/2010.)

With these legislative actions, SIGIR now had authority to review projects and programs funded in part or whole not only by the $20.9 billion in the original IRRF appropriations but by all U.S. funding made available for Iraq's reconstruction in FY 2006 and FY 2007. Among these additional funds were Defense's Iraq Security Forces Fund (ISFF) and Commander's Emergency Response Program (CERP), as well as State's Economic Support Fund (ESF)—a worldwide fund made available in large quantity to Iraq beginning in FY 2006—and its International Narcotics Control and Law Enforcement (INCLE) account.

Projects funded by the ISFF, CERP, ESF, and INCLE were well underway and central to the changing U.S. reconstruction strategy, especially regarding the provinces, through efforts such as the Provincial Reconstruction Team (PRT) program, the Local Governance Program, and the Community Action Program. SIGIR audits reviewed these large multiphase capacity-development efforts, raising concerns about the ability of the U.S. government to measure effective outcomes.

Additionally, SIGIR learned that commanders were using CERP funding to complete large IRRF projects that had experienced cost overruns.

Forensic Auditing Begins

In consultation with the Congress, SIGIR's auditors established a plan to meet the forensic audit requirement of the Iraq Reconstruction Accountability Act. It entailed a complex mix of focused financial reviews of major IRRF contracts and audits of the CERP, ESF, ISFF, and INCLE. The plan responded to the act's requirement for a "final forensic audit report on all funds deemed to be amounts appropriated or otherwise made available to the Iraq Relief and Reconstruction Fund." SIGIR's forensic audit eventually reviewed more than $51.4 billion appropriated or allocated from the five major U.S. reconstruction funds through FY 2011.

SIGIR used a framework entailing multiple audit and investigative approaches in performing the forensic work. This included:

- the examination of major Defense, State, and USAID programs and contracts to determine if the organizations had good internal controls over the expenditure of U.S. reconstruction funds
- the use of internal and external sources to identify fraudulent activities
- the testing of more than 180,000 payment transactions, totaling about $40 billion, to identify irregular or anomalous transactions that could indicate potential fraud

OCTOBER 2006–
MARCH 2007

OCTOBER
- SIGIR receives the Gaston L. Gianni, Jr., Better Government Award

DECEMBER
- P.L. 109-440 extends SIGIR's tenure until 10 months after 80% of all funds made available to the IRRF are expended

JANUARY
- Testimony on SIGIR audits, inspections, and investigations (House Armed Services Committee)

FEBRUARY/MARCH
- Seven testimonies before six different House and Senate Committees on CPA control over the DFI and SIGIR's reports on the Basrah Children's Hospital/Baghdad Police College, on SIGIR oversight, on SIGIR audits of ISF logistics and weapons registration, on SIGIR fraud investigations, on program/project management lessons learned, and on GOI ability to pay for reconstruction
- *Lessons in Program and Project Management*

With the expansion of audit jurisdiction came an increased depth in audit capabilities. SIGIR hired an additional team of eight experienced, former GAO auditors who had been working with the Surveys and Investigations staff of the House Appropriations Committee. One of them became SIGIR's new Assistant Inspector General for Audits, just as the organization began preparations to undergo its first peer review.

Making Oversight a Defense Mission Priority

In 2007, travel to construction sites for inspections became problematic. State provided protective security escorts for travel outside of the Green Zone, but had limited resources. Thus, it denied many requests that SIGIR made for escort. The Commanding General of the Multi-National Force-Iraq, General David Petraeus, rectified the problem by issuing a Fragmentary Order to ensure SIGIR's inspectors could travel to project sites. He directed military units to transport inspection teams to any site in Iraq that SIGIR chose. This new arrangement worked well.

That summer, SIGIR inspectors traveled to one of the most dangerous work sites in Iraq, the Basrah Children's Hospital, where many workers had been killed and others faced daily intimidation. SIGIR inspectors also conducted site visits to some of the 140 primary healthcare centers, the Qudas Power Plant, and the Baghdad Police College (a project emblematic of bad management).

Meanwhile, auditors visited more than 30 PRT and embedded PRT program locations across Iraq. They focused greater attention on the status of the PRT program as it rapidly expanded and changed its strategy to work more closely with military units retaking areas of Iraq.

**APRIL 2007–
SEPTEMBER 2007**

MAY
• Two **testimonies**: on contracting lessons learned (House Appropriations Committee) and on future Iraq relief and reconstruction funding (House Committee on Foreign Affairs)

• P.L. 110-28 adds FY 2007 funding to SIGIR's authority and provides $35 million to SIGIR for operating costs

JUNE
• **Testimony** on anticorruption efforts and proposed war-profiteering legislation (House Judiciary Committee)

JULY
• **Testimony** on the $44.5 billion appropriated for Iraq reconstruction (House Budget Committee)

SEPTEMBER
• **Testimony** on PRT program (House Armed Services Committee)

State managed this program, which facilitated civil-military cooperation to target U.S. funds toward the priorities set by local provincial governments in each of Iraq's 18 provinces. In the spring of 2007, the composition of the PRT staff began to shift when U.S. civilian government employees arrived as part of State's "civilian surge" (which sought to complement the military surge of troops) to fill PRT billets.

Inspection Highlight
Baghdad Police College, Baghdad, Iraq
(PA-06-078.2 and 079.2, 1/29/2007)

In response to a Hotline complaint about a $73 million project performed by Parsons Delaware, Inc., to renovate and build new facilities for the training of Iraqi police, SIGIR inspected the site and immediately observed that diluted feces and urine drained from the ceilings into lighting fixtures and rooms below, causing floors to bow inches off the ground and crack apart.

In response, the U.S. government terminated the Parsons contract for "convenience" in May 2006, with Parsons promising to repair the plumbing issues at no additional cost.

After visiting the project five more times in 2006, SIGIR concluded in its final report that the project was poorly designed and constructed and that the contractor and USACE personnel failed to oversee and manage the project. The Inspections team also found indications of potential fraud and referred those matters to SIGIR's Investigations Directorate.

Communicating Challenges and Proposing Solutions

In FY 2007, the Inspector General testified before the Congress 13 times, answering, among other critical questions, "Is Reconstruction Failing?" He testified on numerous issues, including:

- the development and operation of the PRT program and other capacity-development activities that had transformed the reconstruction strategy's trajectory
- Iraq's ability to begin to pay for its own reconstruction and the fight against corruption
- the many management insights revealed in SIGIR's audits, inspections, and its latest lessons-learned report, *Iraq Reconstruction:*

Lessons in Program and Project Management, released in March 2007

SIGIR's Quarterly Report began presenting a fund-by-fund analysis, using key indicators such as rate of expenditure and obligation, as well as accomplishments by reconstruction sector. The reports summarized the challenges in transitioning projects to the Iraqi government, provided analysis of how much U.S. funding was expended in each of Iraq's provinces (as well as a breakdown of major projects delivered in Baghdad), and a comparison of selected reconstruction-related statutory benchmarks and commitments made by the Iraqi government under the International Compact for Iraq (a conditions-based agreement to provide additional funding from the international community once Iraq met benchmarks set in several areas).

Investigative Collaboration Works

By the beginning of FY 2007, SIGIR had established the value of collaborative task forces to track down and halt criminal activity. SPITFIRE served as an excellent mechanism for integrating cases, sharing information among in-country law-enforcement agencies, and deconflicting investigations.

Newly hired law-enforcement staff ramped up SIGIR's investigative presence in Iraq and across the United States.

In the summer of 2007, the ringleader of another major task-force conspiracy case, U.S. Army Major John Cockerham, was arrested, leading to the first of 23 indictments and 22 convictions that the case would yield over the next six years. Three years into their work in Iraq, SIGIR investigators had arrested 13 suspects, and their cases had contributed to 8 indictments and 5 convictions.

FY 2008: The Rise in Investigations

In January 2008, the Congress again extended SIGIR's termination date and added to SIGIR's oversight authority. The revision gave SIGIR jurisdiction over all funds "appropriated or otherwise made available for the reconstruction of Iraq"—in other words, all money appropriated at any time for Iraq's reconstruction. The law also changed the termination date to "180 days after the date on which amounts appropriated or otherwise made available for the reconstruction of Iraq that are unexpended are less than

$250,000,000." The combined changes in jurisdiction and termination effectively extended SIGIR for years to come.

The Congress further directed SIGIR to develop a comprehensive plan for a series of audits of contracts, subcontracts, and task orders for the performance of security and reconstruction functions relating to Iraq. The Inspector General developed this plan along with the IGs from Defense, State, and USAID.

SIGIR viewed FY 2008 as the "Year of Transfer" of three critical roles from the United States to Iraq:

- responsibility for reconstruction planning, management, and funding
- responsibility for U.S.-provided reconstruction programs, projects, and assets
- responsibility for provincial security in all provinces

Inspection Highlight
Relief and Reconstruction Funded Work at Mosul Dam
(PA-07-105, 10/29/2007)

A SIGIR Inspections team conducted two on-site assessments of a $27 million project at Mosul Dam.

The purpose of the project was to stabilize the soil beneath Iraq's largest dam and thereby reduce the risk of dam failure. SIGIR's team found that the project was poorly designed and inadequately executed and monitored. Almost $20 million worth of equipment and materials for implementing improvements was not being used, with the project showing signs of possible fraud.

In recognition of its response to the urgent need for a comprehensive assessment of the Mosul Dam, SIGIR's inspection team received a President's Council on Integrity and Efficiency Award for Excellence in Evaluations. The award stated: "Despite insurgent activity in the area, the team conducted a thorough on-site inspection and provided significant recommendations for improvement."

New audit work recognized improvements in the process of transferring U.S. projects to the Iraqi government but recommended further changes to avoid waste. Other reports reflected SIGIR's continuing concern about the ability of the Iraqi government to sustain projects after handover. U.S. programs to build capacity in Iraq's ministries and provincial governments worked to address that concern. An audit of the ISFF revealed that transition of funding responsibility for security infrastructure to the Iraqi government was underway, but the Ministry of Defense and the Ministry of Interior needed more U.S. support to reach minimum capabilities for internal and external defense. In reviewing the uses of the CERP, SIGIR found that commanders too often used funds to support large-scale projects—some costing well over $1,000,000—contrary to the original intent of the program.

The Human Cost of Oversight

The professionals who answered the call to serve in Iraq faced extraordinarily dangerous working conditions. In 2007, three separate attacks in the Green Zone wounded five SIGIR staff members:

- Three SIGIR auditors were conducting a planning meeting at a table near the Embassy dining facility when a rocket landed less than 10 meters from where they were sitting. All sustained shrapnel wounds and hearing loss, were treated and released, and went back to work the next day.
- An investigator in his trailer after work was hit in the ankle by a stray AK-47 round fired into the sky during celebratory gunfire that followed an Iraqi national soccer team victory. He was back at work the next day.
- An auditor was wounded when a rocket destroyed his trailer, causing shrapnel wounds and some permanent hearing loss. He also was back at work the next day.

Tragically, on March 24, 2008, a rocket hit a trailer on the Embassy grounds, mortally wounding SIGIR auditor Paul Converse. In October 2008, the President's Council on Integrity and Efficiency posthumously honored him with the Sentner Award for Dedication and Courage.

The Khan Bani Sa'ad Correctional Facility inspection uncovered a gross example of failed construction oversight. The July 2008 report revealed that the U.S. government had spent $40 million of the IRRF to partially complete the project before its termination. An additional $1.2 million in construction materials left at the site by the contractor had been looted by the time SIGIR visited. Further, the GOI had no intention to complete or use the facility. The $40 million was completely wasted. SIGIR's quarterly reporting began providing an update on Iraq to ensure a clear understanding of the deficits that U.S. projects attempted to address in the four main reconstruction areas: security, economy, governance, and essential services. Analyses centered on certain aspects of Iraqi capacity to handle security and pay for reconstruction. The April 2008 Quarterly Report provided a five-year retrospective of the reconstruction program and presented more information on how the U.S. government spent funds in each of the provinces.

Audit Highlight Commander's Emergency Response Program Funds Many Large-Scale Projects (SIGIR 08-006, 1/25/2008)

The Commander's Emergency Response Program (CERP) was created in 2003 to enable U.S. field commanders to respond to urgent humanitarian relief and reconstruction requirements within their areas of responsibility, primarily by executing small-scale, focused projects that met local needs. From October 2005 to April 2007, SIGIR issued four reports finding that, in general, CERP-appropriated funds were properly used for intended purposes, but controls over CERP processes required improvements to ensure accountability. After the CERP program in Iraq had been in place for four years, with allocations for it totaling $2.3 billion, SIGIR auditors again examined CERP-funded projects to determine whether the program was being carried out as intended. They found that the CERP was increasingly being used for development rather than for small-scale urgent humanitarian relief and reconstruction projects. Although 44% of the projects cost no more than $25,000 each, together they used only 4% of the total dollars obligated for CERP projects. Conversely, projects costing $500,000 or more represented only 3% of the project total, but nearly 37% of total dollars obligated. In FY 2006, almost half of the obligated CERP dollars went to these large-scale projects. The audit pointed out planning deficiencies in the CERP program. Field commanders generally were not coordinating their project activities with other U.S. government agencies working in the area, were not adequately planning for the physical handover of completed projects to the Iraqi government upon completion, and were not planning for the long-term maintenance and sustainment of the projects. SIGIR's report resulted in tighter controls over large-scale projects undertaken using CERP funds and better guidance for field commanders.

Energizing the Investigations Directorate

As FY 2008 began, SIGIR's Investigations Directorate began a major strategic shift. While SIGIR's cases had exposed vulnerabilities in cash-based U.S. programs, the rate of convictions for SIGIR cases stalled in FY 2007. But the Congress's significant extension of SIGIR's tenure led the Investigations Directorate to pursue a hiring campaign to bring aboard the expertise necessary for developing cases and processing them faster and more effectively. The Assistant Inspector General who first implemented SIGIR's Inspections program returned to the organization to lead the directorate. SIGIR sought to employ former special agents-in-charge from DCIS, the Department of Agriculture IG, the Drug Enforcement Agency, and the Defense Security Service. Under newly invigorated leadership, SIGIR's investigative team:

- provided extensive experience in investigation of complex international financial transactions and contracting frauds, in computer data manipulation and analysis, and in Defense and State processes and procedures
- identified dozens of cases of criminal activity through financial and document analysis, through computer data analysis, and through the development of new sources of information
- established closer relationships with other key U.S. investigative agencies, such as Army CID and DCIS. The close relationship SIGIR developed with Army CID proved to be the most valuable, as Army CID committed the most resources to joint law-enforcement efforts.
- established relationships with non-U.S. law-enforcement personnel under a 2008 initiative called INTERCEPT (International Criminal Enforcement and Prosecution Team), which conducted criminal investigations of non-U.S. citizens who defrauded the Iraq reconstruction program

OCTOBER 2007–
MARCH 2008

OCTOBER
-100th audit and 100th inspection report released

- Three **testimonies**: on U.S. anticorruption assistance (House Oversight and Government Reform Committee), on SIGIR's third audit of the PRT program (House Armed Services Committee), and on the effectiveness of the U.S. reconstruction program (House Appropriations Committee)

JANUARY
- Testimony on contingency contracting (Senate Homeland Security and Governmental Affairs Committee)
- The **Year of Transfer** to the GOI of:
  – reconstruction funding responsibility
  – U.S.-funded assets
  – security responsibilities

MARCH
- Testimony on controlling corruption, waste, and fraud (Senate Appropriations Committee)
- SIGIR auditor Paul Converse killed in a rocket attack in the Green Zone; PCIE/ECIE honors him with the Sentner Award for Dedication and Courage

• obtained adequate prosecution support by coordinating cases not only with the Department of Justice's Criminal Division but also with U.S. Attorney offices and foreign countries.

SIGIR also began to develop an innovative program called the SIGIR Prosecutorial Initiative (SIGPRO), which is summarized in Section 2 of this report. In 2008, SIGIR Investigations decentralized domestic investigative operations, a move that reflected the fact that the bulk of the work was now scattered across the continental United States. Civilian suspects and witnesses had returned from Iraq, military personnel had returned to U.S. bases, and the company and financial records related to frauds and thefts were now located in the United States. The cases were also increasingly prosecuted by U.S. Attorneys across the country. Consequently, nearly all of SIGIR's investigator positions were moved to satellite locations in Florida, Texas, Pennsylvania, California, New York, Ohio, and Michigan. Over the next five years, these varying innovations and program changes led to the quadrupling of indictments and convictions and a tenfold increase in monetary results.

FY 2009: Revealing Hard Lessons

SIGIR reached peak operations in FY 2009 with 142 people on staff, including 42 audit and 36 investigative professionals. Total U.S. and Iraqi reconstruction funding under SIGIR's oversight stood at $75.67 billion. The Security Agreement and Security Framework Agreement between Iraq and the United States became effective in January 2009, redefining the bilateral relationship between the two nations, and security of the Green Zone became the responsibility of Iraqi forces. The reconstruction program had peaked and was beginning to decline, but oversight was still crucial.

APRIL 2008–
SEPTEMBER 2008

APRIL
• SIGIR Inspectors release an assessment of one of the largest Iraq reconstruction projects—the $277 million Nassiriya Water Treatment Plant

JULY
361
SIGIR investigations initiated since 2004, yielding:

16
Arrests

17
Indictments

8
Convictions

$17.4M
in court-ordered restitution/forfeiture

Applying Hard Lessons to the Work at Hand

In February 2009, SIGIR released *Hard Lessons: The Iraq Reconstruction Experience,* a detailed account of the U.S. effort to rebuild Iraq from prewar planning in mid-2002 through the fall of 2008. Research for this 350-page book included hundreds of interviews with key participants in the reconstruction effort and the review of thousands of documents.

The Inspector General reached out to virtually every senior U.S. official involved in planning and executing the rebuilding of Iraq, and almost all agreed to be interviewed by him or to provide useful responses to questions. In addition, SIGIR staff interviewed rank-and-file members of the military and civilian agencies, as well as private contractors, who carried out the work of Iraq's reconstruction. The Inspector General talked with senior Iraqi leaders, including Prime Ministers Allawi and Ja'afari, to gain their perspectives on the reconstruction program. *Hard Lessons* also drew from the body of SIGIR's audits, inspections, and investigations, as well as reports from other oversight agencies and investigative bodies.

The book presented 13 lessons for current and future contingency relief and reconstruction operations. By the summer of 2009, General David Petraeus, Commander of the United States Central Command had decided to implement most of these recommendations in the Afghanistan rebuilding operations.

Several insights from *Hard Lessons* applied to the U.S. reconstruction program in Iraq in FY 2009 and informed SIGIR's audits and inspections:

1. **Re-evaluating personnel and policy to avoid gaps in program direction.** SIGIR completed an audit requested by Ambassador Ryan Crocker on project reporting, finding weaknesses in processes and systems that led to gaps in what the Chief of Mission, as the leader of the reconstruction program, could see.

2. **Shaping a new reconstruction management structure through a joint State-Defense plan.**

3. SIGIR's inspectors released reports on major infrastructure projects, such as the Falluja Waste Water Treatment System, Missan Surgical Hospital, and Basrah Children's Hospital, exposing the effects of poor management that led to cost overruns and excessive delays. SIGIR's auditors reviewed the extent to which the GOI shared in funding reconstruction projects, finding many weaknesses.

4. **Strengthening security management.** As Iraq's police and military forces assumed full responsibility for security by the end of the year, the increasing use of private security contractors (PSCs) prompted seven audits by SIGIR in FY 2009. Auditors reviewed financial data reporting for PSCs, reporting of incidents involving PSCs, and military commander involvement in controlling and coordinating PSCs. They also reviewed the performance of Aegis Defence Services, Ltd., on a contract with Defense and of Blackwater Security Consulting on the Worldwide Personal Protective Services contract with State.

5. **Completing the security handoff to the GOI, focusing on the use of the ISFF to get Iraq's security forces independently operating.** SIGIR audited a $350 million contract awarded by the Multi-National Security Transition Command-Iraq funded by the ISFF to complete the Taji National Maintenance Depot, determining that the five completed project phases had yet to provide a lasting maintenance capability for Iraq's forces. In other reviews, SIGIR auditors revealed that, although the United States had reduced its funding for the Iraqi Security Forces (ISF), continued support would be needed. However, according to another audit, obtaining reliable data on the status of the ISF to better target that support was not possible.

OCTOBER 2008– MARCH 2009

OCTOBER
- PCIE Award for Excellence in Auditing

- PCIE Award for Excellence in Evaluations (Mosul Dam Inspection)

FEBRUARY
- *Hard Lessons: The Iraq Reconstruction Experience*

- **Testimony** on *Hard Lessons* (Commission on Wartime Contracting in Iraq and Afghanistan)

MARCH
- $13.1 million of the DFI returned to the GOI as a result of SIGIR Investigation
- **Testimony** on how misuse of reconstruction funding affects counterinsurgency efforts in Iraq (House Armed Services Committee)

Audit Highlight
Agencies Need Improved Financial Data Reporting for Private
Security Contractors (SIGIR 09-005, 10/30/2008)
and other reports on PSCs

The use of armed private security contractors (PSCs) proved controversial in Iraq. At the start of the war, there was little guidance on how to control PSCs or track their costs. Seven of the 27 audits that SIGIR completed in FY 2009 addressed these issues. Among the findings:

- The actual total costs of using PSCs was difficult to know because the agencies in Iraq using PSCs were not required to systematically identify the costs, and the agencies' financial management systems did not routinely capture data that would show what had been obligated and spent for PSC services. SIGIR estimated the cost of PSC services in Iraq from April 2003 through March 2008 at roughly $5 billion.
- DoD's contract with Aegis Defense Services was well managed, but there was no central repository that provided a history of the contractor's performance, and there was no process for holding the contractor accountable for equipment lost or damaged due to contractor negligence.
- Day-to-day oversight of the Theater-wide Internal Security Services contract was a problem because the government personnel charged with overseeing the contract had limited experience, training, and time to conduct adequate oversight.
- Although the U.S. military and the U.S. Embassy had established policies for reporting and investigating serious incidents involving PSCs, some of these incidents were not being reported, and the agency responsible for investigating them applied a narrow definition of what constituted a serious incident, which limited the number of investigations.
- Of 109 incidents of weapon discharges by PSCs over a 10-month period, DoD had records for 95% of them, but the database was missing supporting documentation on actions taken for 51% of the incidents.

Harnessing Technology To Catch More Thieves

SIGIR's new Investigations team of 36 was fully formed by FY 2009, working on about 85 cases. About a third of the staff operated in Iraq, while the others were based in nine U.S. locales.

In March 2009, a SIGIR investigation resulted in the return of $13.1 million of the DFI to the Government of Iraq. Investigators had followed a Hotline tip to determine that, at the direction of USACE, several contractors had erroneously submitted vouchers for costs that had not been incurred. No criminal wrongdoing was involved, but the case ensured that the funds were returned to the Iraqi government. The same investigation yielded an additional $300,290 in returned DFI funds in April 2009.

In the summer of 2009, SIGIR developed a task force to focus on individuals involved with U.S. relief and reconstruction programs who had easy access to cash in poorly controlled environments. The Forensic Evaluation Research and Recovery Enforcement Team (FERRET) used data-mining technology to detect suspicious financial transactions by U.S. military and civilian personnel and contractors who had worked in Iraq. With the support of the Department of the Treasury's Financial Crimes Enforcement Network, as well as DCIS, the Naval Criminal Investigative Service, CID-MPFU, and the Air Force Office of Special Investigations, SIGIR followed signs of illicit financial activity, imposing closer scrutiny. These efforts resulted in more than 110 new cases over the next three years.

APRIL 2009–
SEPTEMBER 2009

JUNE
SIGIR Peak Staffing
107 U.S.

35 Baghdad

JULY
431
SIGIR Investigations
initiated since 2004,
yielding:

23
Arrests

29
Indictments

21
Convictions

$35.5M
in court-ordered
restitution/forfeiture

By October 2009, monetary results from SIGIR's investigations had nearly tripled, to more than $49 million. There were 11 indictments and 13 convictions in 2009—about double the number from the previous year—bringing the cumulative number of indictments to 30 and cumulative convictions to 24.

Inspection Highlight Basrah Children's Hospital, Basrah, Iraq (PA-08-160, 7/28/2009)

In January 2009, SIGIR performed an on-site assessment of the Basrah Children's Hospital. The project began in July 2004, and was originally scheduled to be completed by December 2005, at a cost of $50 million. When SIGIR visited the site in January 2009, work was still ongoing, the estimated total cost had increased to almost $166 million, and the hospital was not expected to be fully functional until 2011.

Because of the security situation in Basrah, SIGIR was only able to perform an expedited one-hour assessment. Although a complete review of all work performed was not possible, SIGIR's team had sufficient time to determine that construction appeared to be adequate. However, because of the delays, the end result would not be the state-of-the-art medical facility envisioned at project inception. In its assessment of the project, SIGIR identified several factors that contributed to the escalation of the project's costs and the drastic schedule slippage: unrealistic time frames for design and construction; poor soil conditions; drastically changing security situation at the project site, including the murder of 24 workers; multiple partners and funding sources; and the Government of Iraq's unfulfilled obligations.

Launching a New SIG

SIGIR was the first-ever "Special IG." The Congress believed that this new cross-jurisdictional oversight model was a good one. Thus, in the National Defense Authorization Act for Fiscal Year 2008 (P.L. 110Ǧ181), it replicated the SIGIR model for the U.S. rebuilding program in Afghanistan, creating the Office of the Special Inspector General for Afghanistan Reconstruction (SIGAR). In the summer of 2008, SIGIR began supporting SIGAR, helping to establish its offices in Arlington, Virginia, and Kabul, Afghanistan. The Inspector General met regularly with the new SIGAR, offering insights into operating a special IG mission. He detailed several auditors to the new agency, with some of them deploying to Afghanistan.

SIGIR's security officer helped SIGAR through the process of obtaining Top Secret security clearances, and other SIGIR staff helped them to prepare for deployment overseas. SIGIR's Chief Information Officer traveled to Afghanistan to set up phone and computer communications in Kabul. In total, SIGIR's management and administration staff provided more than 2,900 hours of human resources, budget, contracting, facilities, logistics, policy and program management, and IT services to stand SIGAR up. Auditors provided another 3,800 hours of work. More than $565,000 in staffing and logistics effort went to support SIGAR's start-up.

SIGIR also supported the start-up of the Special Inspector General for the Troubled Asset Relief Program, or SIGTARP, providing staffing and advice to establish SIGTARP's systems.

FY 2010: Losing a Key Partner as Defense Departs

The Congress made more than $2.5 billion in additional U.S. appropriations available for Iraq's reconstruction in FY 2010. This included $1 billion in new funding for the ISFF and more than $700 million for the INCLE account, in anticipation of State assuming responsibility from the U.S. military for training the Iraqi police. As part of a phased withdrawal, approximately 70,000 U.S. combat troops departed Iraq by the end of summer 2010; and USACE, the lead construction agency for the rebuilding effort, drew down its presence to minimal levels.

OCTOBER 2009– MARCH 2010

▸ **OCTOBER**
• **FERRET**—SIGIR's Forensic Evaluation Research and Recovery Enforcement Team formally established; uses advanced financial data-mining techniques, yielding 110 cases and 20 convictions in 3 years

• CIGIE Award for Excellence in Investigations

• CIGIE Sentner Award for Dedication and Courage

▸ **DECEMBER**
• SIGPRO (SIGIR Prosecutorial Initiative) hires three experienced prosecutors to accelerate procurement fraud cases

FEBRUARY
• Two **testimonies** on reforming U.S. approach to SROs/USOCO (Commission on Wartime Contracting and House Foreign Affairs Committee)

• *Applying Iraq's Hard Lessons to the Reform of Stabilization and Reconstruction Operations*

In the wake of Defense's drawdown, the U.S. entities staying behind—including SIGIR—now planned for security and logistical accommodations necessary to replace functions the military had provided. In May 2010, State's Iraq Transition Assistance Office (which had succeeded the Iraq Reconstruction Management Office) transferred most reconstruction program management responsibilities to a third successive temporary entity, the Iraq Strategic Partnership Office. The State-led PRT program reduced in size as U.S. military units departed, heading toward closure in 2011.

SIGIR was still at full operating capacity as the year opened, with a staff of 133 that included 42 audit and 32 investigative professionals. By the end of September 2010, however, total staffing dropped to about 100, with a decrease of another third slated for FY 2011.

Audit Highlight
Department of State Grant Management: Limited Oversight of Costs and Impact of International Republican Institute and National Democratic Institute Democracy Grants (SIGIR 10-012, 1/26/2010)

Although millions of dollars in grants had been awarded during the reconstruction program, it was unclear if agencies were properly overseeing and managing grant activities. To shed light on this subject, SIGIR performed several grant audits in 2010, focusing on 12 grants that the DoS Bureau of Democracy, Human Rights, and Labor (DRL) awarded between 2004 and 2009 to the International Republican Institute (IRI) and the National Democratic Institute (NDI) for democracy-building activities in Iraq. The 12 grants had a combined value of $248 million.

Of the $114 million in grant expenditures that SIGIR examined, almost 60% was spent on security and overhead costs—even though both organizations located themselves in Erbil, probably the safest city in Iraq. DRL officials could not provide documentation showing that DRL had reviewed the reasonableness of security budgets proposed by IRI and NDI, nor could DRL officials explain why the apparent risks associated with these grants, as evidenced by the significant security costs, were accepted. DRL also had no documentation on whether the IRI and NDI grants were meeting their goals and whether the grant money was being used in accordance with requirements or in an effective and efficient manner. Both IRI and NDI stated that they had assessed the impact of their grants, but DRL did not require them to submit reports.

In October 2009, the Council of the Inspectors General on Integrity and Efficiency (CIGIE) presented SIGIR an Award for Excellence in investigations and also the Sentner Award for Dedication and Courage in the conduct of its work in Iraq. In May, the Inspector General received the David M. Walker Excellence in Government Performance and Accountability Award from the National Intergovernmental Audit Forum. Additionally, the Audits Directorate passed its first peer review, receiving the highest grade possible.

Landmark Audits

In 2010, SIGIR released the first four interim reports of its forensic audit series, having reviewed nearly 108,000 transactions valued at approximately $35.8 billion, or more than two-thirds of the $53 billion in U.S. funds appropriated for Iraq reconstruction. It found few specific problems in the agencies' invoice-payment processes. Because of internal control weaknesses, however, there was no certainty that all of the payments they made were for goods and services that were actually received, that they met contractual specifications, that they were in accordance with the contract prices, and that they were competitively priced.

Other identified weaknesses included inadequate reviews of contractor invoices, insufficient numbers of contracting officials, inadequately trained oversight staff, poor inventory controls, high staff turnover, weak record keeping, insufficient price competition by subcontractors, and questionable oversight of cash disbursements.

APRIL 2010–
SEPTEMBER 2010

APRIL 30
• Inspections
Directorate closes

MAY
• Testimony on SIGIR
investigations
(Commission on
Wartime Contracting)

• Inspector General
receives David M.
Walker Excellence in
Government
Performance and
Accountability Award

JUNE
• Testimony on
subcontracting/
proposed
contingency Federal
Acquisition
Regulation (House
Oversight and
Government Reform
Committee)

AUGUST 31
• End of U.S. forces
combat mission; only
advise-and-assist
brigades remain

SEPTEMBER
• Testimony on
challenges facing DoS
reconstruction
leadership (House
Oversight and
Government Reform
Committee)

Three audit findings stood out:

- The U.S. Army's contracting office lacked sufficient experienced personnel to review invoices, leaving the U.S. government vulnerable to undetected overcharges by AECOM Government Services on a $683 million contract. For example, a package of 10 common hardware washers should have cost $1.22 after the allowable markup, but the contractor charged $196.50 for each package.
- The State Bureau for International Narcotics and Law Enforcement Affairs lacked sufficient resources and controls to adequately manage task orders with DynCorp International, LLC, leaving more than $2.5 billion vulnerable to waste and fraud.
- Defense's financial and management controls left it unable to properly account for $8.7 billion of the $9.1 billion in Iraqi DFI funds it received for reconstruction activities. Moreover, the lack of oversight and guidance had contributed to Defense organizations continuing to hold DFI funds long after the end of 2007, when they were to return all unused monies to the Iraqi government.

Inspection Highlight
Basrah Modern Slaughterhouse, Basrah, Iraq
(PA-09-189, 4/27/2010)

In one of its final project assessments, SIGIR inspected the $5.6 million U.S.-funded project to design and build a modern slaughterhouse in Basrah. Inspectors reviewed documentation, interviewed USACE personnel, and performed an expedited on-site inspection. At the time of the site visit, the facility was approximately 45% complete.

SIGIR found that USACE's contract with a local Iraqi company to design and construct the slaughterhouse was so poorly written and confusing that the USACE representatives did not understand the requirements. The completed building was significantly smaller than the contract required, suggesting that the contractor was overpaid. Although reliable supplies of electricity and potable water, as well as means of safely disposing wastewater and blood, are essential to operate a modern slaughterhouse, SIGIR noted that the Basrah facility lacked all three.

New Prosecutors

2010 marked the inception of a major new innovative oversight effort, the SIGIR Prosecutorial Initiative. With concurrence from the Department of Justice, the Inspector General hired three experienced federal prosecutors and detailed them to the Fraud Section of Justice's Criminal Division to handle SIGIR cases. The SIGPRO team worked hand in hand with SIGIR's investigators to ensure that Iraq cases were promptly addressed and resolved. The creation of SIGPRO helped to push prosecutions and convictions up dramatically. By the end of FY 2010, SIGIR investigations had yielded 47 indictments, 37 convictions, and $71.27 million in monetary results.

The End of Inspections

On April 30, 2010, SIGIR closed its Inspections Directorate. During its five-year mission, SIGIR inspectors completed 170 project assessment reports (including 56 reports on sustainment issues) and 96 limited ground surveys. The aerial assessment team continued through FY 2012 in support of SIGIR's audit and investigative teams, providing reports based on satellite imagery.

Applying Hard Lessons for Future SROs

In February 2010, a year after the publication of *Hard Lessons*, SIGIR released its fifth lessons-learned report: *Applying Iraq's Hard Lessons to the Reform of Stabilization and Reconstruction Operations*. In it, SIGIR posited these targeted reforms that could improve the execution of SROs:

1. The National Security Council should lead SRO doctrine and policy development.
2. Integrative SRO planning processes should be developed.
3. New SRO budgeting processes should be developed.
4. Federal personnel laws should be strengthened to support SROs.
5. SRO training should be integrated and enhanced.
6. Uniform contingency contracting practices should be adopted.
7. Permanent oversight for SROs should be created.
8. Uniform SRO information systems should be developed.
9. International organizations should be integrated into SRO planning.
10. Uniform geopolitical boundaries should be implemented.

Most important, SIGIR proposed a new structural solution to address the weaknesses in SRO planning and management: the U.S. Office for Contingency Operations (USOCO).

Drawing on many examples from the first five years of the reconstruction effort in Iraq, SIGIR concluded that the lack of an established SRO management system forced the U.S. government to respond to challenges in Iraq through a series of ad hoc agencies—a virtual adhocracy—that oversaw stabilization and reconstruction activities with, unsurprisingly, generally unsatisfactory outcomes. While State and Defense found many of the specific recommendations SIGIR presented to be useful, neither endorsed USOCO to replace the existing SRO management structure.

FY 2011: Assessing the State-led Program

As FY 2011 opened, CIGIE recognized the oversight work of two of SIGIR's directorates. SIGIR's Inspections Directorate received an award for excellence for its prompt response and resolution of the U.S. Ambassador to Iraq's concern with the lack of progress in the construction of the Missan Surgical Hospital.

CIGIE also presented SIGIR an award for excellence for the Investigations Directorate's work on the Cockerham Task Force. The work of this task force resulted in the indictment of 23 individuals and conviction of 22 of them (with one still at large), monetary penalties of $67.7 million, and the suspension or debarment of 57 companies and individuals as of the end of FY 2013.

OCTOBER 2010–
MARCH 2011

OCTOBER
- CIGIE Award for Excellence in Inspections (Missan Surgical Hospital)

- CIGIE Award for Excellence in Investigations (Cockerham Task Force)

NOVEMBER
- Testimony on proposed Special IG for Contingency Operations (Senate Homeland Security and Governmental Affairs Committee)

MARCH
- Testimony on DoS reconstruction management (House Oversight and Government Reform Committee)

The Investigations team achieved greater monetary results in 2011 than in any previous year, totaling more than $83 million. This included $69 million in criminal and civil penalties levied against Louis Berger Group for inflating invoices relating to work it performed for USAID and Defense. Cumulative monetary results had tripled in two years, reaching almost $155 million by October 2011. The Investigations Directorate also passed a formal peer review with high marks and special commendation of the INTERCEPT, FERRET, and SIGPRO initiatives, which had contributed to SIGIR's cumulative 68 indictments and 58 convictions by the end of the year.

Oversight Concerns as the U.S. Footprint Shrinks

SIGIR's staffing levels continued to drop as the U.S. program in Iraq diminished. By the end of July 2011, 15 personnel remained at the U.S. Embassy in Baghdad, with another 75 working in the United States.

Oversight focused on the status of security support in Iraq as the final withdrawal of all U.S. troops approached. The readiness of Iraq's police to assume responsibility from Iraqi military forces remained a subject of SIGIR's work.

The Congress appropriated an additional $1 billion for the ISFF in FY 2011, which, at $20.194 billion, now rivaled the IRRF. SIGIR auditors found that Defense had used the ISFF to develop a police training force but still did not know its capabilities, a primary concern given that State was preparing to implement an ambitious and potentially expensive Police Development Program by October 2011 as a follow-on to the Defense effort. SIGIR also reviewed the status of Iraq's special forces, finding that they had excellent capabilities developed with a substantial investment from the ISFF.

An audit of the management of private security contractors revealed that, as of the end of July 2011, it had yet to be determined who would be responsible for monitoring PSCs after the departure of the U.S. military. Another audit reported on continuing control weaknesses in the management of the Theater-wide Internal Security Services contract.

In late 2011, SIGIR released an evaluation of the Nassiriya and Ifraz Water Treatment Plants, discussing the project management strengths and weaknesses that led to very different outcomes. The evaluation yielded four recommendations for State and other U.S. government agencies involved in SROs, all dealing with measuring the effectiveness of projects and tying outcomes to U.S. strategic goals.

Oversight Challenges

The departure of the U.S. military from Iraq resulted in several changes that challenged oversight operations. The residual accounting for Defense programs rested with CENTCOM headquarters. As operational units packed up and departed, access to individuals and data for reviews and investigations became more difficult. Defense archived reconstruction data at remote locations. Most personnel who had primary knowledge of programs moved on. Further complicating operations in Iraq, Defense no longer had the capacity to support the movement of civilians to perform oversight; State also lacked that capacity.

Throughout FY 2011, SIGIR reported on a wide range of vulnerabilities in the reconstruction program as State looked to take over for Defense on all fronts. Of greatest concern was the prospect of an exorbitant Police Development Program, which projected significant expenditures for expensive facilities, including an air wing to provide transportation for the program's advisors. When SIGIR raised concerns, it met resistance from State, and working with the department became more difficult.

In testimony before the House Oversight and Government Reform Committee in December 2011, the Inspector General described the arduous process imposed by State that year regarding data requests. It required that all responses to SIGIR's requests—either for the Quarterly Report or for audits—be vetted by State headquarters in Washington, D.C. The Department prohibited direct exchanges between SIGIR and State program managers and Embassy section leaders. The new approval chain added weeks to State's response time on simple matters. The Inspector General also recounted a challenge in a criminal case being investigated jointly by SIGIR and the FBI.

APRIL 2011–
SEPTEMBER 2011

APRIL
• Testimony on improving wartime contracting (Commission on Wartime Contracting)

JULY
563
SIGIR investigations initiated since 2004, yielding:

35
Arrests

64
Indictments

54
Convictions

$153.9M
in court-ordered restitution/forfeiture

Audit Highlight Poor Government Oversight of Anham and Its Subcontracting Procedures Allowed Questionable Costs To Go Undetected (SIGIR 11-022, 7/30/2011)

In September 2007, the Department of Defense (DoD) awarded a $300 million contract to Anham, LLC, to operate and maintain two warehouses and distribution facilities in Iraq. As of June 2011, the contract had incurred obligations of approximately $119.1 million, with Anham subcontractors providing at least $55 million in supplies and services. In its audit of this contract, SIGIR found weak contract oversight practices that left the U.S. government vulnerable to improper overcharges. In four key Anham business systems reviewed, SIGIR found:

- The Defense Contract Audit Agency failed to review Anham's estimating system.
- The Defense Contract Management Agency (DCMA) recommended approval of Anham's purchasing system despite identifying significant gaps in documentation.
- Contracting officer's representatives failed to effectively review invoices.

In conducting a limited review of incurred costs, SIGIR questioned almost 39% of the costs ($4.4 million) reviewed, either because the costs were not properly documented or because they did not appear to be fair and reasonable. For example, an Anham subcontractor charged $900 for a control switch valued at $7.05 and $3,000 for a circuit breaker valued at $94.47. Some of the costs SIGIR questioned resulted from questionable competition practices, inappropriate bundling of subcontractor items, and close working relationships or possible owner affiliations between Anham and certain subcontractors.

OCTOBER 2011–
MARCH 2012

▶ OCTOBER
- CIGIE Award for Excellence for Special Act (Quarterly Report Team)

- CIGIE Award for Excellence—Multiple Disciplines (Schmidt Case)
- SIGIR Issues Its 200th audit

↳ NOVEMBER
- Testimony on DoS Police Development Program (House Foreign Affairs Committee)

↳ DECEMBER
- *Lessons In Inspections of U.S.-funded Stabilization and Reconstruction Projects*
- Testimony on Improving Contingency Oversight (House Oversight and Government Reform Committee)

SIGIR reported that Anham officers held key management positions in five of the six companies awarded subcontracts by Anham worth approximately $55 million. This was a serious concern because prices paid for procurements between affiliated entities must be fair and reasonable and generally may include profit to only one of the entities involved in the transaction. In the transactions reviewed by SIGIR, 39% were characterized by questionable pricing and multiple instances of profit taking as goods and services moved up the chain of these related companies. Anham claimed that only one of the six subcontractors was an affiliate as defined in the Federal Acquisition Regulation (FAR). SIGIR found, however, that all six subcontractors were directly or indirectly owned, wholly or substantially, by one or more of the three family groups (or members of those families) that collectively owned 100% of Anham through subsidiary entities. SIGIR recommended that DCMA—the DoD component charged with monitoring contractors' performance and management systems to ensure that cost, product performance, and delivery schedules are in compliance with the terms and conditions of the contracts—conduct a new review of Anham's purchasing system. DCMA concurred.

Postscript: Whatever Happened to Anham?

In a Comprehensive Contractor Purchasing System Review of Anham dated September 12, 2012, DCMA reported that "there are systemic weaknesses in the contractor's purchasing practices." DCMA concluded that "the contractor fails to meet criteria defining an acceptable purchasing system and the Government is exposed to risk of increased contract cost." DCMA described its findings as "significant deficiencies." As of August 2013, no agency had taken any further action against Anham. As for transactions among affiliates, DCMA reviewed a number of vendors and subcontractors in which Anham had a financial or management interest or relationship, including five of the six subcontractors discussed in SIGIR's audit. Of those five, DCMA accepted Anham's statement that only one of them was an affiliate as defined by the FAR. Without disclosing any independent analysis that DCMA may have done on the issue, DCMA recited Anham's explanation of why it did not consider the other four to be affiliates. Although SIGIR found that all six subcontractors were owned by family groups that owned Anham, DCMA concluded that Anham was not an affiliate of four of those entities. DCMA did not discuss the sixth subcontractor identified by SIGIR as a possible affiliate.

State refused to provide SIGIR's investigator information regarding a potential subject, directing that the investigator use the "audit process" to obtain the information and challenging the SIGIR agent as to whether the information was related to "reconstruction funding," when it clearly was.

Commission on Wartime Contracting Supports SIGIR's Findings

In August 2011, the Commission on Wartime Contracting in Iraq and Afghanistan issued its final report examining the U.S. government's contracting in Iraq and Afghanistan. Drawing on a diverse array of sources, including SIGIR reports and testimony, the CWC estimated that between $31 billion and $60 billion in U.S. taxpayer funds was vulnerable to waste, fraud, and abuse during 10 years of reconstruction work in Afghanistan and Iraq. Among the reasons for these abuses cited by the CWC were poor contract management, inadequate planning, and insufficient government oversight.

The report included more than two-dozen recommendations aimed at reforming the manner in which the U.S. government uses contractors during contingency operations. Several of these suggested changes explicitly echoed recommendations previously made by SIGIR, including establishing a permanent inspector general for contingency operations, developing a deployable cadre of contingency-contracting experts, and improving interagency coordination regarding the use of private security contractors.

APRIL 2012– SEPTEMBER 2012

APRIL
• *Lessons Learned From Investigations*

• *Special Report 1: Leaders' Perceptions of the Commander's Emergency Response Program in Iraq*

JUNE
• *Testimony* on transition from military- to civilian-led reconstruction (House Oversight and Government Reform Committee)

JULY
• *Special Report 2: The Human Toll of Reconstruction or Stabilization During Operation Iraqi Freedom*

FY 2012: The Reconstruction Program Ends

In FY 2012, SIGIR continued to analyze the obligation and expenditure of taxpayer dollars in the five major reconstruction funds and to trace the history of U.S. work by sector through its Quarterly Reports. SIGIR received a second CIGIE award for excellence for its investigative work, and SIGIR's Quarterly Report team received one as well. Total convictions rose to 75, and related monetary results to more than $180 million by October 2012. Additionally, the U.S. Courts of Appeals for the Fourth and Fifth Circuits rendered new legal precedents, which were successfully argued by SIGPRO prosecutors:

- The Wartime Suspension of Limitations Act can suspend the five-year statute of limitations on fraud cases until combat operations cease.
- A foreign national working as a U.S. government employee abroad can be subject to the extraterritorial jurisdiction of the United States and prosecuted for violating U.S. law.

Reconstruction Gives Way to Traditional Assistance

After the last U.S. troops left Iraq on December 19, 2011, the number of ongoing reconstruction projects dwindled. The PRT program had closed during the preceding summer, and the authority to obligate the ISFF expired at the end of FY 2012. New amounts made available to the Foreign Military Financing programs for Iraq would be used to provide continuing support for the Ministries of Defense and Interior. SIGIR Quarterly Reports and audits in FY 2012 analyzed Defense's final spend plan for the ISFF and reported on the unmet capacity-building priorities that would need to be addressed by the Foreign Military Sales and Foreign Military Financing programs. These funds fall under the purview of the Defense and State IGs.

INL's Police Development Program was the last remaining major reconstruction effort. SIGIR's FY 2011 audits had raised several concerns about planning for the program, the rising costs associated with its activities, and the lack of commitment by Ministry of Interior leadership to the program. During their FY 2012 audit of the program, SIGIR auditors met significant resistance, thus warranting a rare letter to the Secretary of State (with copies to several congressional committees) from the Inspector General urging her to break the logjam on SIGIR data requests. Stonewalling soon stopped, and information began to flow, allowing auditors to complete their work. In the audit, SIGIR raised questions about the program's continued viability, endorsing the State decision to reduce its scope and size in the face of weak

MOI support and other problems. In an interview with SIGIR's Deputy Inspector General published in the October 2011 Quarterly Report, the acting Minister of Interior expressed grave doubts about the PDP. This report and SIGIR's audits eventually led to closure of the program by March 2013, saving billions of taxpayer dollars. Had the program continued, SIGIR's analysis estimated that support costs would have comprised 94% of the program's funding in FY 2013, and the cost for each police advisor would have doubled from an already exorbitant $2.1 million to $4.2 million per year.

Audit Highlight
Iraqi Police Development Program: Opportunities for Improved Program Accountability and Budget Transparency (SIGIR 12-006, 10/24/2011)

On October 1, 2011, DoD transferred responsibility for managing the training of Iraqi police to INL. DoS had been planning for the transfer since 2009 and originally envisioned its Police Development Program (PDP) to be a 5-year, multibillion-dollar effort with 350 police advisors—the largest single DoS program worldwide.

SIGIR undertook this audit to determine whether the transfer was supported by sound planning. Initially, the audit was impaired by DoS's lack of cooperation, which resulted in limited access to key officials and documents. After an exchange of letters on this issue, the access problems were mitigated.

The audit found major issues in DoS's planning, raising questions about the PDP's viability:

- DoS had not assessed Iraqi police capabilities and thus had an insufficient basis for developing the detailed program.
- DoS did not have a comprehensive PDP strategic plan that provided specifics on what was to be accomplished, performance milestones, and transparency and accountability for program costs and performance.
- Only a relatively small portion of program funds (about 12%) paid for advising, mentoring, and developing police forces. Most money funded security and life support.
- DoS had not secured written commitment from the GOI regarding either its support for the PDP or its planned financial contributions.

After the issuance of this audit report, DoS wisely reduced the scope and size of the program; the number of in-country advisors was reduced to 36. In October 2012, CIGIE presented SIGIR's Iraq Police Development Program Audit Team with an Award for Excellence in Auditing, citing the team's "exceptional audit work ... that contributed to major changes in the scope of the program and approximately $1.7 billion put to better use."

A Plan for Closure and Transition

Although two of the major funds under SIGIR's purview, the ESF and INCLE, continued to receive new appropriations to fund activities in Iraq in FY 2013, the Inspector General had earlier concluded that the special oversight mission in Iraq was largely complete and that any remaining duties could be transitioned to State and Defense IG offices. Thus, SIGIR and the Office of Management and Budget submitted a proposal to the Congress for SIGIR's drawdown, aiming for a December 2012 closure. The Consolidated Appropriations Act, 2012 (P.L. 112-74), provided $19.5 million for FY 2012 SIGIR operations, but the Congress did not support the proposal for SIGIR's closure in December, instead directing the organization to continue to work into FY 2013.

After further discussions, the Congress determined that SIGIR should conclude its audit work in calendar 2012 and finish its investigative work by the end of FY 2013. Reports released at the close of 2012 provided summary reviews of SIGIR's entire body of audit work on the DFI and of the forensic audit initiative requested by the Congress. SIGIR released another capping report in April—the seventh in its series— *Iraq Reconstruction: Lessons Learned From Investigations.*

A new special-report series presented in-depth studies of issues that no other agency had been able to fully capture:

OCTOBER 2012–
MARCH 2013

OCTOBER
· CIGIE Award for Excellence in Auditing (Iraq Police Development Audit)

· Lessons From Auditing U.S.-funded Stabilization and Reconstruction Activities

JANUARY
· Audits Directorate closes

· Special Report 3: Interagency Rebuilding Efforts in Iraq: A Case Study of the Rusafa Political District

MARCH
· Learning From Iraq

- In April 2012, the first special report, *Leaders' Perceptions of the Commander's Emergency Response Program in Iraq*, presented the results of SIGIR's survey of U.S. military battalion commanders— both Army and Marine Corps—and USACE, USAID, and PRT leaders who nominated, executed, and monitored reconstruction activities funded by the CERP. Among other things, the report examined the extent to which commanders used the CERP, the outcomes commanders tried to achieve, and the measures of effectiveness used to assess projects. It also revealed effective coordination among commanders, their headquarters, and other U.S. government agencies, as well as the severity of fraud and corruption in CERP projects.

- In July 2012, the second special report, *The Human Toll of Reconstruction or Stabilization During Operation Iraqi Freedom*, gathered together all available data regarding casualties sustained in reconstruction-related work during Operation Iraqi Freedom. After consulting with Defense, all the military services, State, USAID, USACE, the Department of Labor, and several insurance carriers and private companies, SIGIR determined that 719 people were killed in connection with reconstruction activities.

- In January 2013, SIGIR's final special report, *Interagency Rebuilding Efforts in Iraq: A Case Study of the Rusafa Political District,* looked at the hundreds of projects accomplished in the Rusafa District in Baghdad. It found that interagency discontinuities prevented program managers from effectively assessing the collective impacts of these projects.

FY 2013: Final Convictions and Closeout

In October 2012, 61 staff remained at SIGIR, including 9 auditors wrapping up SIGIR's final 6 audits. CIGIE recognized their work with an award for excellence for their audit of the Police Development Program. At the end of January 2013, the Audits Directorate closed, releasing its final set of reports. One reviewed the progress achieved by State through its rule-of-law programs in Iraq, while two others recapped lessons learned on Defense's CERP program and on U.S. agency management of Iraqi funds for relief and reconstruction. SIGIR's last audit provided a macroscopic accounting for all U.S. reconstruction projects, detailing weaknesses in data collection and data management that prevented more detailed reviews. SIGIR's audit history yielded numerous best practices, which were conveyed in the eighth report of the lessons-learned series, released in October 2012, entitled *Iraq Reconstruction: Lessons From Auditing U.S.-funded Stabilization and Reconstruction Activities.*

Learning From Iraq

In March 2013, SIGIR released *Learning From Iraq*, its final lessons-learned report, which comprised a complete study of Iraq's reconstruction. The book-length review provided more than a recapitulation of what the reconstruction program accomplished and what SIGIR found in the interstices. It captured the effects of the rebuilding program as derived from 44 interviews with the recipients (the Iraqi leadership), the executors (U.S. senior leaders), and the providers (members of Congress). These interviews offered an instructive picture of what was the largest stabilization and reconstruction operation ever undertaken by the United States (until recently overtaken by Afghanistan).

Learning From Iraq revealed countless details about the use of more than $60 billion in taxpayer dollars and articulated numerous lessons derived from SIGIR's 220 audits and 170 inspections, and listed the varying consequences meted out from the 90 convictions achieved through SIGIR's investigations. It concluded with seven final lessons, the most important of which again urged the Congress to consider the creation of the U.S. Office for Contingency Operations.

The Inspector General appeared before the House Committee on Foreign Affairs on July 9, 2013, to present the findings from *Learning From Iraq*. Further, Representatives Steve Stockman and Peter Welch introduced H.R. 2606, which would create USOCO.

APRIL 2013–
SEPTEMBER 2013

APRIL
· Testimony on
reconstruction
program
failures/proposed
solutions (House
Oversight and
Government Reform
Committee)

JULY
· Testimony on SIGIR's
Learning From Iraq
report (House Foreign
Affairs Committee)

SEPTEMBER
639
SIGIR investigations
initiated, yielding:

42
Arrests

112
Indictments

90
Convictions

$192M
in court-ordered
restitution/forfeiture

Audit Highlight
Government Agencies Cannot Fully Identify Projects Financed
with Iraq Relief and Reconstruction Funds (SIGIR 13-006, 3/6/2013)

In its final audit report, SIGIR reviewed the entire reconstruction program, seeking to construct a picture of how the $51.6 billion appropriated to five major Iraq relief and reconstruction funds was used. But, because of poor data, SIGIR was only able to identify a plurality of the projects paid for with the funds.

SIGIR's effort was limited by several factors:

- In their record keeping, the agencies had no common definition of "project." For example, a single record in a database might represent an entire facility or just one component or phase of the facility.
- The costs reported for individual projects often did not match across databases and internal agency records.
- Data on obligations and expenditures was incomplete. For example, 15% of the IRRF obligations were not accounted for in agency databases—suggesting careless record keeping or possible fraud.

Because of these deficiencies, the disposition of billions of dollars for projects remains unknown because the U.S. government agencies involved in the relief and reconstruction effort did not maintain project information in any uniform or comprehensive manner. The audit concluded that a full accounting, if even possible, would require combing through mountains of disordered electronic and paper records accumulated since 2003 that are currently stored in multiple locations across many agencies. The audit estimated that at least $8 billion in U.S. funds was wasted in Iraq.

SIGIR's LEGACY

The Iraq rebuilding mission pushed oversight of reconstruction and stabilization operations into new territory. The nine-year relief and reconstruction program, the second-largest in U.S. history (as measured by taxpayer dollars expended), took place in a frequently perilous environment. It demanded a strengthening of traditional methods for auditing and investigating programs and projects. The entire oversight experience points to a single key lesson: the need for reform of the U.S. approach to SROs.

Early in the program, the Congress recognized the need for an independent inspector general with cross-cutting jurisdictional authority. In November 2003, it acted to create such: the CPA-IG came into statutory existence, and the new inspector general was appointed in late January 2004.

Audit by audit, inspection by inspection, Quarterly Report by Quarterly Report, SIGIR documented the full Iraq reconstruction story, providing on-site oversight every step of the way. Through thousands of pages of published work, the organization provided the Congress, the agencies, the taxpayers, and the Iraqis with insights into an overseas operation of enormous import. The agency's high productivity was rooted in the strong work ethic of SIGIR's auditors, inspectors, investigators, and prosecutors, supported by innovative leadership, special legislative authorities, and an unwavering dedication to achieving the mission.

The Audits Directorate produced 220 reports in nine years with a staff that never exceeded 42 auditors. This voluminous output yielded $1.6 billion in financial benefits: $973 million in funds put to better use and $640 million in questioned costs.

SIGIR issued most of its audits in less than 120 days from the initiation of work to the publication of final report. The Audits Directorate performed its work in accordance with U.S. generally accepted government auditing standards.

The Inspections Directorate issued 170 project assessments through a unique blend of engineering and audit talent. Inspection teams operated at a high production rate, traveling across Iraq during the most dangerous periods of the reconstruction operation to provide on-site project assessments. Innovative practices, such as the use of satellite imagery, allowed SIGIR to advance and strengthen accountability. The directorate averaged more than eight reports a quarter.

The Investigations Directorate initiated 639 investigations that, with the support of SIGIR's prosecutors, led to 112 indictments, 90 convictions, and more than $192 million in monetary results. Innovative ideas—including the FERRET program, which used special electronic means to identify criminal activity, and the SIGPRO initiative, which placed SIGIRpaid prosecutors at the Department of Justice to work SIGIR cases—helped drive good outcomes.

SIGIR's success stemmed from a collective commitment to its core values: professionalism, productivity, and perseverance. These values infused a unifying effort to realize the organization's vision—to be the best IG office possible—and to meet the mission—to provide transparency and accountability for $60 billion in taxpayer dollars. The organization's functional polestars were to "always improve" and to ensure that every report was better than the last.

The capacity to succeed depended on support from the Congress and the Departments of State and Defense. Capitol Hill was generous in its interest in and provision for SIGIR, requesting testimony 37 times over 9 years and consistently meeting appropriations requests. Cooperation from State and Defense, which SIGIR received most of the time, was also key to mission accomplishment. Success resulted from flexibilities conferred by SIGIR's authorizing legislation and a culture of innovation.

The agency benefited from flexible hiring standards and, in general, bore fewer restrictions on its operations than permanent IG organizations.

SIGIR's Strategies for Success

Several important strategies contributed to SIGIR's success:

Flexible Hiring

The SIGIR team's overall professional experience level contributed greatly to its capacity to produce high-quality work. SIGIR was authorized to exercise a special employment provision (5 USC 3161) that allowed the hiring of personnel without the constraints most agencies bear. This authority permitted three benefits:

- the rapid hiring of experienced staff to meet exigent objectives
- the ability to require deployment to Iraq as a condition of employment
- limited appointment periods

Importantly, SIGIR could hire government annuitants (retirees) who possessed substantial experience in audits or investigations and still allow them to collect their pensions. This permitted the securing of a highly competent staff in very short order. SIGIR's auditors had an average of 24 years experience; its investigators, about the same.

Proactive Approaches

The Inspector General set a standard of productivity that aimed to supply reconstruction managers with a bounty of audits as fast as possible. This stemmed from a recognition that these reports provided intelligence on what was actually occurring in the field, which amounted to guidance on how to improve the rebuilding mission. The Inspector General emphasized that oversight had a consultative component that, when prudently exercised, could further the mission's ultimate success. This approach enabled SIGIR to earn the trust of State and Defense senior leaders, which opened doors to program improvements.

Rapid Audit Reporting

The uncertain duration of the Iraq war drove an early management decision to aim for near-realtime reporting. This led to a production rate of six audits per quarter, with audits published usually within 120 days of announcement.

Producing highly technical reports in so tight a time span required special provisions:

- careful scoping to ensure rapid production
- constant monitoring to ensure audits stayed on schedule
- senior audit managers closely overseeing every audit

Auditors constantly pushed to get critical issues before agency management. SIGIR recognized that, in an environment in which tens of millions of dollars were being spent every day, the importance of providing accurate and usable information rapidly to reconstruction managers required good scoping, careful monitoring, and senior-level attention. The Inspector General monitored audit production weekly to ensure that goals were met. Further, he took the initiative to inform agency leadership if problems arose that required rapid attention.

Innovative Inspections

In an unprecedented innovation, SIGIR created auditor-engineer inspection teams that conducted hundreds of inspections at reconstruction sites all across Iraq. The resulting body of 170 reports proved instrumental in producing better quality-assurance programs, improved quality-control programs, and stronger program-management practices across the board. The use of engineers on an inspection team proved salutary, leading to the discovery and repair of numerous project defects, some during the course of the inspection visit. This produced immeasurable savings and better outcomes.

Other innovations included the use of Iraqi engineers to conduct on-site inspections in dangerous locations. The use of satellite imagery to produce aerial assessment reports allowed the preliminary inspection of sites too dangerous to visit.

Data Mining to Detect Crime

In 2009, DCIS and SIGIR began collaborating with the Department of the Treasury's Financial Crimes Enforcement Network (FinCEN) to access information on financial transactions from Iraq. This process revealed more than 110 instances of apparent abuse in Iraq reconstruction contracting. In 2010, the FERRET program combined traditional investigative and audit techniques with sophisticated data analysis to identify irregular financial activity related to persons involved in Iraq's reconstruction. This innovative approach yielded 21 indictments and 20 convictions in the four years it operated.

Cooperation and Coordination

SIGIR's productive relationships with counterpart law-enforcement agencies were key to the investigative program's success. Agents collaborated with many federal investigative entities, but especially Army CID-MPFU and DCIS. Additional working relationships with foreign investigative organizations led to the filing of charges against citizens in South Korea, the United Kingdom, and Iraq for crimes involving U.S. funds.

SIGIR agents teamed with investigative counterparts to manage the FERRET initiative and cooperated with the Department of Justice to create the SIGPRO initiative. FERRET tracked illicit funds coming out of Iraq, yielding numerous cases. SIGPRO allowed SIGIR to fund its attorneys and place them within the Department of Justice's Fraud Section, which expedited prosecution. In its first year of operation, SIGPRO contributed to a 90% increase in the number of indictments and convictions from the previous year. The International Contract Corruption Task Force was established for Iraq and Kuwait cases, and it subsequently was expanded to include Afghanistan. When SIGPRO came into being, the ICCTF successfully utilized it as a resource for prosecuting cases arising in Iraq.

The Iraq Inspectors General Council and the Iraq Accountability Working Group exemplified effective teaming with other agencies to improve oversight. The IIGC served for seven years as the key forum for formal coordination among all of the oversight entities operating in Iraq. As SIGIR began to wind down, the work of the IIGC was transitioned to the Southwest Asia Joint Planning Group, led by the Defense IG, to ensure integrated oversight planning continued.

Data Collection

No agency developed a reliable centralized data system for tracking projects in Iraq. This left significant gaps regarding oversight of funds. SIGIR's ability to meet its mandate for reporting on projects varied by appropriated fund, but there was generally poor data with which to work.

In the face of these data limitations, SIGIR developed and maintained its own integrated database on the use of reconstruction funds. Because of the questionable quality, accuracy, and completeness of the project records feeding this database, the agency often had to make judgments when assigning costs to programs and projects.

In the end, the data SIGIR amassed and analyzed helped to put the entire reconstruction effort in context, providing the status of programs and their effects. The nine-year effort to collect and organize this data may constitute the most complete gathering of information on the Iraq reconstruction and stabilization effort for posterity's use. It is certainly more complete than the IRMS, the ostensible uniform database. SIGIR audits found that the IRMS captured about 70% of all project data for Iraq.

Lessons Learned

Publishing nine major reports, SIGIR's Lessons Learned Initiative highlighted the many challenges in staffing, contracting, and managing SROs and provided solutions for advancing the likelihood of future success. SIGIR provided regular testimony to the Congress on the Iraq reconstruction program, addressing the findings arising from its lessons-learned work. The Inspector General or other senior officials testified 37 times before 12 House or Senate committees and 3 times before the Commission on Wartime Contracting to communicate promptly the challenges facing the reconstruction program and to promote recommendations for improved performance both in the Iraq theater and in future contingency operations.

Effects of SIGIR Oversight

SIGIR Audits

SIGIR's audit staff was relatively small, yet highly productive, providing meaningful contributions to U.S. reconstruction policies and programs:

- A 2006 report found that the award-fee process for cost-plus contracts was not being properly managed and that there were not adequate criteria in place for the implementation of award fees. In response, the managing agency quickly reformed the process so that only documented performance exceeding expectations would be rewarded.
- After SIGIR issued three reports in 2006 finding that U.S. agencies had no policies in place to ensure the Iraqi ministries would accept responsibility for sustaining completed U.S.-funded projects, the Congress called for agencies to certify that they had secured Iraqi commitments to maintain the transferred assets.
- A January 2008 SIGIR report showing that commanders were spending an increasing amount of CERP funds on very large projects caused the Congress to respond. For example, the National Defense Authorization Act for FY 2009 set a limit of $2 million for any CERP project in Iraq.
- In 2012, SIGIR issued two reports on the Iraqi Police Development Program. State originally envisioned a five-year multibillion-dollar program involving 350 mentors and advisors. SIGIR found numerous problems with State's plans, including that it did not have a current assessment of the Iraqi police force's capabilities or a comprehensive plan with specifics on what was to be accomplished. It also had no buy-in from the Iraqi government. During FY 2009–FY 2012, State reduced the size of the program from 350 trainers to 36 because of the Ministry of Interior's lack of interest and because of security concerns. This resulted in a decrease in estimated FY 2012 costs from an initial $500 million to $76.3 million. Program reductions did not occur, however, until after State had already spent $206 million constructing training facilities that will not be used by the program.

SIGIR Summary of Performance
As of August 31, 2013

Audits	Cumulative
Reports Issued	220
Recommendations Issued	487
Potential Savings if Agencies Implement SIGIR Recommendations To:	
Put Funds to Better Use ($ Millions)	$973.62
Disallow Costs SIGIR Questioned ($ Millions)	$640.68
Inspections	
Project Assessments Issued	170
Limited On-site Assessments Issued	96
Aerial Assessments	923
Investigations	
Investigations Initiated	639
Investigations Closed or Referred	639
Open (Active) Investigations	-
Arrests	42
Indictments	112
Convictions	90
Sentencings	76
Monetary Results ($ Millions)	$192.6
Hotline Contacts	
Email	413
Fax	19
Mail	30
Referrals	26
SIGIR Website	200
Telephone	84
Walk-in	112
Total Hotline Contacts	884
Other Products	
Congressional Testimony	37
Lessons Learned Reports	9
Special Reports	3
Evaluation Reports	1
Quarterly Reports	37

SIGIR Inspections

The relationships forged by the SIGIR Inspections Directorate with Defense Department personnel epitomized a productive civil-military partnership. Defense transport capacity made possible SIGIR's on-site inspection program, and, through the employment of satellite imagery and local Iraqi contractors, SIGIR's reach extended anywhere in Iraq—at any time. Audit and engineering teams worked together to establish a model for operations that accomplished several outcomes:

- early identification of deficiencies in meeting contractual specifications that stemmed from, among other things, inadequately trained personnel, inferior materials, and lack of oversight on the part of the contractor or the government
- opportunities to take corrective action prior to completing projects to improve design, construction, quality assurance, and probability of sustainment once projects were transferred to Iraqi control
- identifying and forwarding to-investigators indications of potential fraud

SIGIR Investigations and Prosecutions

Although some of the criminal investigations coming out of the reconstruction effort involved very large sums of money, many did not. But catching and deterring wrongdoers of any stripe had larger strategic implications. Each conviction sent a message to the Iraqis that the United States was serious about addressing corruption. This engendered trust and promoted good will with the host-nation's leadership. SIGIR's aggressive investigative teams across the United States and Iraq, supported by a highly productive prosecutorial team, rooted out a lot of wrongdoing:

- employing the latest technical forensic techniques available
- working independently or hand in hand with other law-enforcement agencies
- providing prosecutorial support to their colleagues in Justice's Fraud Section and at several U.S. Attorney's offices around the country
- arguing appellate cases that resulted in the suspension of the statute of limitations during the pendency of war and making foreign nationals working as U.S. government employees outside of the United States subject to the extraterritorial jurisdiction of the United States. (See Section 3 of this report for the details of both cases: *U.S. v. Pfluger* and *U.S. v. Ayesh.*)

Investigations still open when SIGIR terminates in late September 2013 will be transferred to other federal law-enforcement agencies. These cases will continue to produce indictments, convictions, and monetary recoveries in addition to those already achieved by SIGIR.

SIGIR Lessons-learned Reports

SIGIR published nine reports in its lessons-learned series. They underscored the views of those involved in the relief and rebuilding effort and recapped the findings of SIGIR's audits, inspections, and investigations. In addition to informing and broadening the conversation of SROs, these reports prompted lasting change in the programs and operations of U.S. agencies in Iraq, in Afghanistan, and for future operations. For example:

- Personnel practices in Iraq changed after SIGIR's January 2006 report on human-capital management. Changes included improved management of tour lengths and better handoffs between transitioning personnel to avoid loss of institutional memory. The need for developing a "civilian reserve corps" recommended in that report received support in the agencies and from the Congress.
- SIGIR's July 2006 contracting report exposed Defense's weak contingency contracting resources, practices, and procedures, and the Congress responded in these ways: (1) The John Warner National Defense Authorization Act for 2007 required Defense to develop policies and procedures that defined contingency contracting requirements, identified a deployable cadre of contracting experts, and provided training in contingency contracting; (2) the Congress required contracting training for personnel outside the acquisition workforce because of the broad reach of contracting activities in Iraq (particularly regarding the CERP); and (3) the Accountability in Government Contracting Act of 2007 strengthened the federal acquisition workforce by establishing a contingency contracting corps and providing specific guidance to encourage accountability and limit fraud, waste, and abuse.
- SIGIR's March 2007 report on program and project management helped in the development of an updated Emergency Acquisitions Guide issued by OMB's Office of Federal Procurement Policy. The guide included a number of best practices that agencies should consider when planning for contingency operations.
- SIGIR's February 2009 *Hard Lessons: The Iraq Reconstruction Experience* provided a detailed primary-sourced narrative and analysis of the U.S. reconstruction program, presenting 13 lessons applicable

to SROs. After reviewing *Hard Lessons*, General David Petraeus concluded that the U.S. Central Command would apply 9 of the 13 lessons in Afghanistan.

- Building on *Hard Lessons,* SIGIR issued its fifth lessons-learned report in February 2010, *Applying Iraq's Hard Lessons to the Reform of Stabilization and Reconstruction Operations*. This study proposed an innovative solution to the question of who should be accountable for planning and executing SROs.

- *Learning From Iraq,* SIGIR's final report issued in March 2013, led to the introduction of H.R. 2606, which would establish a single office for the planning, execution, and oversight of SROs. The House Foreign Affairs Committee's Subcommittee on the Middle East and North Africa conducted a hearing on the report, at which the USOCO concept received a favorable reception.

SIGIR Lessons Learned

- **Find good leaders.** Oversight leadership in a war zone requires certain character. The most important trait is a reasonable ease with working in unstable, fluid environments. Several of SIGIR's successful leaders in Iraq had prior Vietnam experience. This background may account for their capacity to function well in a very dangerous Iraq.
- **Operate transparently**. SIGIR was perhaps the most transparent audit entity in Iraq. It published a weekly report to State and Defense documenting ongoing jobs and providing information on progress. This kept departmental leadership informed and prevented surprises.
- **Resolve audit and inspection findings before publication.** The Inspector General directed his audit leadership to begin working with agencies
- on resolving findings immediately upon their discovery. "Gotcha" is always a bad game to play in a conflict zone. The best report is one that indicates that all findings were resolved before publication.
- **Engage with host-country leadership.** Sometimes the best information for SIGIR reports came from Iraqi officials. Access to this information stemmed from relationships that were built over time. Early and ongoing engagement with host-nation officials is crucial and can lead to important information.

- **Start deterrent initiatives early.** A pouncing effect early on provides the best deterrence. Many of SIGIR's early cases lacked the benefit of an experienced or focused prosecutor. Ensuring effective early prosecutions will deter potential criminals.
- **Employ personnel with expertise in contingency operations.** Reach out to professional engineering organizations to hire inspectors, reach out to Assistant U.S. Attorneys' offices to hire prosecutors, and reach out to law-enforcement circles to find investigators with the needed specialized skills and good connections. The importance of hiring bilingual cultural advisors with links to the host country is critical. Many doors opened for SIGIR once these professionals were incorporated into the office.
- **Rotate personnel to maintain productivity.** An Inspector General needs to have an aggressive in-country presence to promote performance. But life in a conflict zone can be exhausting. Rotating personnel in and out can obviate loss of productivity due to exhaustion.

Impact of Quarterly Reports

Aggressive timelines, highly refined data collection, and sophisticated analytical methods allowed SIGIR to produce comprehensive reviews of the entire Iraq reconstruction program through its Quarterly and Semiannual Reports to the Congress. Most of these reports were over 200 pages in length, containing in-depth analysis performed on a mountain of gathered data. The reports were all posted on the SIGIR website in Arabic and English and have been widely relied upon by civilian and military managers and leaders, as well as the Congress, academic institutions, the general public, and the Iraqi government.

Among other things, the Quarterly Reports provided:

- summaries of all audit and inspection findings
- lists of criminal convictions and sentencing information, as well as all suspensions and debarments arising from criminal investigations associated with Iraq
- coverage of all congressional activity related to SIGIR
- detailed analyses of particular subjects critical to the understanding of Iraq's reconstruction
- observations from the Inspector General of the most important issues in Iraq

- a comprehensive list of Iraq reconstruction contracts from FY 2004 through FY 2012
- a listing of the report work of other U.S. oversight agencies on Iraq reconstruction

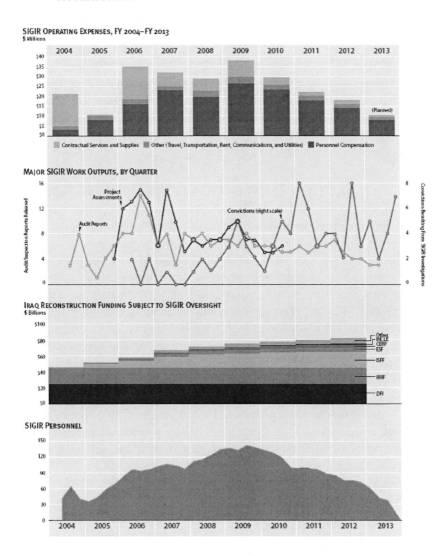

SIGIR OPERATING EXPENSES, FY 2004–FY 2013
$ Millions

Contractual Services and Supplies ■ Other (Travel, Transportation, Rent, Communications, and Utilities) ■ Personnel Compensation

MAJOR SIGIR WORK OUTPUTS, BY QUARTER

IRAQ RECONSTRUCTION FUNDING SUBJECT TO SIGIR OVERSIGHT
$ Billions

SIGIR PERSONNEL

Conclusion

One lesson from the SIGIR experience stands above all others: Oversight matters.

In 2003, the Congress spotted the oversight shortfall in Iraq and acted to rectify it. The vehicle it created, like so much in Iraq, was novel: the CPA-IG. The mission it took on in 2004 had no precedent. It continued under the aegis of SIGIR through 2013.

Ten years ago, there was no manual for a war-zone watchdog. Now there is. It has been written in the blood, sweat, and tears shed by the SIGIR personnel who strived to meet our mission in Iraq with bravery, commitment, and success. Their collective success is SIGIR's legacy.

SECTION 2. INVESTIGATIONS UPDATE

Investigative Accomplishments

Throughout the summer of 2013, the Investigations Directorate pursued allegations of fraud, waste, and abuse in the Iraq reconstruction program. During this reporting period, SIGIR had 10 investigators in offices in Pennsylvania, Florida, Texas, Oklahoma, and California; 5 investigative personnel at SIGIR headquarters in Arlington, Virginia; and 1 investigator in Baghdad. As of August 31, 2013, the work of SIGIR investigators had produced 112 indictments, 90 convictions, 76 sentencings, and more than $192 million in fines, forfeitures, recoveries, restitution, and other monetary results (see Figure 2.1).

As SIGIR moved toward closure, 14 defendants in SIGIR cases awaited trial, and an additional 15 convicted individuals awaited sentencing. At least 20 investigations were ongoing where charges had not yet been filed or prosecutorial decisions had not been made. These cases will be transferred to the agencies with which SIGIR partnered over the years.

The successful conclusion of these cases potentially could achieve an additional 30 indictments, 44 convictions, and more than $100 million in monetary results, which would bring the total number of indictments to as many as 142, total convictions to as many as 134, and total monetary recoveries to about $300 million.

For SIGIR convictions, by affiliation of wrongdoer at the time of criminal activity, see Figure 2.2. For the monetary results of SIGIR investigations, by affiliation of wrongdoer, see Figure 2.3.

The work of SIGIR investigators also led to 106 contractor suspensions, 184 proposals for debarment, and 139 debarments.

For a comprehensive list of convictions compiled by the Department of Justice (DoJ), see Table 2.5 at the end of this section.

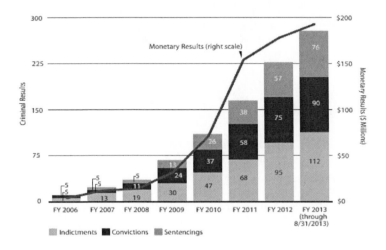

Figure 2.1. SIGIR Investigations Criminal and Monetary Results, Cumulative to Date, by Fiscal Year.

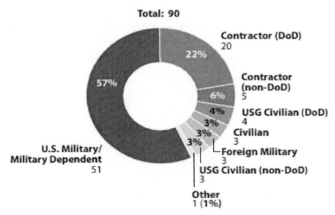

Note: Percentages a_ected by rounding.

Figure 2.2. SIGIR Convictions, by Affiliation of Wrongdoer, as of 8/31/2013.

$ Millions

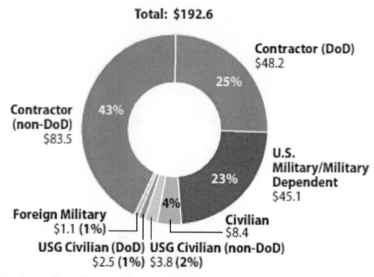

Note: Numbers affected by rounding.

Figure 2.3. SIGIR Investigations Monetary Results, by Affiliation of Wrongdoer, as of 8/31/2013.

Activity during This Reporting Period

Investigative accomplishments since SIGIR's April 2013 Quarterly Report include 7 indictments, 7 convictions, 4 sentencings, and more than $540,000 in fines, recoveries, restitution, forfeitures, and other monetary results (see Tables 2.1 and 2.2). During this period, SIGIR's investigative work led to 1 suspension from government contracting, 17 proposals for debarment, and 24 debarments.

Convictions
Seven convictions occurred this reporting period, with one of the individuals convicted also sentenced.

Former U.S. Army Warrant Officer Pleads Guilty to and Sentenced for Conspiracy to Supplement Salary
On May 16, 2013, Shawn Lueders, a former chief warrant officer in the U.S. Army, pled guilty to a one-count criminal information charging him with

conspiring to illegally supplement his salary as a government employee. He was sentenced on July 11, 2013, to three years of probation and ordered to pay a $1,000 fine and a $100 special assessment.

In January 2008, while stationed at Camp Victory in Baghdad, Lueders sought to enrich himself by entering into a scheme involving a government contractor that provided parts and repair services at the base's transportation motor pool. When the company needed parts, it would inform Lueders, who then purchased the parts himself and resold them to the company at a profit.

Lueders continued to supply parts to the company after departing Iraq in April 2008 and returning to Fort Hood, Texas. From January to July 2008, he received almost $50,000 in payments from various co-conspirators in exchange for his services.

According to Lueders' plea agreement, the conspiracy included the owner and four employees of the company, as well as the U.S. government contracting officer's representative for the contract.

This case was prosecuted by the U.S. Attorney's Office for the Western District of Texas.

Former U.S. Army Officer Pleads Guilty to Failing to Report Foreign Bank Account

On June 5, 2013, Azubuike Ukabam, a former U.S. Army captain, pled guilty to willfully failing to notify the Internal Revenue Service (IRS) that he had a financial interest exceeding $10,000 in a foreign bank account.

While serving at Forward Operating Base (FOB) Justice in 2007, Ukabam was a pay agent responsible for receiving and processing invoices from Iraqi contractors who performed work for the Army. Ukabam altered invoices or caused them to be altered so that they showed incorrect or inflated amounts due. He then paid the contractor the original invoice amount and kept the difference—approximately $110,000—for himself.

In November 2007, Ukabam was redeployed to Germany, where he opened at least two bank accounts, made cash deposits, and then had funds sent via wire transfer to another of his accounts in the United States. The investigation identified approximately $60,000 in cash deposits or wire transfers from two of Ukabam's accounts in Germany to his account in the United States from November 2007 to December 2008.

Table 2.1. Legal Actions in Cases Investigated by Sigir and Partner Agencies, 5/1/2013–8/31/2013

ACTION	NAME	CRIMES	DATE	INVESTIGATING AGENCIES						
				SIGIR	DCIS	NCIS	ARMY CID-MPFU	FBI	IRS-CI	DCAA
Sentencing	Ulysses Hicks	Conspiracy to accept illegal gratuities	5/29/2013	x	x		x			
	Shawn Lueders	Conspiracy to supplement salary of government employee	7/11/2013	x	x		x			
	Ramy Elmery	Making false statements	7/12/2013	x	x		x	x		
	Richard Gilliland	Bribery	8/19/2013	x						
Conviction	Shawn Lueders	Conspiracy to supplement salary of government employee	5/16/2013	x	x		x			
	Azubuike Ukabam	Failure to file foreign bank account report	6/5/2013	x	x		x			
	Timothy Benton	Accepting a gratuity for performing an official act while on active duty	6/6/2013	x	x		x			
	Bradley Christiansen	Conspiracy (kickbacks)	7/2/2013	x	x			x	x	x
	Mario Khalil	Giving illegal gratuities	7/9/2013	x						
	Edward Knotts	Bribery	7/10/2013	x	x		x			
	Harold Broeck	Conflict of interest	7/23/2013	x	x			x		
Indictment	Shawn Lueders	Conspiracy to supplement salary of government employee	4/18/2013	x	x		x			
	Timothy Benton	Accepting a gratuity for performing an official act while on active duty	4/23/2013	x	x		x			
	USA Sergeant	Bribery	6/5/2013	x			x	x		
	Mario Khalil	Giving illegal gratuities	6/18/2013	x						
	Eric Schmidt	Making a false statement	7/5/2013	x	x	x				
	Edward Knotts	Bribery	7/10/2013	x	x					
	Harold Broeck	Conflict of interest	7/19/2013	x	x		x	x		

Table 2.2. Sentences and Settlements Imposed in Cases Investigated by Sigir, 5/1/2013–8/31/2013

NAME	TIME	MONETARY ($)				
		FINE	RESTITUTION	FORFEITURE	SPECIAL ASSESSMENT	TOTAL
Ulysses Hicks	5 years probation	5,000	65,409		100	70,509
Shawn Lueders	3 years probation	1,000			100	1,100
Ramy Elmery	30 days in prison, 3 years supervised release, 50 hours community service	20,000			100	20,100
Richard Gilliland	5 months in prison followed by 3 years supervised release	27,200			100	27,300
Edward Knotts*				91,500		91,500
Sentencing Total		53,200	65,409	91,500	400	210,509
Civilian Settlement						331,378
Grand Total						541,887

*Although Knotts was not scheduled to be sentenced until October 8, 2013, the court ordered a forfeiture on July 10, 2013.

Marine Corps Master Sergeant Indicted and Pleads Guilty to Accepting Gratuity

On June 6, 2013, Timothy Benton, a master gunnery sergeant in the U.S. Marine Corps, pled guilty to accepting a gratuity for performing an official act while on active duty. He had been indicted on April 23, 2013.

From June 2007 to December 2008, Benton served as deputy chief of staff for his Marine Corps unit in Iraq. In addition to having direct knowledge of the process used by his unit to make cash purchases from government contractors, he had a romantic and financial relationship with the owner of a Florida-based company that was doing business with the military in Baghdad. In his plea agreement, Benton admitted that he:

- escorted this contractor's trucks (some loaded with furniture, others with gravel) on numerous occasions in 2008 through Camp Liberty in exchange for cash payments totaling between $2,500 and $3,000
- issued government purchase orders to the contractor, including orders for two televisions costing a total of $6,400 and for 100 video cables totaling $5,500
- designed military-style notebooks, called "sand books," and sold them for a profit through the contractor's store located on Camp Victory

After returning to the United States in December 2008, Benton continued his romantic relationship with the company's owner. In mid-2009, they went together to the Bahamas on a vacation paid for with company funds, and, later that year, the owner gave Benton a $5,000 interest-free loan, which he paid back in full.

Early in 2010, Benton used his position at the Pentagon to draft two official memorandums on Marine Corps letterhead that sponsored and endorsed the company and its owner to conduct business at Camp Victory. He also drafted an official email requesting information about the Defense Finance Accounting Service's payment process relative to the company and its owner.

Benton was scheduled to be sentenced on September 4, 2013, and faced a maximum of two years in prison and a fine of $250,000.

Former Officer of Defense Contractor Pleads Guilty to Conspiracy, Kickbacks, and Tax Evasion

On July 2, 2013, Bradley Christiansen, a former officer of Laguna Construction Company, Inc. (LCC), pled guilty to criminal charges arising from his role in a kickback scheme, as well as his efforts to evade federal taxes on the money and assets he received in kickbacks.

Christiansen's conviction was the first to result from a 91-count indictment that a federal grand jury returned on February 28, 2012. That indictment also charged seven other individuals for their alleged roles in the fraud and money-laundering scheme: two other former LCC officers, Neal Kasper and Tiffany White; Christiansen's wife, Sara; and four foreign nationals.

LCC was a minority disadvantaged business wholly owned by the Pueblo of Laguna in New Mexico. Early in the Iraq rebuilding program, the United States Air Force Center for Engineering and the Environment awarded LCC two prime contracts for reconstruction projects. From 2003 through 2009, LCC received and administered almost $400 million for these projects, which included repairing defective work at the Baghdad Police College and renovating the Ministry of Defense headquarters.

In his plea agreement, Christian admitted that he, Kasper, White, and others submitted invoices under false pretenses. Although they repeatedly certified to the U.S. government that all subcontracts were awarded pursuant to competitive bidding procedures, Christiansen acknowledged that they, in fact, were accepting kickbacks from the foreign companies in return for awarding them the subcontracts. He admitted accepting numerous kickbacks from four foreign nationals and asserted that he had personal knowledge of Kasper accepting numerous kickbacks from the foreign nationals and directing them to send money to White, who worked as the contract compliance manager out of LCC's San Antonio office.

Christiansen received almost $819,000 from foreign contractors: approximately $360,000 in monetary kickbacks, a 2006 Porsche Cayenne valued at $65,163, a Ford GT350 Shelby valued at $290,000, and several watches collectively worth $103,800. Christiansen admitted that he willfully failed to declare the kickback payments and assets he received from the foreign nationals as personal income when filing his federal income tax returns in 2006, 2007, and 2008. As a result, he evaded approximately $389,413 in federal taxes.

At sentencing, Christiansen faces a maximum penalty of 10 years in prison. The plea agreement requires Christiansen to pay full restitution to the victims of his criminal conduct, including $389,413 in restitution to the IRS. It also requires that Christiansen agree to the imposition of a money judgment against him in the amount of $1,687,310.84 and that he forfeit all assets derived from his criminal conduct, including his residence, which was substantially remodeled with kickbacks from the foreign nationals.

Kasper and White had been scheduled for trial on October 7, 2013. However, the U.S. District Court, Albuquerque, New Mexico, issued an order on August 23, 2013, vacating the trial because of the complexity of the case and an impending superseding indictment of Kasper, White, and three of the four foreign nationals. On August 27, the grand jury issued the superseding indictment, which incorporated additional information about the kickback scheme, including information obtained from Christiansen's plea agreement and subsequent guilty plea.

The foreign nationals have not been arrested and are considered fugitives. Christiansen's wife was indicted for money laundering, but the United States filed a motion to dismiss all charges against her as required by his plea agreement, which was so ordered by the court on July 9, 2013.

On July 30, 2011, the shareholders of LCC voted to "completely and permanently cease doing business and dissolve once [LCC] has completed existing projects and taken all actions necessary for the winding up of the Company, including but not limited to the collection of outstanding amounts due to it, and resolution of its legal and auditing issues with the federal government."

This case is being prosecuted by the U.S. Attorney's Office for the District of New Mexico.

Business Manager for Iraqi Company Pleads Guilty to Illegal Gratuities Scheme

On July 9, 2013, Mario Khalil, a U.S. citizen who had been employed by an Iraqi company, pled guilty to giving thousands of dollars in illegal gratuities to a U.S. Army pay agent in Iraq.

From 2007 to 2009, Khalil worked at Camp Liberty as the business manager for Golden Company, an Iraqi firm that had several contracts with the U.S. military to provide logistical services and supplies. Seeking to obtain more business for his company, as well as to acquire used and non-working generators from the Defense Reutilization and Marketing Office, Khalil gave $10,000 in cash and a laptop computer to U.S. Army Sergeant Richard Gilliland, who at the time was a pay agent in the Civil Affairs Unit at Camp Victory.

Khalil is scheduled to be sentenced on October 3 and faces up to two years in prison and a $250,000 fine. For his role in the bribery scheme, Gilliland was sentenced on August 19, 2013. His sentencing is discussed later in this section.

The Khalil case was prosecuted by two SIGIR Prosecutorial Initiative (SIGPRO) attorneys on detail to the Fraud Section of DoJ's Criminal Division and the U.S. Attorney's Office for the Southern District of Texas. One of the SIGPRO attorneys is now DoJ's Director of Procurement Fraud Litigation.

Former U.S. Army Reserve Captain Pleads Guilty to Bribery Scheme
On July 10, 2013, Edward Knotts, a former U.S. Army Reserve captain, pled guilty to accepting more than $90,000 in bribes from contractors while he was deployed to Iraq.

From December 2005 until December 2007, Knotts was stationed at Camp Buehring, Kuwait, as a contracting officer's representative for contracts between the U.S. Army and local contractors to provide services to support the operations at Camp Buehring and another U.S. facility in Kuwait.

In November 2006, Knotts entered into an agreement to receive a monthly fee from a Kuwait-based corporation in return for providing confidential bidding information about U.S. Army contracts. Between November 2006 and November 2007, the corporation paid him approximately $31,500 in cash. Also during this period, a representative of the corporation paid Knotts $40,000 at a hotel in Las Vegas in return for his promise to provide confidential bid information and in anticipation of the corporation hiring him. In August 2008, Knotts accepted another cash payment of $20,000 at a different Las Vegas hotel.

Knotts faces a maximum penalty of 15 years in prison when he is sentenced on October 8, 2013. On the date of his guilty plea, the court ordered Knotts to forfeit $91,500.

This case is being prosecuted by a SIGPRO attorney (now DoJ's Director of Procurement Fraud Litigation) and a trial attorney in the Fraud Section of DoJ's Criminal Division.

Retired U.S. Army Lieutenant Colonel Pleads Guilty to Conflict of Interest in Contracting Scheme
On July 23, 2013, retired U.S. Army Lieutenant Colonel Harold Broeck pled guilty to a criminal information charging him with one count of conflict of interest. He was charged on July 19, 2013.

In 2007, while serving as the Chief of Contracting at the Tikrit Regional Contracting Center at FOB Camp Speicher, Broeck developed a friendly relationship with Rohit Goel, the principal of Avalon International Limited, a company doing business with the U.S. government in Iraq. Broeck left Iraq in August 2007; but before doing so, he signed a waiver and shortened the deadline on a competitive procurement for the purchase and delivery of line-of-sight radios. This action effectively ensured that Avalon would win the contract. Less than two weeks later, one of Broeck's subordinates awarded the Commander's Emergency Response Program (CERP)-funded contract, valued at $162,151, to Avalon.

Before departing Iraq, Broeck also began taking steps to form a company, called Global Motion, in his home state of Washington. This company would be staffed by members of his immediate family—his wife, his brother (also a member of the U.S. Army), and his sister-in-law. Under an agreement between Goel and Broeck, Goel would subcontract work for the U.S. government to Global Motion, pay Broeck's company 30% of the profits from the prime contracts, and front necessary funds or provide financing to enable Broeck's company to purchase goods and perform services under the contracts.

In September 2007, about a month after Broeck returned to Washington State, Avalon fronted almost $99,978 to Global Motion. Broeck's company then spent $58,733 to purchase line-of-sight radios and ship them to Iraq, keeping the balance of the front money in its account. Global Motion's records show that its profit from this one subcontract was $29,871.90, and its tax returns for 2007 and 2008 showed profits totaling $52,440.

Contracting officers and their families are prohibited from benefiting from government contracts and from relationships with government contractors. In addition, Broeck was required to disclose financial information regarding potential conflicts of interest.

Under the terms of his plea agreement, Broeck will make restitution in the amount of $52,400.16. He faces up to five years in prison and a maximum fine of $250,000.

This case is being prosecuted by the U.S. Attorney's Office for the Western District of Washington.

Sentencings

Four individuals investigated by SIGIR were sentenced since the April 2013 Quarterly Report. One of them, Shawn Leuders, was also convicted during this time, and his case is discussed above.

U.S. Army Major Sentenced for Defrauding U.S. Government

On May 29, 2013, U.S. Army Major Ulysses S. Hicks, was sentenced to serve five years probation and to pay a fine of $5,000 and restitution of $65,409. Hicks's co-conspirator, former Army Master Sergeant Julio Soto, Jr, received an almost identical sentence in December 2012. The two of them were convicted for accepting illegal gratuities from contractors.

While Hicks and Soto were deployed to Iraq in 2007 and 2008, they unlawfully sought, received, and accepted thousands of dollars in gratuities for helping Iraqi contractors gain U.S. government contracts related to the construction of a government building at FOB Hammer. They then purchased U.S. postal money orders with the illegal proceeds and mailed them back to the United States.

This case was prosecuted by a trial attorney on detail from SIGIR to the Fraud Section of DoJ's Criminal Division and the U.S. Attorney's Office for the District of South Carolina.

Former U.S. Army Interpreter Sentenced for Making False Statements

On July 12, 2013, Ramy Elmery, a former U.S. Army interpreter, was sentenced for making false statements about his financial transactions with an Iraqi contractor. He was sentenced to 30 days in prison, followed by 3 years of supervised release and 50 hours of community service, and ordered to pay a $20,000 fine.

While stationed in Iraq in 2007, Elmery served as an interpreter in contract negotiations between the U.S. Army and the Iraqi contractor. After returning to the United States in 2008, he asked the Iraqi contractor to pay him $500,000, and the contractor began wiring payments to two Egyptian bank accounts—one that belonged to Elmery's brother and another that Elmery opened in his own name. In total, Elmery received approximately $47,000 from the Iraqi contractor.

In 2011, when Elmery applied for a top-secret security clearance for work with a defense contractor, he failed to disclose the relationship with the Iraqi contractor and claimed that he had no foreign bank accounts.

This case was prosecuted by a SIGPRO attorney on detail from SIGIR to the Fraud Section of DoJ's Criminal Division and the U.S. Attorney's Office for the Eastern District of Virginia.

Former U.S. Army Staff Sergeant Sentenced for Bribery Scheme

On August 19, 2013, Richard Gilliland, a former U.S. Army staff sergeant, was sentenced to 5 months in prison, followed by 3 years of supervised release, and ordered to pay a fine of $27,200. He had pled guilty on February 12, 2013, to accepting thousands of dollars in bribes from contractors while deployed to Iraq.

From October 2007 through November 2008, Gilliland was a pay agent at Camp Victory. During that time, he received approximately $27,200 and a laptop computer from the U.S. representatives of two Iraqi companies in return for his attempt to influence the award of contracts to those firms and assist them in acquiring used and non-working generators from the Defense Reutilization and Marketing Office.

The case was prosecuted by a SIGPRO attorney on detail from SIGIR to the Fraud Section of DoJ's Criminal Division and the U.S. Attorney's Office for the Eastern District of Tennessee.

Indictments

Seven individuals investigated by SIGIR were indicted since the April 2013 Quarterly Report. Five of them were also convicted during this time and are discussed above.

Army Sergeant Arrested for and Charged With Accepting Bribes From a Contractor

On June 5, 2013, SIGIR and Army Criminal Investigation Command-Major Procurement Fraud Unit (CID-MPFU) agents arrested a U.S. Army sergeant first class (SFC) at Fort Bragg, North Carolina, for accepting more than $16,000 in bribes from a contractor in Iraq during 2009–2010.

The contractor provided security protection services, such as armor plating for vehicles, and fire protection for buildings. The SFC was turned over to base authorities who charged him with bribery under the Uniform Code of Military Justice (UCMJ). The SFC was confined to the base pending judicial action.

Retired U.S. Marine Corps Captain Faces General Court Martial

On August 2, 2013, retired U.S. Marine Corps Captain Eric Schmidt was transferred from U.S. Bureau of Prisons custody in Taft, California, to the Marine Corps correctional facility in Camp Pendleton, California. Schmidt was charged on July 5, 2013, with conduct unbecoming an officer under the UCMJ and faces a general court-martial on October 11, 2013. The charge includes dereliction of duty, wrongful and dishonorable conduct to obtain personal financial gain, and false writings. Schmidt faces an additional charge for trying to ship his illegal proceeds back to the United States.

While deployed to Iraq in 2008, Schmidt used his position in the contracting process to steer contracts to an Iraqi contractor, al-Methwad Company, which was to furnish goods to the U.S. Marines in Iraq. Captain

Schmidt also arranged for al-Methwad to obtain those goods from companies set up by his wife, Janet Schmidt, in the United States. She would then purchase the products—but often in lesser quantities or lower quality than required by the contract—and have them delivered. Captain Schmidt then falsely certified that al-Methwad had provided the required goods.

Schmidt was sentenced on February 7, 2011, in U.S. District Court, Riverside, California, to 72 months in federal prison, and his wife was sentenced to 12 months of home confinement followed by 36 months of probation. The Schmidts were also ordered to pay full restitution to the Department of Defense (DoD) and IRS.

If convicted of the new charges under the UCMJ, Captain Schmidt faces a loss of his military retirement.

The original case was investigated by SIGIR's Forensic Evaluation Research and Recovery Enforcement Team (FERRET) and is discussed further in the FERRET Update later in this section.

Other Legal Actions

Court of Appeals Upholds Convictions of Pressleys
On May 2, 2013, the U.S. Court of Appeals for the Eleventh Circuit upheld the convictions of former U.S. Army Major Eddie Pressley and his wife, Eurica Pressley.

In March 2011, a federal jury convicted the Pressleys on 22 counts of bribery and money laundering for their roles in the widespread corruption scheme at Camp Arifjan in Kuwait known as the Cockerham Conspiracy. Eddie Pressley was subsequently sentenced to 12 years in prison, and Eurica Pressley was sentenced to 6 years in prison. Together, they were required to forfeit real estate, several automobiles, and $21 million.

Extradition to the United States Ordered for Former British Soldier
On July 15, 2013, the British Home Secretary upheld her previously issued surrender order, clearing the way for the extradition of former British soldier David McIntyre to the United States. In August 2012, a criminal information and subsequent guilty plea of Robert N. Boorda, the former Chief of Party in Iraq for the U.S. Institute of Peace (USIP), revealed a conspiracy to commit fraud involving McIntyre and his security-services firm.

Boorda admitted that he recommended USIP award a $1.165 million contract for the lease of a villa in Baghdad and security services at a fraudulently inflated price to a company owned by McIntyre. For his role,

Boorda received a purported consulting and marketing agreement with the company for a monthly fee of $20,000 for the term of the USIP contract. According to plea documents, some of that fee was made possible by falsely representing to USIP headquarters that the villa owner would not agree to a monthly rental payment of less than $22,000, whereas the owner had actually agreed to $13,000. Boorda's sentencing awaits McIntyre's extradition and trial proceedings.

McIntyre was arrested in the United Kingdom on July 6, 2012, under a warrant issued as the result of an eight-count indictment charging wire fraud and gratuities conspiracy, wire-fraud scheme, agreement to pay a gratuity to a public official, and payment of a gratuity to a public official. His extradition was originally ordered to take place by December 7, 2012, but he filed multiple appeals in Britain's court system only to be denied permission to appeal to the Supreme Court. Pending further appeal, McIntyre faces extradition under the Home Secretary's ruling.

Investigators Recover Additional Iraqi Funds

On August 20, 2013, as a result of SIGIR's investigative work, $331,378.06 in Iraqi funds were recovered for return to the Iraqi people. This was the final settlement in an investigation that had previously led to the return of more than $13 million in Iraqi funds. The returned money was part of the Development Fund for Iraq, which consisted of Iraqi oil proceeds used for reconstruction projects in 2003 and 2004. The unused funds discovered by SIGIR were from the U.S. Army Corps of Engineers (USACE) Restore Iraqi Electricity contracts and were supposed to have been returned to the Iraqi government by the end of 2007.

Tipped off by a complaint to the SIGIR Hotline, SIGIR determined that these funds were being improperly held in various accounts belonging to the U.S. government and some U.S. contractors.

In March 2009—following coordination with USACE, the Federal Reserve Bank of New York, and the Government of Iraq—USACE returned $13.1 million to the Central Bank of Iraq. An additional $300,290 was returned in April 2009.

This investigation was conducted jointly by SIGIR, CID-MPFU, and the Defense Criminal Investigative Service (DCIS), with audit assistance from the Defense Contract Audit Agency (DCAA).

Sigpro Update

Prosecuting "white collar" crimes committed in a war zone in another country can be challenging and broaches the following significant legal issues:

- Does the governing criminal statute provide for extraterritorial jurisdiction?
- Can the normal tools of law enforcement— interviews, grand jury or Inspector General subpoenas, or undercover operations—be used overseas?
- What if the case involves non-U.S. citizens?
- Is the evidence that is gathered admissible in U.S. federal court?
- In what venue should the crime be prosecuted?
- Does any statute of limitations apply?
- Can the U.S. government compel foreign witnesses to testify in court?
- In cases involving government contractors, would suspension or debarment adequately vindicate the government's law-enforcement interests?

Most DoJ attorneys, including Assistant U.S. Attorneys (AUSAs) in districts throughout the United States, understandably focus on domestic cases. As SIGIR built its investigative capabilities and uncovered more and more instances of corrupt behavior in the Iraq reconstruction program, it saw the need for forming a dedicated team of prosecutors with the necessary expertise to work difficult war-zone prosecutions and bring cases to their proper resolution.

Senior DoJ and SIGIR officials worked collaboratively in 2009 to develop an innovative solution: the SIGIR Prosecutorial Initiative, or SIGPRO. Through SIGPRO, SIGIR hired respected former federal prosecutors and detailed them to the Fraud Section of DoJ's Criminal Division to work exclusively on cases in SIGIR's jurisdiction. This arrangement enabled SIGIR to field an aggressive prosecution team focused on its mission. It established a more efficient and productive way of doing business, achieving the following:

- By working hand in hand with SIGIR agents from the earliest stages of their investigations, SIGPRO lawyers helped develop cases in ways that ensured the likelihood of successful prosecution.

- By working within DoJ, SIGPRO lawyers gained an inside track to advance Iraq cases, streamlining charging decisions and developing important relationships with DoJ's Office of International Affairs.
- By working closely with the AUSAs and other DoJ attorneys on SIGIR cases, SIGPRO lawyers provided guidance and support that comes from a sound understanding of criminal activity in overseas contingency operations, as well as a deeper appreciation of the larger good that can be served by pursuing these types of cases.

SIGPRO focused on results. If an AUSA in a particular district was in the best position to prosecute a case, SIGPRO would defer to that AUSA and provide whatever support was needed. In some cases, the prosecutions were joint efforts. In others, a SIGPRO attorney took the lead.

Once SIGPRO was in place, prosecutions of investigations related to the Iraq reconstruction program drastically increased. During the more than three years of its operations, SIGPRO was instrumental in achieving 33 indictments, 27 convictions, and more than $8.3 million in fines, forfeitures, recoveries, restitution, and other monetary results.

The benefits of SIGPRO—in terms of tangible monetary results and the less tangible deterrence effects—certainly would have been even greater had SIGIR started the initiative earlier. In the first two years of the reconstruction program, Iraq was almost a "free fraud" zone, and SIGIR was still clarifying its investigative authorities as late as 2007. Experienced prosecutors collaborating with experienced investigators in the early years undoubtedly would have identified and stopped more criminal activity. This is a lesson that SIGIR was able to share with the Special Inspector General for Afghanistan Reconstruction, giving that organization a jump-start in establishing its own focused prosecutorial capability.

At least three barriers to greater prosecutorial success were beyond SIGIR's control:

- **Lack of mutual legal assistance treaty with Iraq.** Mutual legal assistance treaties provide a framework for exchanging evidence and information, such as banking and other financial records, between treaty partners in criminal and related matters. In money-laundering cases, they can be extremely useful as a means of obtaining banking and other financial records from our treaty partners. The United States has mutual legal assistance treaties with more than 50 countries, but it has not successfully negotiated one with Iraq. This made it difficult for SIGIR investigators to obtain records from Iraqi banks for use in court.

- **Uncertain status of extradition treaty with Iraq.** Although the United States and the Republic of Iraq signed an extradition treaty in 1934, no one has ever been extradited under it. In the few cases where the United States requested extradition from Iraq, Iraqi courts determined that extradition in those cases was not permitted by their domestic laws and avoided directly addressing the treaty. There is some question today about the viability of extraditing persons of any nationality from Iraq, which in turn can thwart the government's desire to bring all accountable persons to justice.

- **Inadequate access to financial records in third countries.** SIGPRO prosecutors and the agents learned that parties engaged in procurement fraud in Iraq sometimes moved the financial proceeds of their crimes to banks in Jordan. Because Jordan, as a matter of policy, does not provide U.S. law enforcement with access to financial records in non-terrorism cases, prosecutors sometimes were hampered in developing the necessary evidence for prosecution.

First SIGPRO Conviction of a SIGIR Investigation: The Razo Case

In February 2011, a SIGPRO attorney obtained a guilty plea from Richard Razo, a former U.S. government contractor and Department of State (DoS) employee who collected more than $106,000 in kickbacks by fraudulently providing Iraqi contractors with confidential bidding information. Razo was sentenced to 33 months in prison and ordered to pay $106,820 in restitution. This was the first SIGIR investigation to be prosecuted by SIGPRO.

First Major SIGPRO Precedent: The Ayesh Case

In February 2011, Osama Esam Saleem Ayesh, a former DoS employee who worked and lived at U.S. Embassy-Baghdad, was convicted by a jury of stealing nearly $250,000 intended for the payment of shipping and customs services for the embassy. Ayesh established a phony email account in the name of an actual Iraqi vendor, used an embassy computer to impersonate the vendor in communications with procurement officials at the embassy, and submitted fraudulent invoices and requests for wire-transfer payments to a personal bank account in Jordan. After Federal Bureau of Investigation (FBI) and DoS Inspector General agents discovered the scheme, they arrested Ayesh by luring him to the United States under the pretext of attending a training seminar. A SIGPRO attorney prosecuted the case in collaboration with the U.S. Attorney's Office for the Eastern District of Virginia.

The district court sentenced Ayesh to 3.5 years in prison and ordered him to pay $243,416 in restitution and a $5,000 fine. In addition, citing "the need for general deterrence," the court ordered the U.S. government to inform the court about steps taken to publicize Ayesh's conviction and sentence to U.S. Embassy personnel in Baghdad and elsewhere. DoS responded by issuing a cable to all diplomatic and consular posts detailing the facts of the case.

Ayesh appealed the conviction on the grounds that, because all of his offenses occurred outside of the United States, he was not subject to the extraterritorial jurisdiction of the United States. But a SIGPRO attorney successfully argued before the U.S. Court of Appeals for the Fourth Circuit that Ayesh, as a U.S. government employee, was subject to U.S. conflict-of-interest laws and could be prosecuted in the United States for violating them. As a result of this case, there now exists , for the first time, judicial precedent upholding extraterritorial jurisdiction to prosecute criminal conflicts of interest on the part of U.S. government employees that occur outside of the United States, as well as stronger precedent to prosecute the overseas theft of U.S. government property and funds.

Second Major SIGPRO Precedent: The Pfluger Case

In March 2011, David Pfluger, a retired lieutenant colonel with the U.S. Army National Guard, pled guilty to conspiracy, accepting gratuities, and, as a public official, converting property of another to his own use. From October 2003 through April 2004, Pfluger was stationed at FOB Ridgeway in Iraq. During most of that time, he served as the "mayor" of the base and had authority over the day-to-day operations of the base's physical assets and security—a status that he used to enrich himself.

Pfluger accepted more than $10,000 in cash, as well as gifts of jewelry and clothing, from contractors. In return, Pfluger encouraged awarding projects to specific contractors, bypassed or relaxed security procedures at the base for specific contractors, issued weapon permits without legal authority, and converted government property in his control for use by these contractors.

Pfluger's illegal activities were identified during a Joint Terrorism Task Force (JTTF) investigation, conducted out of New York, into the possession of classified U. S. government documents by an Iraqi employed as an interpreter by the U. S. military in Iraq. After the interpreter provided incriminating evidence, Pfluger admitted to the JTTF that he accepted bribes while serving in Iraq at FOB Ridgeway. The interpreter was ultimately sentenced in March 2008.

Beginning in 2008, Army CID-MPFU in Texas pursued the Pfluger case and asked SIGIR agents to assist in preparing the case for prosecution. SIGIR and CID-MPFU agents met with a prosecutor from the U. S. Attorney's Office for the Northern District of Texas during 2008 and 2009 to work on the matter. Because that office had a large workload during late 2009, it asked SIGPRO to take the lead role in prosecuting Pfluger, and a SIGPRO attorney was instrumental in obtaining the March 2011 guilty plea. Four months later, the court sentenced Pfluger to 18 months in prison.

Pfluger subsequently appealed the conviction to the U.S. Supreme Court on the grounds that the government waited too long to indict him. The court denied certiorari. The SIGPRO attorney helped set an important legal precedent by arguing that the Wartime Suspension of Limitations Act suspended the five-year statute of limitations during the pendency of the war in Iraq.

SIGPRO Prosecutes Major Fraud: The Newell, Hunt, and Kazzaz Cases

In April and May 2012, a SIGPRO attorney obtained guilty pleas from three individuals—Gaines Newell, Billy Joe Hunt, and Ahmed Kazzaz—for conspiring to defraud the U.S. government. Newell was the program manager on Parsons Corporation's contract to implement the Coalition Munitions Clearance Program in Iraq, and Hunt was his deputy. Kazzaz, a British citizen, paid them more than $947,500 in unlawful kickbacks to obtain lucrative subcontracts for his company, Leadstay. For their crimes, the three conspirators were collectively sentenced to 57 months in prison, fined $15,000, and ordered to pay restitution of more than $2.1 million and forfeit almost $1.2 million.

Ferret Update

Established in October 2009, SIGIR's Forensic Evaluation Research and Recovery Enforcement Team used data-mining technology to detect suspicious financial transactions by U.S. military and civilian personnel and contractors who worked in Iraq. FERRET investigators focused particularly on individuals involved with U.S. relief and reconstruction programs that provided easy access to cash and had weak controls over expenditures.

To root out wrongdoers, SIGIR coordinated its efforts with the Department of the Treasury's Financial Crimes Enforcement Network (FinCEN) and also worked closely with DCIS, the Naval Criminal Investigative Service (NCIS), CIDMPFU, and the U.S. Air Force Office of Special Investigations (AFOSI). FinCEN supported SIGIR by providing access to financial data, analysis, and case support.

During its almost four-year lifespan, the FERRET team uncovered more than 110 cases that exhibited signs of illicit financial activity and called for closer scrutiny. As of September 2013, the ensuing investigations resulted in 21 indictments (a 19% success rate), 20 convictions, 17 sentencings, more than 15 years of imprisonment, and more than $5.5 million in monetary results.

With training provided by SIGIR investigators, the Special Inspector General for Afghanistan Reconstruction established a similar effort to identify potentially fraudulent activity in the U.S. reconstruction program in Afghanistan.

FERRET's Biggest Catch: The Schmidt and Hamilton Cases

Weaknesses in internal controls open the door to opportunities for fraud and other illegal activities. The tangled tales of Captain Eric Schmidt and Staff Sergeant Eric Hamilton, two U.S. Marines who served at Camp Fallujah, provide a case study in how FERRET investigative techniques can bring these activities to light and the wrongdoers to justice.

In 2008 and 2009, Captain Schmidt was a logistics officer at Camp Fallujah, responsible for managing reconstruction contracts using Iraq Security Forces Fund and CERP funds. Schmidt played multiple roles in the procurement process— establishing requirements, identifying contractor sources, and validating the receipt of goods. There was no institutional check to balance his broad powers.

Egregiously choosing criminality, as SIGIR later proved, he steered contracts to favored contractors, requiring them to purchase supplies from companies established by his wife. He further conspired to benefit financially from these contracts by directing the delivery of substandard goods, while charging standard prices, and then falsely certifying that the U.S. government received the higher standard.

Captain Schmidt's perfidy included the resale of property stolen from military storage yards in Iraq. In all, Schmidt and his wife garnered about $1.7 million in illicit gains. By delving into confidential information about the Schmidts' financial transactions, SIGIR investigators were able to expose the couple's misdeeds.

In 2011, Captain Schmidt was sentenced to 72 months in federal prison followed by 36 months of supervised release, his wife was ordered to serve 12 months of home confinement, and they were ordered to pay $2.15 million in restitution.

When interrogated by SIGIR's investigative team, the Schmidts implicated Staff Sergeant Hamilton, Captain Schmidt's subordinate at Camp Fallujah who managed the storage yard. By again analyzing confidential financial information, the investigators were able to develop corroborating evidence that led to Hamilton's conviction for conspiring to steal more than 70 electrical generators from two U.S. bases in Iraq. In the scheme he developed with Schmidt, Hamilton would mark the generators to be stolen by painting a red circle on them and would then unlock the gate to allow the contractors and their trucks access to the yard, whereupon they would steal the designated generators.

For his participation in this scheme, Hamilton received more than $124,000 from Schmidt and the contractors. He received the funds through checks that Schmidt's wife sent to Hamilton's wife in the United States, wire transfer payments to a bank account in the United States, and cash payments in Iraq. Hamilton sent home approximately $43,000 of the cash he received by concealing it among American flags contained in foot lockers that he mailed from Iraq to his wife.

In February 2012, Hamilton was sentenced to 18 months in prison, followed by 3 years of supervised release, and ordered to pay almost $125,000 in restitution.

FERRET's Punitive Impact: The Charpia Case

Of all the individuals caught by FERRET investigators, Jill Charpia earned one of the largest monetary penalties.

Charpia gained extensive knowledge of government contracting during her eight years in the U.S. Air Force. While deployed to Afghanistan, she served as a Warranted Contracting Officer at the Joint Contracting Command-Iraq/Afghanistan (JCC-I/A) office at Baghram Air Base. After her discharge from the Air Force, she accepted a position as an independent contractor assigned to the JCC-I/A in Iraq.

In 2008, she became a co-owner of Texas-based Sourcing Specialists, LLC, a company that won a contract in September of that year to provide "Business Transition Services" in Iraq for the DoD Task Force for Business Stability Operations. Specifically, her company was to provide a turnkey housing facility outside the International Zone for use by multinational firms that wanted to develop business opportunities in Iraq.

On September 26, 2008, Charpia submitted an invoice to the JCC-I/A in the amount of $1,270,075.50 for "mobilization" costs under that contract. She subsequently provided two supporting invoices, one claiming that she had paid $700,000 for the rental of two villas in Baghdad and the other claiming that she had paid $570,075.50 for the purchase of three armored vehicles.

In court, Charpia admitted that she did not purchase any armored vehicles and paid only half the submitted cost for the villas. She fabricated both supporting invoices and forged the signatures on the documents. For her crime, Charpia was sentenced on January 24, 2013, to 30 months in prison followed by three years of supervised release. She also was ordered to pay $920,000—the amount of her fraudulent overbilling—plus interest in restitution to the United States.

Suspensions and Debarments

Since December 2005, SIGIR has worked closely with DoJ, Army CID-MPFU, DCIS, and the Army Legal Services Agency's Procurement Fraud Branch to support their efforts to suspend and debar contractors and government personnel for fraud or corruption within the Army. Many of these cases arise from criminal indictments filed in federal district courts or allegations of contractor irresponsibility that require fact-based examination by the Army's Suspension and Debarment Official.

Suspension and debarment are effective tools for preventing criminals from continuing to defraud the government. When individuals or companies are suspended or debarred, their income decreases or stops, potentially putting them out of business. In SIGIR's experience, these tools are more effective against U.S. companies than small foreign companies. The foreign companies are harder to track and can more easily resurface under new names after they are debarred.

From April 1, 2013, to July 31, 2013, the Army suspended 1 contractor based on allegations of fraud in Iraq and Kuwait. In addition, the Army proposed 33 contractors for debarment and finalized 32 debarments of individuals and companies during that same period based on fraudulent activity in Iraq and Kuwait.

Since 2003, the Army has suspended 182 individuals and companies involved in sustainment or reconstruction contracts supporting the Army in

Iraq and Kuwait and proposed for debarment 285 individuals and companies, resulting in 218 finalized debarments that range in duration from 9 months to 10 years. Suspension and debarment actions related to reconstruction and Army support-contract fraud in Afghanistan are reported to the Special Inspector General for Afghanistan Reconstruction. For a list of debarments, see Table 2.3. For a complete list of suspensions and debarments, see www.sigir.mil.

Table 2.3. Debarment List

Name	Debarred
Mohammed Shiahaden Amin	7/3/2013
Gregory S. Light	7/3/2013
Lighthouse Consulting	7/3/2013
Gaines Ray Newell	6/21/2013
Billy Joe Hunt	6/21/2013
Ahmed Sarchil Kazza	6/21/2013
Leadstay Company	6/21/2013
Al Zuhoor Al Nassaa Company	6/21/2013
Total General Trading and Contracting Company	6/21/2013
Faris Nasir	6/21/2013
ASK Group of Companies	6/21/2013
ABD Allah ABD Allah Ghanim	6/21/2013
Garo Chacmajian	6/21/2013
Al Mahran Group	6/21/2013
Francisco Mungia	6/12/2013
Robert Nelson	5/30/2013
Abdual Mustafa	5/30/2013
Sabah H. Ali	5/30/2013
Alzab Company	5/30/2013
Durmus Sahin	5/30/2013
Tara International Construction & Trade Company of Iraq	5/30/2013
James Momon Jr.	5/7/2013
Omega Construction and Support Services	5/7/2013
Ismail Salinas	5/2/2013
The Technical Group	5/2/2013
Hozan General Construction Company, Ltd.	5/2/2013
Al-Barea Company	5/2/2013
Jill Charpia	4/29/2013

Table 2.3. (Continued)

Name	Debarred
Sourcing Specialist, LLC	4/29/2013
Monther "Mike" Majeed Naji	4/9/2013
Harith "Harry" Naji Al Jabawi	4/9/2013
Phoenix Construction	4/9/2013
Joshua Construction	4/9/2013
Jacy Singleton	3/26/2013
Calvin Glass	3/26/2013
Peter Logiotatos	3/26/2013
Roberto Martino	3/26/2013
Mahir Needham Company for General Contracting and Trading	3/7/2013
Areebel Engineering & Logistics	3/7/2013
Fadyah Taj Musa Ivy	3/7/2013
Scott Allan Ivy	3/7/2013
Bryant Williams	1/17/2013
Sadeq Sewaiseh	12/20/2012
Kendall Johnson Caige	12/20/2012
Global Innervisionary Network, Inc.	12/20/2012
Felisa Ilao Castillo	12/20/2012
Geraldine Knighten	12/20/2012
Derrick Shoemake	12/20/2012
Kamel Nayef al-Balawi	11/27/2012
David John Welch	11/27/2012
River Mississippi	10/25/2012
Horaa Kamel	10/25/2012
Amasha King	10/25/2012
Delmus Eugene Scott, Jr.	10/25/2012
Ashleigh Woods	9/17/2012
MACR Construction, LLC	9/17/2012
Al-Batat Construction Co.	8/24/2012
Hayder al-Batat	8/24/2012
Yahya al-Batat	8/24/2012
Ahmed Alssabari	8/24/2012
Hawks of Iraq	8/24/2012
Richard Lopez Razo	8/24/2012
Charles Bowie	7/12/2012

Name	Debarred
Peter Dunn	6/14/2012
Global Procurement, Inc.	6/14/2012
World Wide Procurement and Construction, LLC	6/14/2012
Michelle Lynn Adams	6/14/2012
Matrix International	5/17/2012
Jose Flores	5/17/2012
Barry Steven Szafran	5/17/2012
Jossey Varghese	5/17/2012
Specialised Security Systems	5/17/2012
Thomas Aram Manok	5/17/2012
SIMA International	5/17/2012
Ali Amer Huissein	5/17/2012
Majeed Sahdi Majeed	5/17/2012
Al-Sald Company for General Contracts	5/17/2012
C Buildling	5/17/2012
Al-Andalus/A Cap Company	5/17/2012
Al-Baqier Company	5/17/2012
Mohammed Baqier	5/17/2012
Frederick Manfred Simon	5/17/2012
Manfred Otto Simon	5/17/2012
Railway Logistics International, Inc.	5/17/2012
Engineering International Corporation	5/17/2012
Eric Hamilton	4/30/2012
Mike Atallah	2/25/2012
Marta Atallah	2/25/2012
Theresa Baker	2/25/2012
Theodore Williams	2/17/2012
Ozgen Kacar	2/17/2012
Mezin Kacar	2/17/2012
Ayfer Atilan	2/17/2012
Al-Amal al-Mushrig Company	2/15/2012
Charles Sublett	1/19/2012
Ali Hatham Soleiman	12/15/2011
Al-Anbar Trucking Association	12/15/2011
Abed Errazak Soleiman	12/15/2011
Saad Soleiman	12/15/2011
Taleb Alirfan	12/15/2011
Shalan Alirfan	12/15/2011

Table 2.3. (Continued)

Name	Debarred
David Pfluger	12/6/2011
Ehsan Hassan al-Ameli	11/29/2011
Al-AALI General Contracting Co.	11/28/2011
Mahmoud Shakier Mahmoud	10/14/2011
Ahmad Muhammed Hassan	10/13/2011
Al-Ula Iraq	10/12/2011
Al-Ula FZCO	10/12/2011
Al-Ula Global Trading, LLC	10/12/2011
Chet Fazand	9/13/2011
Chad Fazand	9/13/2011
Fazand International Trading, LLC	9/13/2011
Al-Dalla Co.	9/13/2011
Faustino Gonzales	9/7/2011
Chasib Khazal Mehadi al-Mosawi	9/7/2011
Quasay Shamran Mehdi al-Mosawi	9/7/2011
The Economical Group	9/7/2011
Jenna International, Inc.	8/4/2011
Al-Methwad Company	7/21/2011
Tariq Zadan Dawood	7/21/2011
Tareq Zaidan Dawod	7/21/2011
Tariq Zaidan Dawod	7/21/2011
Tariq Zaidon Dawod	7/21/2011
Tarik Zaidon Dawood	7/21/2011
Abd al-Alim Abbod	7/21/2011
Frankie Joseph Hand	7/21/2011
Richard Joseph Harrington	7/21/2011
Janet Schmidt	6/22/2011
Mariam Steinbuch	6/6/2011
Mark Carnes	6/3/2011
Terence Walton	6/3/2011
Al-Aali Future Mario Company	5/11/2011
Eric Schmidt	4/20/2011
Mark Fuller	4/1/2011
Ahmad Mustafa	1/25/2011
Mubarek Hamed	1/25/2011
Ali Mohammed Bagegni	1/25/2011

Name	Debarred
Abdel Azzim El-Saddig	1/25/2011
Mark Deli Siljander	1/25/2011
Precy Pellettieri	1/12/2011
Salvatore Pepe	1/12/2011
Ammar Tariq al-Jazrawi	1/10/2011
Ammar Tareq al-Jazrawi General Contracting Company	1/10/2011
Liberty al-Ahlia General Trading and Contracting Company	12/13/2010
Bronze al-Taqoos al-Afjan	12/13/2010
International Quality Kitchens Ardiya	12/13/2010
John Napolian	12/13/2010
Joseph Sebastian	12/13/2010
N.K. Ismail	12/13/2010
Biju Thomas	12/13/2010
Combat General Trading Company	12/13/2010
Jank Singh	11/24/2010
Blue Marine Services	11/24/2010
Blue Marines General Trading, LLC	11/24/2010
Blue Marines	11/24/2010
Blue Marines Group	11/24/2010
BMS Logistics	11/24/2010
BMS Group	11/24/2010
BMS General Trading, LLC	11/24/2010
Christopher Murray	11/10/2010
Curtis Whiteford	10/22/2010
William Driver	10/22/2010
Allied Arms Company, Ltd.	9/28/2010
Allied Arms Company, W.L.L.	9/28/2010
Shahir Nabih Fawzi Audah	9/28/2010
Defense Consulting and Contracting Group, LLC	9/28/2010
Amwaj al-Neel Company	9/22/2010
Baladi Company	9/22/2010
Desert Moon Company	9/22/2010
Ameer S. Fadheel	9/22/2010
Oday Abdul Kareem	9/22/2010
Maytham Jassim Mohammad	9/22/2010
Michael Dung Nguyen	8/19/2010
Michael Wheeler	7/28/2010

Table 2.3. (Continued)

Name	Debarred
Austin Key	7/14/2010
Marko Rudi	5/26/2010
Ashraf Mohammad Gamal	4/16/2010
Triple A United General Trading and Contracting	4/16/2010
Jeff Thompson	3/29/2010
John Cockerham	3/17/2010
Melissa Cockerham	3/17/2010
Carolyn Blake	3/17/2010
Nyree Pettaway	3/17/2010
Robert Young	3/9/2010
Elbert Westley George III	1/21/2010
Roy Greene	1/21/2010
Ofelia Webb	1/21/2010
Patrick Faust	1/21/2010
Ali Jabak	9/30/2009
Liberty Jabak	9/30/2009
Liberty's Construction Company	9/30/2009
Tharwat Taresh	9/30/2009
Babwat Dourat al-Arab	9/30/2009
Dourat al-Arab	9/30/2009
Hussein Ali Yehia	9/30/2009
Amina Ali Issa	9/30/2009
Adel Ali Yehia	9/30/2009
Javid Yousef Dalvi	9/25/2009
Mohamed Abdel Latif Zahed	9/10/2009
Gerald Thomas Krage	9/4/2009
Andrew John Castro	9/4/2009
Airafidane, LLC	9/4/2009
Kevin Arthis Davis	8/20/2009
Jacqueline Fankhauser	8/7/2009
Debra Harrison	8/7/2009
Nazar Abd Alama	7/1/2009
San Juan Company	7/1/2009
Mississippi Company for the General Contract	7/1/2009
Lee Dynamics International	6/17/2009
Lee Defense Services Corporation	6/17/2009

Name	Debarred
George Lee	6/17/2009
Justin Lee	6/17/2009
Oai Lee	6/17/2009
Mark Anthony	6/17/2009
Levonda Selph	6/17/2009
Starcon Ltd., LLC	6/17/2009
Cedar Lanmon	6/3/2009
D+J Trading Company	5/14/2009
Jesse Lane, Jr.	1/30/2009
Jennifer Anjakos	1/30/2009
Carlos Lomeli Chavez	1/30/2009
Derryl Hollier	1/30/2009
Luis Lopez	1/30/2009
Mohammed Shabbir Kahn	10/10/2008
Kevin Andre Smoot	9/30/2008
Green Valley Company	9/17/2008, 5/18/2007
Triad United Technologies, LLC	9/17/2008
Dewa Europe	9/17/2008
Dewa Trading Establishment	9/17/2008
Al-Ghannom and Nair General Trading Company	9/17/2008
Dewa Projects (Private), Ltd.	9/17/2008
Future AIM United	9/17/2008
First AIM Trading and Contracting	9/17/2008
Vasantha Nair	9/17/2008
K. V. Gopal	9/17/2008
Falah al-Ajmi	9/17/2008
Trans Orient General Trading	9/17/2008
Zenith Enterprises, Ltd.	9/17/2008
Peleti "Pete" Peleti	6/15/2008
Al-Sawari General Trading and Contracting Company	3/13/2008
John Allen Rivard	1/14/2008
Samir Mahmoud	11/29/2007
Robert Grove	10/30/2007
Steven Merkes	9/27/2007
Bruce Hopfengardner	9/20/2007
Robert Stein, Jr.	8/16/2007
Philip Bloom	8/8/2007

Table 2.3. (Continued)

Name	Debarred
Global Business Group S.R.L.	8/8/2007
Stephen Lowell Seamans	7/27/2007
Gheevarghese Pappen	6/28/2007
Faheem Mousa Salam	6/28/2007
QAH Mechanical and Electrical Works	6/27/2007
Abdullah Hady Qussay	6/27/2007
Al-Riyadh Laboratories and Electricity Co.	1/26/2007
Thomas Nelson Barnes	1/24/2007
Danube Engineering and General Contracting	12/28/2006
Alwan Faiq	12/28/2006
Christopher Joseph Cahill	11/9/2006
Ahmed Hassan Dayekh	9/26/2006
Diaa Ahmen Abdul Latif Salem	5/14/2009, 6/2/2006
Jasmine International Trading and Service Company	5/14/2009, 6/2/2006
Custer Battles	3/17/2006
Robert Wiesemann	3/6/2006
Glenn Allen Powell	2/16/2006
Amro al-Khadra	1/12/2006
Dan Trading and Contracting	1/12/2006
Steven Ludwig	9/29/2005
DXB International	9/29/2005

Other Agency Investigations

SIGIR regularly coordinated with other government agencies conducting investigations in Iraq. For statistics of investigative activities from other agencies, see Table 2.4.

Table 2.4. Status of Investigative Activities of Other U.S. Agencies, As of 8/31/2013

AGENCY	INVESTIGATORS IN IRAQ	INVESTIGATORS IN KUWAIT	OPEN/ONGOING CASES*
U.S. Army Criminal Investigation Command, Major Procurement Fraud Unit	–	2	23
Defense Criminal Investigative Service	–	2	109
Department of State Office of Inspector General	3	–	13
Federal Bureau of Investigation	–	–	40
Naval Criminal Investigative Service	–	–	–
U.S. Air Force Office of Special Investigations	–	–	16
USAID Office of Inspector General	1	–	24
Total	**4**	**4**	**225**

* Numbers include pending cases worked with other agencies within the Joint Operations Center.

Table 2.5. Convictions (As Compiled by the Department of Justice)

Name/Title at Time of Conviction	Charges	Date of Conviction	Sentence
Harold Broeck	Conflict of interest	7/23/2013	Pending
Edward Knotts III, former USAR Captain	Bribery	7/10/2013	Pending
Mario Khalil, business manager for an Iraqi company	Giving illegal gratuities	7/9/2013	Pending
Bradley Christiansen, operations manager and vice president of operations of Laguna Construction Co.	Conspiracy (kickbacks)	7/2/2013	Pending
Timothy Benton, USMC master gunnery sergeant	Accepting a gratuity for an official act while on active duty	6/6/2013	Pending

Table 2.5. (Continued)

Name/Title at Time of Conviction	Charges	Date of Conviction	Sentence
Azubuike Ukabam, former USA captain	Failure to file foreign bank account report	6/5/2013	Pending
Kurt Bennett, USA chief warrant officer	Conspiracy and theft of government property	6/4/2013	Pending
Shawn Lueders, former USA chief warrant officer (W-4)	Conspiracy to supplement salary of U.S. government employee	5/16/2013	3 years probation; $1,000 fine; $100 special assessment
Ramy Elmery, USA sergeant	Making false statements	4/12/2013	30 days in prison; 3 years supervised release; 50 hours community service; $20,000 fine; $100 special assessment
Richard Gilliland, USA staff sergeant	Bribery	2/20/2013	5 months in prison; 3 years supervised release; $27,200 fine; $100 special assessment
Ulysses Hicks, USA major	Conspiracy to accept illegal gratuities	1/3/2013	5 years probation; $5,000 fine; $65,409.53 restitution; $100 special assessment
Gregory Light, owner Lighthouse Consulting (and former USAR lieutenant colonel)	Tax evasion	12/17/2012	5 years probation, which includes 12 months of house arrest; $3,000 criminal fine; $81,886 restitution; $100 special assessment
Gilbert Mendez, USMC staff sergeant	Bribery	12/6/2012	Pending
Robert Walker, USA sergeant first class	Conspiracy and theft of government property	11/14/2012	Pending
Sean Patrick O'Brien, former USA captain	Accepting illegal gratuities	11/9/2012	23 months prison; 3 years supervised release; $37,500 restitution; $200 special assessment
Daniel Hutchinson, former USA sergeant	Receiving stolen funds from Iraq	9/14/2012	Time served (post arrest) in prison; 1 year probation; $12,000 restitution; $100 special assessment

Name/Title at Time of Conviction	Charges	Date of Conviction	Sentence
Mohammed Shihaden Amin, former KBR employee	Bribery	9/10/2012	6 months in prison; 6 months house arrest; $47,000 restitution; $100 special assessment
John Markus, former USACE civilian employee	Wire fraud, money laundering, failure to report foreign bank and financial accounts	9/7/2012	13 years in prison; 3 years supervised release; $75,000 fine; $3.7 million forfeiture
Julio Soto Jr., retired USA master sergeant	Conspiracy to accept illegal gratuities	8/29/2012	5 years probation; $5,000 fine; $62,542 restitution; $100 special assessment
Jill Charpia, former co-owner Sourcing Specialists, LLC (former USAF contracting officer)	Providing false statements to a government agency	8/9/2012	30 months in prison; 3 years supervised release; $920,000 restitution; $100 special assessment
Robert Boorda, former USIP chief of party	Conspiracy to commit wire fraud	8/6/2012	Pending
Hutchinson co-conspirator, former USA specialist	Conspiracy	6/29/2012	Pretrial diversion program
Crystal Martin, former U.S. base concession operator	Conspiracy, money laundering	6/25/2012	5 years probation; $600 special assessment
Richard Evick, USA sergeant first class	Conspiracy, bribery, money laundering, obstructing an agency proceeding	6/25/2012	12 months and 1 day in prison on each count to run concurrently; $1,100 special assessment
Ahmed Kazzaz, owner Leadstay Company	Conspiracy, kickbacks, wire fraud, mail fraud	5/21/2012	15 months confinement; 2 years supervised release; $947,585 restitution; $15,000 fine; $947,585 forfeiture; $1,200 special assessment
Nicole Luvera, former USA captain	Theft of government property	5/17/2012	Pending
Billy Joe Hunt, former Parsons Global Services, Iraq, program manager	Conspiracy, filing false tax returns	5/8/2012	15 months in prison; 3 years supervised release; $66,212 restitution to the IRS; $236,472 forfeiture; $200 special assessment

Table 2.5. (Continued)

Name/Title at Time of Conviction	Charges	Date of Conviction	Sentence
Gaines Newell, former Parsons Global Services, Iraq, deputy program manager	Conspiracy, filing false tax returns	4/10/2012	27 months in prison; 3 years supervised release; $1,102,115 restitution ($861,027 to USACE and $241,088 to the IRS); $861,027 forfeiture; $200 special assessment
Christopher Bradley, USA major	Gratuities	4/9/2012	6 months in prison; 1 year supervised release; $20,000 restitution; $200 special assessment
David Welch, former Fluor Corporation employee	Conspiracy to steal government property	4/2/2012	2 years in prison; 3 years supervised release; $160,000 restitution
Michael Rutecki, USA captain	Gratuities	3/7/2012	3 years probation; $10,500 restitution; $2,000 fine; $100 special assessment
Amasha King, USAR sergeant	Conspiracy to defraud	2/14/2012	3 months in prison; 5 years probation; $20,500 restitution; $100 special assessment
John Hayes, former DoS contractor employee	Conspiracy	11/10/2011	5 months in prison; 2 years supervised release; $12,000 restitution
Brian Cornell, former USACE civilian employee	False statements	10/27/2011	3 months confinement; 2 years supervised release; $1,000 fine; $100 special assessment
Robert Nelson, former USA sergeant	Conspiracy to steal public property	6/28/2011	4 years probation with the first 6 months in home confinement; $44,830 restitution; $100 special assessment
Thomas Manok, former USACE civilian employee	Conspiracy	9/19/2011	20 months in prison; 3 years supervised release; $73,500 forfeiture; $100 special assessment

Name/Title at Time of Conviction	Charges	Date of Conviction	Sentence
Tamimi Global Company LTD	Kickbacks	9/16/2011	$13 million to resolve criminal and civil allegations through a deferred prosecution agreement
Eric Hamilton, USMC gunnery sergeant	Conspiracy	8/10/2011	18 months in prison; 3 years supervised release; $124,944 restitution
Francisco Mungia III, associate of a USMC contracting officer	Conspiracy	7/22/2011	4 months in prison; 3 years supervised release; $30,000 restitution
Barry Szafran, former prime contractor employee	Illegally receiving a gratuity	7/15/2011	1 year probation with the first 4 months in home confinement; $7,169 restitution; $100 special assessment
Justin Lee, former president of Lee Dynamics International	Conspiracy, bribery	7/15/2011	Pending
Derrick Shoemake, retired USA lieutenant colonel	Bribery	6/13/2011	41 months in prison; 2 years supervised release; $68,100 forfeiture; $181,900 restitution
David Pfluger, retired USA lieutenant colonel	Conspiracy, accepting gratuities, converting the property of another to his own use	3/25/2011	18 months in prison; 3 years supervised release; $24,000 restitution
Charles Bowie, retired USA major	Engaging in monetary transactions in property derived from specified unlawful activity	5/11/2011	2 years in prison; 3 years supervised release; $400,000 restitution; $100 special assessment
Eddie Pressley, former USA major	Bribery, conspiracy to commit bribery, honest services fraud, money-laundering conspiracy, engaging in monetary transactions with criminal proceeds	3/1/2011	12 years in prison; 3 years supervised release; forfeiture of $21 million, real estate, and several automobiles

Table 2.5. (Continued)

Name/Title at Time of Conviction	Charges	Date of Conviction	Sentence
Eurica Pressley, former contractor and military spouse	Bribery, conspiracy to commit bribery, honest services fraud, money-laundering conspiracy, engaging in monetary transactions with criminal proceeds	3/1/2011	6 years in prison; 3 years supervised release; forfeiture of $21 million, real estate, and several automobiles
Richard Razo, former DoS contractor (and DoS civilian employee)	Wire fraud, wire-fraud conspiracy	2/28/2011	33 months in prison; 2 years supervised release; $106,820 restitution; $200 special assessment
Kevin Schrock, USA major	Money laundering	2/8/2011	3 years probation; $47,241 restitution
Osama Ayesh, former U.S. Embassy-Baghdad civilian employee	Theft of public money, engaging in acts affecting a personal financial interest	2/2/2011	42 months in prison; 36 months supervised release; $243,416 restitution; $5,000 fine
Bryant Williams, former USA captain	Honest services fraud, accepting bribes	12/17/2010	3 years in prison; 3 years supervised release; $57,030 forfeiture; $200 special assessment
Mark Carnes, USAF master sergeant	Bribery	12/16/2010	20 months in prison; 3 years supervised release; $40,000 fine
Michelle Adams, co-owner Global Procurement, Inc., and owner Worldwide Procurement and Construction LLC	Bribery	12/7/2010	15 months in prison; 3 years supervised release; $757,525 forfeiture; $100 special assessment
Frankie Hand Jr., retired USN lieutenant commander	Fraud, bribery, receiving illegal gratuities	12/7/2010	3 years in prison; $757,525 forfeiture
Peter Dunn, former DoD contractor	Bribery	11/19/2010	14 months in prison; 2 years supervised release
Louis Berger Group, Inc.	Major fraud statute	11/5/2010	Agreed through a deferred prosecution agreement to $18.7 million in criminal penalties;

Name/Title at Time of Conviction	Charges	Date of Conviction	Sentence
			civil settlement of $50.6 million; full restitution to USAID; adoption of effective standards of conduct, internal control systems, and ethics training for employees; employment of an independent monitor to evaluate and oversee the company's compliance with the agreement for 2 years
Salvatore Pepe, former Louis Berger Group chief financial officer	Conspiracy to defraud	11/5/2010	Pending
Precy Pellettieri, former Louis Berger Group controller	Conspiracy to defraud	11/5/2010	Pending
Roderick Sanchez, USA major	Bribery	10/27/2010	5 years in prison; 3 years supervised release; $15,000 fine
Richard Harrington, USMC major	Receiving illegal gratuities	10/18/2010	1 year and 1 day in prison; forfeiture of jewelry and rugs
Bruce Gillette, USAR lieutenant colonel	Acts affecting a personal financial interest	10/6/2010	1 year probation; $2,000 fine; 160 hours community service; inability to possess a firearm
Mariam Steinbuch, former USMC staff sergeant	Bribery	10/5/2010	5 years probation and $25,000 restitution
Ismael Salinas, Laguna Construction Company employee	Kickbacks	10/1/2010	9 months in prison (time served); 2 years supervised release; $7,500 fine; $807,904 forfeiture; $300 special assessment
Dorothy Ellis, former senior DoD contractor employee	Conspiracy	9/2/2010	37 months in prison; 3 years probation; $360,000 restitution

Table 2.5. (Continued)

Name/Title at Time of Conviction	Charges	Date of Conviction	Sentence
Wajdi Birjas, former DoD civilian contract employee	Bribery, money laundering	8/11/2010	35 months in prison; 3 years supervised release; $650,000 forfeiture; $200 special assessment
Mark Fuller, USMC major	Structuring financial transactions	8/4/2010	1 year and 1 day in prison; $198,510 fine; $200 special assessment
Charles Sublett, USA major	False statements	7/7/2010	21 months in prison; 2 years supervised release; forfeiture of $107,900 and 17,120,000 Iraqi dinar
Faustino Gonzales, USA captain	Receipt of a gratuity by a public official	6/24/2010	15 months in prison; 1 year supervised release; $10,000 fine; $25,500 restitution; $100 special assessment
Terrance Walton, USMC master sergeant	Bribery, graft, failure to obey a direct order	5/17/2010	Reprimand; reduction in rank from E-8 to E-3; $65,000 fine; 62 days confinement
Eric Schmidt, USMC captain	Wire fraud, filing a false federal tax form	5/17/2010	6 years in prison; 3 years probation; $2,150,613 restitution
William Collins, USA civilian employee	Bribery	4/21/2010	42 months in prison; 3 years supervised release; $1,725 fine; $5,775 forfeiture; $200 special assessment
Ryan Chase, USA sergeant first class	Illegal gratuities, money laundering, false statements	4/21/2010	1 year and 1 day in prison; 2 years probation; $1.4 million restitution
Marcus McClain, former USAR captain	Acceptance of illegal gratuities	4/15/2010	Pending
Kevin Davis, retired USA colonel	Acceptance of illegal gratuities	4/13/2010	Pending
Janet Schmidt, wife of Eric Schmidt and co-owner of Jenna International, Incorporated	Filing a false tax return, fraud	3/18/2010	1 year home confinement; 3 years probation; $2,150,613 restitution

Name/Title at Time of Conviction	Charges	Date of Conviction	Sentence
Terry Hall, owner of Freedom Consulting and Catering Company and Total Government Allegiance	Conspiracy, bribery	2/17/2010	39 months in prison; 1 year supervised release; forfeiture of $15,757,000
Theresa Russell, former USA staff sergeant	Money laundering	1/28/2010	5 years probation; $31,000 restitution
Michael Nguyen, USA captain	Theft, structuring financial transactions	12/7/2009	30 months in prison; 3 years supervised release; $200,000 restitution; forfeit of interest in all personal property bought with the stolen money as well as the remaining funds seized by the government at the time of arrest
Ronald Radcliffe, retired USA master sergeant	Bribery, money laundering	10/16/2009	40 months in prison; $30,000 fine
Joselito Domingo, USACE resident engineer	Bribery	11/19/2009	39 months in prison; 2 years supervised release; $70,000 fine
Gloria Martinez, USACE supervisory contract specialist	Bribery, conspiracy	8/12/2009	5 years in prison; $210,000 restitution
Robert Jeffery, former USN master chief petty officer	Conspiracy, theft	8/11/2009	4 years in prison
William Driver, military spouse	Money laundering	8/5/2009	3 years probation, to include 6 months home confinement; $36,000 restitution
Nyree Pettaway, John Cockerham's niece	Conspiracy to obstruct justice	7/28/2009	1 year and 1 day in prison; 2 years supervised release; $5 million restitution
Michel Jamil	Conspiracy	7/27/2009	40 months in prison; 2 years supervised release; $75,000 forfeiture; $27,806,879 restitution

Table 2.5. (Continued)

Name/Title at Time of Conviction	Charges	Date of Conviction	Sentence
Robert Young, contractor (and former USA captain)	Conspiracy, theft of government property	7/24/2009	8 years and 1 month in prison; 3 years supervised release; $1 million forfeiture; $26,276,472 restitution
Samir Itani, owner of American Grocers, Inc.	Conspiracy	7/21/2009	2 years in prison; 3 years supervised release; $100,000 fine; $100 special assessment
Tijani Saani, former DoD civilian employee	Filing false tax returns	6/25/2009	110 months in prison; 1 year supervised release; $1.6 million fine; $816,485 restitution to the IRS
Jeff Thompson, former Environmental Chemical Corporation field supervisor	Kickbacks	6/16/2009	5 years probation; $144,000 restitution; $100 special assessment
Diane Demilta, Global-Link Distribution LLC president	Wire fraud	5/27/2009	6 months in prison; 12-month house arrest; 2 years supervised release; $20,000 fine; $70,000 restitution
Benjamin Kafka, Alchemie Technology Group representative	Misprision of a felony	5/18/2009	Pending
Elbert George III, USA captain	Theft of government property, conspiracy	5/18/2009	60 days intermittent confinement; 2 years supervised release; $103,000 forfeiture; pay jointly and severally with co-conspirator Roy Greene $52,286.60 restitution
Roy Greene Jr., USA sergeant first class	Theft of government property, conspiracy	5/18/2009	3 years supervised release; $103,000 forfeiture; pay jointly and severally with co-conspirator Elbert George $52,286.60 restitution
Frederick Kenvin, former American Grocers, Incorporated employee	Conspiracy	4/30/2009	3 years probation; $2,072,967 restitution

Name/Title at Time of Conviction	Charges	Date of Conviction	Sentence
Stephen Day, Logistics Group International, Incorporated, owner and president	Conspiracy to defraud the United States by misrepresentation	4/13/2009	3 years probation; $41,522 restitution; $2,000 fine
Jeff Alex Mazon, former KBR employee	Major fraud against the United States, wire fraud	3/24/2009	1 year probation; 6 months home confinement; $5,000 fine
Carolyn Blake, John Cockerham's sister	Conspiracy, money laundering	3/19/2009	70 months in prison; 3 years of supervised release; $3.1 million restitution
Michael Carter, Force Protection Industries project engineer	Violating the Anti-Kickback Act	1/24/2008	61 months in prison; 3 years supervised release
Harith al-Jabawi, DoD contractor	Conspiracy, bribery, false statements	1/22/2009	Pending
Christopher Murray, retired USA major	Bribery, false statements	1/8/2009	57 months in prison; 3 years supervised release; $245,000 restitution
Theresa Baker, USAR major	Conspiracy, bribery	12/22/2008	70 months in prison; $327,192 restitution; 5,000 fine
Curtis Whiteford, USAR colonel	Conspiracy, bribery, wire fraud	11/7/2008	5 years in prison; 2 years supervised release; $16,200 restitution
Michael Wheeler, USAR lieutenant colonel	Conspiracy, bribery, wire fraud, interstate transportation of stolen property, bulk cash smuggling	11/7/2008	42 months in prison; 3 years supervised release; $1,200 restitution; $100 special assessment
David Ramirez, contractor, Readiness Support Management, Inc.	Bulk currency smuggling, structuring transactions	10/9/2008	50 months in prison; 3 years supervised release; $200 special assessment
Lee Dubois, contractor, Future Services General Trading and Contracting Company	Theft of government property	10/7/2008	3 years in prison; $450,000 restitution
Robert Bennett, contractor, KBR	Violating the Anti-Kickback Act	8/28/2008	1 year probation; $6,000 restitution

Table 2.5. (Continued)

Name/Title at Time of Conviction	Charges	Date of Conviction	Sentence
James Momon Jr., USA major	Conspiracy and bribery	8/13/2008	18 months in prison; 3 years supervised release; $5.8 million restitution; $300 special assessment
Debra Harrison, USA lieutenant colonel	Conspiracy, bribery, money laundering, wire fraud, interstate transportation of stolen property, smuggling cash, preparing false tax returns	7/28/2008	30 months in prison; 2 years supervised release; $366,640 restitution
Cedar Lanmon, USA captain	Accepting illegal gratuities	7/23/2008	1 year in prison; 1 year supervised release
Jacqueline Fankhauser, mother of Major Theresa Baker	Receipt of stolen property	6/30/2008	1 year probation; 180 days home confinement; 104 hours community service; $10,000 fine; $100 special assessment
John Cockerham Jr., USA major	Bribery, conspiracy, money laundering	6/24/2008	210 months in prison; 3 years of supervised release; $9.6 million restitution
Melissa Cockerham, John Cockerham's wife	Conspiracy, money laundering	6/24/2008	41 months in prison; 3 years of supervised release; $1.4 million restitution
Levonda Selph, USAR lieutenant colonel	Conspiracy, bribery	6/10/2008	12 months in prison; 3 years supervised release; $5,000 fine; $9,000 restitution
Raman International Corporation	Conspiracy, bribery	6/3/2008	$500,000 fine; $378,192 restitution
Austin Key, USA captain	Bribery	12/19/2007	2 years confinement; 2 years supervised release; $108,000 forfeiture; $600 assessment
John Rivard, USAR major	Bribery, conspiracy, money laundering	7/23/2007	10 years in prison; 3 years supervised release; $5,000 fine; $1 million forfeiture order

Name/Title at Time of Conviction	Charges	Date of Conviction	Sentence
Kevin Smoot, Eagle Global Logistics, Inc., managing director	Violating the Anti-Kickback Act, making false statements	7/20/2007	14 months in prison; 2 years supervised release; $6,000 fine; $17,964 restitution
Anthony Martin, KBR subcontractor administrator	Violating the Anti-Kickback Act	7/13/2007	1 year and 1 day in prison; 2 years supervised release; $200,504 restitution
Jesse Lane, Jr., former DoD civilian employee (and former CA Army National Guard soldier)	Conspiracy, honest services wire fraud	6/5/2007	30 months in prison; $323,228 restitution
Steven Merkes, former DoD civilian employee	Accepting illegal gratuities	2/16/2007	12 months and 1 day in prison; $24,000 restitution
Peleti "Pete" Peleti Jr., USA chief warrant officer	Bribery, smuggling cash	2/9/2007	28 months in prison; $57,500 fine; $50,000 forfeiture
Jennifer Anjakos, former CA Army National Guard	Conspiracy to commit wire fraud	11/13/2006	3 years probation; $86,557 restitution; $100 assessment
Carlos Lomeli Chavez, former CA Army National Guard sergeant	Conspiracy to commit wire fraud	11/13/2006	3 years probation; $28,107 restitution; $100 assessment
Derryl Hollier, former CA Army National Guard sergeant	Conspiracy to commit wire fraud	11/13/2006	3 years probation; $83,657.47 restitution; $100 assessment
Luis Lopez, former CA Army National Guard sergeant	Conspiracy to commit wire fraud	11/13/2006	3 years probation; $66,865 restitution; $100 assessment
Bonnie Murphy, former DoD civilian disposal officer	Accepting unlawful gratuities	11/7/2006	1 year supervised release; $1,500 fine
Samir Mahmoud, employee of U.S. construction firm	Making false statements	11/3/2006	1 day credit for time served; 2 years supervised release
Gheevarghese Pappen, retired USACE civilian	Soliciting, accepting illegal gratuities	10/12/2006	2 years in prison; 1 year supervised release; $28,900 restitution
Bruce Hopfengardner, former USAR lieutenant colonel	Conspiracy, conspiring to commit wire fraud and money laundering, smuggling currency	8/25/2006	21 months in prison; 3 years supervised release; $200 fine; $144,500 forfeiture

Table 2.5. (Continued)

Name/Title at Time of Conviction	Charges	Date of Conviction	Sentence
Faheem Mousa Salam, former DoD contractor interpreter	Violating anti-bribery provisions of the Foreign Corrupt Practices Act	8/4/2006	3 years in prison; 2 years supervised release; 250 hours community service; $100 special assessment
Mohammad Shabbir Khan, former director of operations for Kuwait and Iraq, Tamimi Global Co., Ltd.	Violating the Anti-Kickback Act	6/23/2006	51 months in prison; 2 years supervised release; $10,000 fine; $133,860 restitution; $1,400 assessment
	Witness tampering	8/10/2009	15 months in prison; 2 years supervised release; $6,000 fine; $200 special assessment
Philip Bloom, owner of Global Business Group, GBG Holdings, and GBG-Logistics Division	Conspiracy, bribery, money laundering	3/10/2006	46 months in prison; 2 years supervised release; $3.6 million forfeiture; $3.6 million restitution; $300 special assessment
Stephen Seamans, former KBR subcontracts manager	Wire fraud, money laundering, conspiracy	3/1/2006	12 months and 1 day in prison; 3 years supervised release; $380,130 restitution; $200 assessment
Christopher Cahill, former Eagle Global Logistics, Incorporated, regional vice president for the Middle East and India	Major fraud against the United States	2/16/2006	30 months in prison; 2 years supervised release; $10,000 fine; $100 assessment (a civil settlement with EGL arising from the same facts resulted in a settlement of $4 million)
Robert Stein, former DoD comptroller and funding officer	Felon in possession of a firearm, possession of machine guns, bribery, money laundering, conspiracy	2/2/2006	9 years in prison; 3 years supervised release; $3.6 million forfeiture; $3.5 million restitution; $500 special assessment
Glenn Powell, KBR subcontracts manager	Major fraud, violating the Anti-Kickback Act	8/1/2005	15 months in prison; 3 years supervised release; $90,973.99 restitution; $200 assessment

SECTION 3. DEVELOPMENTS IN IRAQ

Resurgent Violence

Iraq has become significantly more dangerous since SIGIR's last report. Indeed, the last four months have been the most violent period in the country since the summer of 2008.

Among the parade of horrible events, the killings at Hawija on April 23 stand out. According to press and government reports, more than 50 people died when security forces raided an encampment of Sunni protesters near Kirkuk.

In the tense days that followed this tragedy, dozens of Sunni tribesman and Iraqi police were killed in skirmishes in Kirkuk and the nearby provinces of Salah Al-Din, Anbar, and Ninewa—predominantly in the cities of Ramadi and Mosul. Kurdish *Peshmerga* troops moved farther south around Kirkuk to take up guard posts vacated by Iraqi Security Forces (ISF) near the northern oil fields, further escalating tensions between the Kurdistan Regional Government (KRG) and the Government of Iraq (GOI). Fighting in Syria has further complicated security in these areas, rendering control of the Syria-Iraq border beyond difficult. The disorder has facilitated the cross-border movements of personnel from al-Qaeda in Iraq (now called the Islamic State of Iraq and Sham, or ISIS) between the two countries.

According to the United Nations (UN), 963 civilians were killed and 2,191 were wounded in May, making it the deadliest month since 2008. May also saw the deadliest day in Iraq in five years—at least 86 people killed in bombings of both Shia and Sunni areas on May 20. As Figure 3.1 shows, July casualties rivaled the deaths in May, with relentless bombing, gunfire, and improvised explosive device (IED) attacks in several provinces each day.[1]

A Very Bloody Ramadan
According to press reports, the month of Ramadan in Iraq—which began July 9 and culminated with the Eid al-Fitr celebrations on August 10—saw more than 1,000 killed in attacks around the country. Bombings in multiple cities killed worshippers exiting or entering mosques during the day and at cafes in the evenings, where Muslims gathered to break their fast. The final day of Ramadan proved to be bloodier than May 20. The Eid al-Fitr celebrations were marred by coordinated attacks across Iraq that killed at least 94 people. Baghdad sustained more than half of the casualties, and ISIS reportedly claimed responsibility for the attacks.

Although car and suicide bombings contributed most to the death toll, more than a third of the victims died by gunfire or IEDs. There were numerous reports of gunmen setting up fake checkpoints to target specific groups, including transportation convoys. On July 24, for example, 14 truck drivers were killed in an ambush in Salah Al-Din.

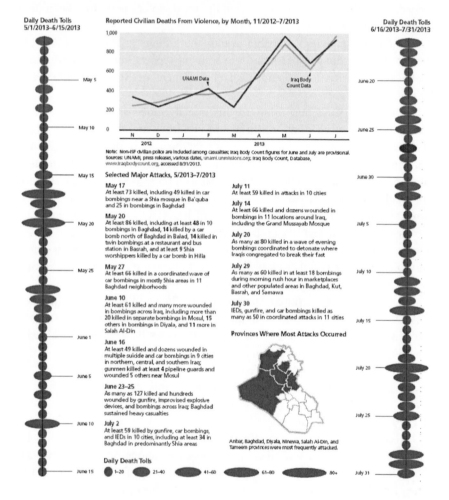

Figure 3.1. Recent Civilian Deaths and Security Incidents.

On Friday, August 1, the U.S. Department of State (DoS) announced that U.S. embassies in several countries (including Iraq) would be closed the following Sunday, citing reports of specific threats against facilities. The next day, DoS issued a worldwide travel warning to alert all U.S. citizens of the potential for terrorist attacks by al-Qaeda operatives, particularly in the Middle East and North Africa, through the end of August. U.S. Embassy-Baghdad reopened for business on Monday, August 5, but warnings for U.S. citizens traveling in Iraq continued.[2]

GOI Responses

In the face of the escalating civilian death tolls and the armed attacks against the ISF and transportation convoys, the GOI reshuffled several senior security posts within the Ministries of Defense and Interior over the summer, including leadership of the Ground Forces Command, Tigris Operations Command, Baghdad Operations Command, and three military divisions.

According to GOI statements, several operations purportedly resulted in the identification and capture or killing of dozens of terrorists. For example, on May 25, GOI forces launched Operation Phantom, employing 20,000 security personnel from various services to locate and neutralize terrorists in Anbar. The Iraqi Ground Forces Commander announced that troops had discovered the largest al-Qaeda base in the western desert. Operations in Diyala and Salah Al-Din, led by the Tigris Operations Command in August, reportedly led to the capture of 81 suspects wanted on terrorism charges, as well as the destruction of two vehicles and a house packed with explosives.

Critical state-threatening security challenges persist in Iraq. During August meetings with U.S. officials in Washington, D.C., on the subject, Iraqi Foreign Minister Hoshyar Zebari requested greater assistance from the United States to fight the resurgence of al-Qaeda in Iraq, including a limited number of additional security advisors, more intelligence support, and the sale to Iraq of lethal drones.[3]

Mass Prison Breaks

Al-Qaeda front group ISIS claimed responsibility for July 21 coordinated attacks that freed hundreds of inmates from Abu Ghraib Prison in Baghdad and Taji Prison north of Baghdad. During the attacks, inmates reportedly set fires and rioted as suicide bombers broke through. As many as 20 security personnel and 21 prisoners were reportedly killed during the attacks.

The damage from these attacks is incalculable. Up to 500 inmates, many affiliated with al-Qaeda, may have escaped. Iraqi officials claim to have killed more than 100 and recaptured more than 300, but these are unconfirmed numbers. Reports of vendetta killings carried out by escaped prisoners surfaced a few days later. As many as 100 escapees may have crossed into Syria.

Prime Minister Nuri al-Maliki subsequently fired the head of Iraq's prisons directorate and ordered senior police officers negligent in their duties to be detained. Several suspicious events reportedly occurred prior to the attacks at Abu Ghraib Prison, signaling possible conspiracies, including the disabling of the prison's cell-phone jamming devices and the smuggling of phones into the prison.[4]

Refuge from Syria

From January 2012 through August 2013, the civil unrest in Syria drove an estimated 2 million Syrians from their homes into neighboring countries. While the vast majority crossed the border into Lebanon, Jordan, and Turkey, about 200,000 Syrian refugees sought protection in Iraq, primarily in the Kurdistan Region. Almost one-fourth of this refugee population in Iraq arrived during the last two weeks of August 2013.

As shown in Figure 3.2, the number of Syrian refugees registered by the United Nations High Commissioner for Refugees (UNHCR) in Iraq rose steadily from July 2012 through May 2013. In the first four months of this year alone, the Syrian refugee population in Iraq doubled.

Al-Qaim border crossing in Anbar province was closed to new Syrian arrivals in October 2012, except to allow individuals to be treated for medical emergencies or to be reunited with their families. Those restrictions were further tightened in late March 2013, when the ISF closed the crossing to all entries into Iraq, while leaving it open to Syrians wanting to return to their home country.

In January 2013, the refugee population in al-Qaim stood at almost 9,000; by July, this number had dropped to slightly more than 5,000 because of the growing number of Syrians opting to return home.

What had been the busiest entry point into Iraq, the Peshkapor border crossing in the Kurdistan Region, was closed on May 19, though exceptions were made for humanitarian and family-reunification cases. Despite the closure, UNHCR reported that a relatively small number of Syrian refugees continued to approach its offices in the region during June and July for registration. Some of those people probably crossed the border legally, while others may have entered illegally by crossing the river or paying smugglers.

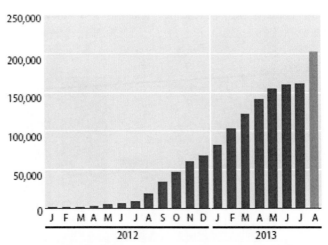

Note: August 2013 number includes UN estimate of new arrivals as of August 29.
Sources: UNHCR, Syria Regional Refugee Response Inter-agency Information
    Sharing Portal, data.unhcr.org/syrianrefugees/
country.php?id=103.

Figure 3.2. Syrian Refugees in Iraq, 1/2012–8/2013.

On August 15, the growth trend that had been stifled in late May dramatically reasserted itself. The KRG opened a new pontoon bridge at Peshkapor. Within three days, an estimated 20,000 Syrians had streamed across the bridge into Iraq. The KRG then closed the bridge to refugee traffic, but allowed the influx to continue at the Sahela crossing south of Peshkapor. By the end of August, as many as 50,000 Syrians had crossed the border into Iraq. UNHCR called it "a major exodus ... unlike anything witnessed entering Iraq previously."

In response, UNHCR and its partners scrambled to erect shelters with plastic tarps to protect the refugees from the sun and heat. Relief agencies established an emergency refugee camp, with a planned capacity of 20,000, at Kowergosk in Erbil province. On August 20, Iraq's Council of Ministers (CoM) agreed to allocate 15 billion dinar (about $13 million) in emergency funds to the GOI's Ministry of Migration and Displacement to aid Syrian refugees in the Kurdistan Region.

Most of the new refugees apparently were Kurds escaping the escalating violence between al-Qaedaaffiliated groups and Kurdish militias vying to control Syria's northeastern provinces. One new arrival told a reporter, "We fled because there is war, beheadings, and killings, and in addition to that, there is no work."

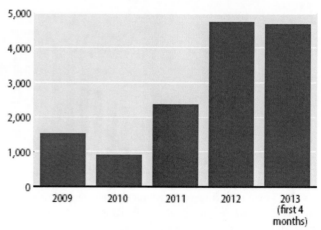

Source: UNHCR, "Iraq Operation: Monthly Statistical Update on Return," 12/2009, 12/2010, 12/2011, 12/2012, and 4/2013..

Figure 3.3. Average Monthly Returns of Iraqi Refugees from Syria, 2009–2013.

In addition to the Syrians who fled to Iraq, more than 75,000 Iraqis who sought a safe haven in Syria after the 2003 invasion returned to Iraq between January 1, 2012, and April 30, 2013. As shown in Figure 3.3, the number of returnees in 2012 was twice what it was in 2011, and the accelerated return rate continued during the first four months of 2013.[5]

GOI-KRG Talks

On June 9, 2013, and then again on July 7, GOI Prime Minister Nuri al-Maliki and KRG President Masoud Barzani met to discuss the unresolved issues that have long created tensions between their two governments. The meetings, held in Erbil and Baghdad, were the first between the two leaders in more than two and a half years. Although neither the GOI nor the KRG issued a statement suggesting substantive progress, both the U.S. Embassy in Baghdad and the UN Special Representative of the Secretary-General for Iraq "welcomed" the talks as encouraging steps.

Control of Iraq's vast oil resources, as well as the Kurdistan Region's disputed border with neighboring provinces, is at the core of the long-simmering power struggle. Although draft legislation setting out a basic framework for the hydrocarbon sector was approved by the CoM in 2006, it has yet to be enacted because of political differences. Meanwhile, the KRG has signed contracts with international companies to explore for and develop its oil and gas resources, but the GOI does not recognize the contracts, asserting that only the central government's Ministry of Oil is authorized to enter into such agreements. As a result, oil companies operating in the Kurdistan Region have not always been paid, KRG and GOI officials have exchanged claims and counterclaims about how much money who owes whom, and oil exports from the Region have been on again, off again.[6]

Provincial Elections

Iraq held elections for Provincial Council seats in 12 of its 18 provinces on April 20, 2013, and then held elections in Anbar and Ninewa on July 20. Elections in Tameem (Kirkuk) have been delayed indefinitely because of its "disputed territory" status, while elections in the Kurdistan Region's three provinces are scheduled for November 21.

According to Iraq's Independent High Electoral Commission, 51% of the eligible voters participated in the April 20 elections, while 50% voted in Anbar and 38% voted in Ninewa on July 20.

Candidates in the 14 provinces were contending for 447 Provincial Council seats. Prime Minister al-Maliki's State of Law Coalition won 97 seats, more than any other political block, but suffered an overall 24-seat loss. The Islamic Supreme Council of Iraq's Citizen's Alliance, headed by Shia cleric Amar al-Hakim, finished second with 61 seats, up from 58 seats in the 2009 elections. Former Prime Minister Ayad Allawi's al-Iraqiya list won just 16 seats, down from 26 in 2009.

As of mid-August, the new Provincial Councils had all held their inaugural sessions and elected governors and council chairs.[7]

Energy

In mid-June, the GOI released its new Integrated National Energy Strategy (INES), which aims to develop Iraq's deteriorated energy sector to meet domestic energy needs, foster the growth of a diversified national economy, improve the standard of living of Iraqi citizens, create employment, and position Iraq as a major player in regional and global energy markets.

To achieve this vision, the INES lays out a longterm plan of policy commitments, infrastructure development, and institutional reform. The plan covers upstream and downstream oil, natural gas, electric power, and industries that consume large quantities of energy either as fuel or as feedstock for production processes. The INES identifies six currently underdeveloped industries—petrochemicals, fertilizers, steel, aluminum, cement, and bricks— that could develop into significant and profitable producers if they were built to sufficient capacity and provided sufficient energy resources.

According to the INES, the recommended energy development program will require an investment of approximately $620 billion (in 2011 dollars) between 2012 and 2030. Over the same period, this investment is expected to generate $6 trillion in government revenues. And by 2022, domestic demand for energy (including demand for oil and gas as an industrial feedstock) is expected to be completely met through domestic production.

To ensure successful implementation, the INES calls for the establishment of special task forces within the Oil, Electricity, and Industry and Minerals Ministries; management "ownership" by the Prime Minister's Office; a steering committee chaired by either the Deputy Prime Minister for Energy Affairs or the Chairman of the Prime Minister's Advisory Commission (PMAC); and monitoring by the Council of Representatives (CoR).

The INES, developed by Booz & Company under a contract with the PMAC, took three years to complete. The World Bank provided $6.9 million for the project.[8]

Oil Production and Exports: Federal Iraq

During the first six months of 2013, crude oil production in the "Southern 15" provinces (that is, Iraq exclusive of the Kurdistan Region) averaged 3.00 million barrels per day (MBPD), an 8% increase from the first half of 2012 but a 3% drop from the second half. More than three-fourths of this year's production came from Iraq's oil-rich southern fields. One field alone, supergiant alRumaila in Basrah, reportedly was producing more than half of the southern output.

Figure 3.4 shows the trends in production during the four-year period ending June 30, 2013.

Under the middle of three growth scenarios in the INES, oil production in federal Iraq would increase from the current average of 3.00 MBPD to 4.50

MBPD by the end of 2014 and 9.0 MBPD in 2020. These targets are higher than the levels deemed realistic by the International Energy Agency in an October 2012 study but less ambitious than the GOI's previous projections.

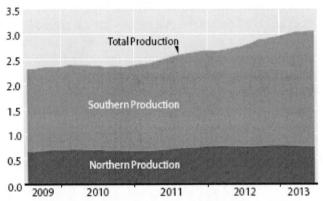

Note: Does not include oil produced in the Kurdistan Region.
Source: GOI, Ministry of Oil, "Domestic Consumption," www.oil.gov.iq.

Figure 3.4. Crude Oil Production, 7/2009–6/2013; MBPD, 12-month Rolling Average.

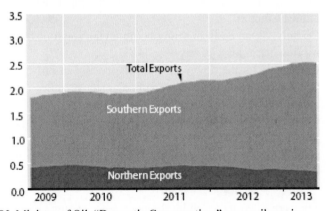

Source: GOI, Ministry of Oil, "Domestic Consumption," www.oil.gov.iq.

Figure 3.5. Crude Oil Exports, 7/2009–6/2013; MBPD, 12-month Rolling Average.

In line with these downward revisions, the GOI has been trying to renegotiate contracts it signed in 2009 with international oil companies to develop its oil fields. The aim is to lower the plateau production targets and extend output over a longer period of time. As of mid-August, the GOI had reached an agreement with the Eni-led consortium to lower the target at the Zubair field and with the Lukoilled consortium to do the same at West Qurna-2. It reportedly was still in discussions with ExxonMobil to reduce the targeted output at West Qurna-1; with Shell, at Majnoon; and with BP, at al-Rumaila.

Exports of crude oil during the first half of 2013 averaged 2.46 MBPD and followed almost the same pattern as production—up almost 7% from the first half of 2012, but down more than 3% from the second half. Almost 90% of this year's exports were shipped by tanker from Iraq's facilities in the south.

Starting in early May, successive attacks on the country's northern export pipeline continually disrupted the flow of oil destined for the Turkish port of Ceyhan:

- On May 6, an attack in Ninewa province shut the pipeline down for five days.
- On May 13, insurgents bombed the pipeline in Salah Al-Din, halting the flow for another three days.
- On May 17, pumping again was stopped by an attack southwest of Mosul.
- On June 4, a bombing shut the line down for three days.
- On June 21, an attack near Mosul put the pipeline out of service for almost a month.
- On July 28, an early morning bomb attack south of Mosul halted the oil flow for at least 10 days.
- On August 13, the flow was again stopped by an early morning blast.
- On August 16, a roadside bomb planted 40 miles south of Mosul disabled the pipeline for almost three days.
- On August 22, explosions in Ninewa and Salah Al-Din damaged four separate sections of the pipeline, not only shutting down the line, but also spilling oil into the Tigris River and threatening water supplies over a wide area.

Repairs were often impeded by the poor security situation in Ninewa and Salah Al-Din. These attacks, combined with leakages caused by the poor condition of the Kirkuk-Ceyhan pipeline and the KRG's December 2012 decision to stop exporting oil produced in the Region through that pipeline, resulted in a 24% drop in northern exports during the first half of 2013, compared with the first half of 2012. In May and June, these exports fell to their lowest levels in more than five years. In June, northern exports averaged

0.19 MBPD, compared with 0.55 MBPD during the same month in 2011—a 65% decrease.

Figure 3.5 shows the trends in exports during the four-year period ending June 30, 2013.

The INES envisions that pipelines and offshore loading facilities in southern Iraq will be expanded to an overall capacity of 6.8 MBPD by 2014 and that pipelines in northern Iraq will be rehabilitated and expanded to allow the export of 3.75 MBPD by 2017. To provide greater flexibility in choosing export routes and markets, the INES also calls for the rehabilitation and expansion of Iraq's internal system of pipelines linking the north and the south.[9]

Oil Production and Exports: Kurdistan Region

The KRG has continued on its independent path to increase the Kurdistan Region's oil production and exports. Crude-oil production in mid-2013 averaged about 200,000 barrels per day, and KRG Minister of Natural Resources Ashti Hawrami expected production to grow to 1 MBPD by 2015 and 2 MBPD by 2019.

Ignoring the GOI's concerns, several major Western oil companies— including ExxonMobil, Chevron, Total, and a Turkish company (apparently a public-private venture)—have agreed to help the KRG develop its oil resources. Because the GOI's Ministry of Oil did not approve the contracts for oil exploration in the Kurdistan Region, the GOI considers them to be illegal and has withheld payments to the KRG that would cover the oil companies' costs. Furthermore, two of the exploration blocks recently awarded to the Turkish company extend into Iraq's disputed territory.

Because of its disagreement with the GOI about oil-revenue sharing and payments to oil companies, the KRG stopped exporting its crude oil through the federal government's Kirkuk-Ceyhan pipeline in December 2012. Since then, it reportedly has been trucking oil to Turkey, with estimates varying from 30,000 to 65,000 barrels per day (BPD).

At the same time, the KRG has been building its own oil-export pipeline connecting the Taq Taq field in Erbil and Fishkabur on the Turkish border and will likely complete it this year. The GOI claims that the KRG is prohibited from exporting oil without first getting permission from the Ministry of Oil. However, in April 2013, the KRG Parliament passed a law—the Law of Identifying and Obtaining Financial Dues to the Kurdistan Region of Iraq from Federal Revenue—justifying the export of crude oil. According to Dr. Hawrami, if the GOI defaults on its payments to the KRG, "then the KRG is authorized to sell oil produced in the Region to recover unpaid dues." Dr. Hawrami expects the Kurdistan Region to be exporting 2 MBPD of crude oil by 2019.[10]

Refineries

In June, the Ministry of Oil awarded French-based Technip a follow-on contract to manage the engineering, procurement, and construction phase of the 200,000 BPD Kerbala refinery. Two months later, the ministry reported that 13 companies had been qualified to participate in the bidding round, scheduled for December 2013, for development of the Nassiriya oil field and construction of an accompanying refinery. With a capacity of 300,000 BPD, the refinery would be Iraq's largest.

Currently, the country's refineries produce too much low-grade fuel oil and too little higher-grade products, such as gasoline. According to the INES, the upgrade of existing and construction of new refineries will approximately double Iraq's current refining capacity (to 1.4 MBPD) and, equally significant, allow for a mix of petroleum products that matches domestic demand.

Until those projects are completed, Iraq will continue to require imported petroleum products to meet domestic needs. In March 2013, the National Iranian Oil Refining and Distribution Company agreed to supply Iraq with 2 million liters (about 525,000 gallons) of diesel fuel per day for an unspecified period of time. The contract was revised in May to allow Iraq to import up to 5 million liters per day.[11]

Natural Gas

The Basrah Gas Company—a joint venture between the Ministry of Oil's South Gas Company, Shell, and Mitsubishi—commenced formal operations in May 2013. Its mandate is to capture the natural gas that is produced along with crude oil at al-Rumaila, West Qurna-1, and Zubair, thereby reducing wasteful and environmentally damaging flaring and providing gas to fuel Iraq's combustion-turbine power plants.

According to the INES, all of Iraq's domestic gas requirements will be satisfied by domestic production by 2015. After that time, however, continued growth in production will result in surplus gas, which will have to be either exported or flared.[12]

Electricity

Inadequate electricity supplies have plagued Iraq since the 1990s. Outages and poor power quality, particularly in the hot summer months, have created widespread public discontent and occasional violent demonstrations. The GOI has promised to close the supply-demand gap, but these promises remain unkept.

In mid-June, the Ministry of Electricity (MOE) reported that total generating capacity on its national grid, including electric power imported from Iran, had climbed to 10,000 megawatts (MW). More than one-fifth of that capacity, however, was unproductive because of lack of fuel, low water levels at hydroelectric plants, and temporary shutdowns for maintenance. As a result, actual supply at the point of generation averaged about 7,800 MW. Furthermore, because of Iraq's inefficient power transmission and distribution networks, the amount of electricity that reached end users likely was less than 5,500 MW. In contrast, according to the MOE's own estimate, demand for electric power at the time totaled about 14,700 MW.

As it has done each summer over the past few years, the MOE said that the shortfall in power supplies was made worse by the Ministry of Oil's inability to provide sufficient fuel of the needed quality to existing power plants and also by contractors (some of whom apparently blamed the security situation or technical obstacles) falling behind schedule in the construction of new plants.

This year's increase in violence has resulted in relatively minor disruptions in electricity service. On May 21, bomb attacks destroyed seven transmission towers on a high-capacity line running between Baghdad and Baiji. The MOE returned the line to service in two weeks.

Although most of the MOE's new power-plant projects were progressing more slowly than planned, the ministry did report two significant milestones this reporting period:

- In March, Shanghai Electric completed the first generating unit, with a capacity of 330 MW, at al-Zubaidya thermal plant in Wassit. According to the MOE, the plant's capacity will reach 1,320 MW by the end of 2013 and 2,540 MW by March 2016, which would then likely make it the largest power plant in the Middle East.
- In April, Çalık Enerji of Turkey completed construction of the first power plant that uses combustion turbines purchased in the December 2008 "Mega Deal" with General Electric. Although the GOI bought 56 GE turbines with a total nameplate capacity of 7,000 MW in 2008, none came out of storage until more than three years later. Çalık Enerji began building the 1,250 MW al-Qaryat power plant in Kerbala in May 2012 and completed it on schedule.

Because the MOE stopped publishing daily statistics on Iraq's electricity situation in 2012, it is difficult to determine if these new plants have actually entered service and resulted in increased supplies on the national grid.

As it has done for the past several years, the CoM approved a plan on May 21 to help compensate for the MOE's inability to meet demand during the summer months. Under the plan, which will be in effect from June 1 until September 30, the Ministry of Oil will provide limited quantities of free fuel to owners of off-grid generators who deliver at least 10 hours of electricity per day at reasonable prices to residential customers.

At the direction of Prime Minister al-Maliki, the CoM postponed the regular agenda for its July 9 session so it could focus exclusively on the electric power situation. The CoM discussed the reasons— including identifying the parties responsible—for the delays in reaching planned production levels. This session was followed by a meeting in which Deputy Prime Minister for Energy Affairs Hussein al-Shahristani apparently directed the Ministry of Oil to provide additional quantities of oil and gas to MOE plants and called on security agencies to provide additional protection for the pipelines carrying fuel to these plants.

Later in July, Prime Minister al-Maliki publicly criticized Deputy Prime Minister al-Shahristani and MOE officials for providing overoptimistic assessments about Iraq's current and expected electricity-generation capabilities. He also said that the Mega Deal contracts with GE and Siemens— contracts that al-Maliki personally signed—were based on "defects and stupidity." The 72 combustion turbines that the GOI purchased under those two contracts have a combined nameplate capacity of more than 10,000 MW and operate best when fueled by natural gas. But, as the Prime Minister pointed out, Iraq is still unable to supply gas to many of its power plants, so the plants burn oil (when available) instead. By capturing associated gas in Iraq's southern oil fields, the Basrah Gas Company is meant to solve this supply problem, but that project is still in its early stages. Meanwhile, the MOE signed a contract on July 22 to purchase 25 million cubic meters (about 850 million cubic feet) of gas per day from Iran for a period of four years once a gas pipeline currently being constructed by an Iranian firm is completed.

Both before and after al-Maliki's comments, the MOE issued press releases reiterating its message that the supply-demand gap would be closed by the end of 2013. The INES offered a more tempered, but still optimistic, view: The power plants currently planned or under construction will more than triple effective generating capacity between now and 2016—from 7 gigawatts to 22 gigawatts— an amount sufficient to meet peak demand and end Iraq's need for imported electricity.[13]

Water

Iraq continues to contend with the diplomatically delicate issue of water scarcity, and, ironically, it suffered this year from its most damaging flooding in decades.

In late January, torrential rains caused the Tigris River flowing from Turkey to rise to its highest level in 50 years and overflow its banks, submerging several villages in north-central Iraq and displacing an estimated 5,000 people. Then, in May, the southern provinces of Thi-Qar, Missan, and Wassit were hit hard, with floodwaters coming from mountainous areas of Iran covering highways and destroying agricultural lands. The GOI declared a state of maximum alert over these floods.

This year's flooding, however, was not the norm. Since 2007, Iraq has suffered from drought conditions that have diminished the productivity of croplands and devastated livestock populations. Ensuring adequate supplies of water for drinking, agriculture, and other uses therefore remains a pressing, long-term problem for Iraq, and one with regional political implications.

Iraq depends primarily on surface water, predominately from the Tigris and Euphrates Rivers, to meet is needs. In a typical year, precipitation in Iraq contributes little to its surface water, with annual precipitation averaging just 8.5 inches (but ranging from 47 inches in the Kurdistan Region to less than 4 inches in most of the south). While some of Iraq's surface water originates in Syria and Iran, most comes from Turkey, where the average annual precipitation exceeds 23 inches.

Since the mid 1970s, Turkey has been planning and developing the Southeastern Anatolia Project, which includes 22 dams, 19 power plants, and numerous networks of irrigation canals within the Tigris-Euphrates basins. The entire project is scheduled for completion in 2023. The largest of the dams, the Ilisu, is being built on the Tigris and is expected to be completed in mid-2014. Turkey asserts that the dam will help Iraq by limiting the amount of water flowing downstream during the flood season, while increasing it during droughts. However, environmentalists and others in Iraq are concerned that the dam will further cut Iraq's water supply and stop the rebuilding of the country's marshes, which were heavily depleted during the Saddam era.

Iran has its own ambitious program for building dams, including on tributaries of the Tigris River. In mid-2013, 135 new dams were under construction throughout the country. One of them, Bakhtiari Dam, was being built in the Zagros Mountains of southwestern Iran and reportedly will be the world's tallest concrete dam. Precipitation in the area averages about 44 inches annually. If unimpeded, the waters of the Bakhtiari River eventually flow to the Shatt al-Arab, the withering, increasingly saline waterway along Iraq's southernmost border with Iran. Various Iraqi provincial leaders and members of the CoR have criticized Iran for already reducing river flows into Iraq. In mid-July, the Governor of Diyala reportedly accused Iran of committing "a crime against humanity and a violation of traditions and divine religions" for allegedly drying up a river that enters Diyala from Iran.

Prime Minister al-Maliki stressed that the water issue should be resolved through dialogue with Iraq's neighbors. On July 8, the Prime Minister chaired a meeting of the High National Commission on Water, which focused on securing Iraq's needs for water. Al-Maliki reportedly discussed the need to work with Turkey, Iran, and other neighboring countries on the management of shared water resources. He also addressed the demand side, saying that Iraqis needed to minimize waste by adopting modern irrigation and water-conservation techniques.[14]

Corruption and Integrity

In June, the GOI's Commission of Integrity (COI), with the support of the Central Statistics Office, released the findings of its study of corruption and integrity in Iraq's public sector. The study was based on analyses of a 2011 survey of 31,000 civil servants, another 2011 survey of 29,000 households, and COI data on corruption cases from 2006 through 2011. The study provides further evidence that corruption remains a major challenge in Iraq:

- Slightly more than half the people surveyed believed corruption was on the rise, while one-third perceived it to be decreasing.
- Almost 12% of Iraqis who had contact with a public official during the preceding year said that they paid a bribe.
- On average, citizens who paid bribes did so almost four times during the year.
- The prevalence of reported bribery was highest amongst citizens dealing with police, land registry, and tax and revenue officers.

- In absolute terms, bribes reportedly were most frequently paid to nurses in public health facilities, public utilities officers, and police officers.
- Citizens reported that almost two-thirds of bribes paid are requested by the civil servant involved either by an explicit request (41%) or in an indirect and implicit way (23%), 14% of the bribes are requested by a third party, and 19% are initiated by the citizen.
- Almost 60% of civil servants said they had been offered bribes.
- 35% of civil servants were hired without undergoing a formal selection process.
- More than 66% of the civil servants reportedly did not feel comfortable reporting instances of corruption.
- Less than 7% of civil servants said that they had ever attended integrity and anticorruption training.[15]

International Relations

U.S.-Iraq Strategic Partnership Meetings
As of the end of August, three meetings were held in 2013 as part of the ongoing implementation of the U.S.-Iraqi Strategic Framework Agreement (SFA). Signed by the United States and the GOI in November 2008, the SFA provides the basis for the bilateral relationship between the two countries. Issues covered by the SFA include political relations and diplomacy, defense and security, trade and finance, energy, judicial and law-enforcement issues, services, science, culture, education, and the environment. The joint U.S.-GOI Higher Coordinating Committee has overall responsibility for the SFA, while the work of implementing the agreement is managed by seven sector-specific Joint Coordinating Committees (JCCs).

On August 15, 2013, the Political and Diplomatic JCC met at the Department of State in Washington, D.C. The meeting was co-chaired by U.S. Secretary of State John Kerry and Iraqi Foreign Minister Hoshyar Zebari.

During the meeting, the U.S. delegation offered its full support for Iraq's efforts to strengthen ties with Kuwait and other regional partners, emphasizing the importance of working together to bolster moderate forces and isolate extremists in the region. The United States also affirmed its strong commitment to help the GOI defeat al-Qaeda and other terrorist groups that continue to threaten Iraq and the entire region.

According to their joint statement at the close of the meeting, both delegations emphasized their commitment to close and ongoing security cooperation, pledged to enhance this cooperation in pursuit of their joint interests in denying terrorists safe haven anywhere in Iraq, and explored areas of potential cooperation relative to the ongoing crisis in Syria, particularly on humanitarian issues and border security. The U.S. delegation emphasized the importance of providing refuge and services to people fleeing the violence in Syria, and the Iraqis reiterated their commitment to deter the transit of weapons through its territory and welcomed the recent notification to the U.S. Congress of the GOI's potential purchase of an integrated air-defense system to protect its airspace. Both sides said they were committed to a "Syrian-led political transition leading to a pluralistic political system representing the will of the Syrian people."

The U.S. delegation also pledged to assist Iraq in implementing the national elections scheduled for 2014 and to continue supporting GOI efforts to combat trafficking in persons and provide security for all Iraqis.

The other two JCC meetings this year were held in Baghdad. The first took place on March 6 and was the inaugural meeting of the Trade and Finance JCC. The stated goal of this JCC is to strengthen the GOI's "capacity to build a diversified and advanced economy that ensures Iraq's integration into the international community and meets the needs of the Iraqi people." The Iraqi delegation was jointly headed by Deputy Prime Minister for Economic Reform Dr. Rowsch Shaways and Minister of Trade Khair Allah Babakir, while Assistant U.S. Trade Representative Michael Delaney led the U.S. delegation. They reaffirmed each country's commitment to increasing bilateral trade and U.S. investment in Iraq.

On June 4, Acting Higher Judicial Council Chairman Judge Hassan al-Humairy and Assistant Chief of Mission Ambassador James Knight co-chaired a meeting of the Law Enforcement and Judicial Cooperation JCC. The two sides said that they emphasized the importance of continued close cooperation on law-enforcement and judicial matters, and they discussed ways to expand cooperation to advance the GOI's efforts to strengthen the administration of justice for women, children, and other vulnerable groups; prevent gender-based violence; combat trafficking in persons; and enhance the effectiveness of police-training institutions.[16]

Easing of Chapter VII Sanctions

On June 27, the UN Security Council voted unanimously to further ease the sanctions placed on Iraq after its 1990 invasion of Kuwait by moving the issue of missing Kuwaitis and Kuwaiti property from Chapter VII to Chapter VI of the UN Charter. Before this change, Iraq was obligated to release all Kuwaiti and third-country nationals detained in Iraq, return the remains of any of them who were deceased, and return all Kuwaiti property seized by Iraq; and failure to do so could subject Iraq to sanctions or military intervention. The resolution adopted in June called on the GOI to continue searching for missing persons and remains, as well as seized property, but removed the threat of military action.

Two and a half years earlier, in December 2010, the United Nations ended trade sanctions related to weapons of mass destruction, extended protection of Iraqi oil funds until December 2011, and ended all activities related to the Oil for Food program. The recent move leaves only a limited arms embargo and repayment of the final $11 billion of the $52 billion in compensation owed by Iraq to Kuwait under Chapter VII. Iraq expects to pay off the remainder by 2015.

The GOI has been pushing for several years to be removed from the international sanctions. Until recently, however, Kuwait continued to urge the United Nations not to lift them. With the resolution of some remaining issues and continued diplomatic work, particularly over the past year, Kuwait agreed to support Iraq's request.[17]

Extension of DFI Protection

On May 17, 2013, President Obama continued for one year the national emergency with respect to the stabilization of Iraq originally declared by President George W. Bush a decade earlier. Executive Order 13303, which President Bush signed on May 22, 2003, protected the Development Fund for Iraq (DFI), Iraqi petroleum and petroleum products, and certain other financial instruments in which Iraq has an interest from attachment or judicial processes. The stated purpose of the order was to help ensure these assets would be available for "the orderly reconstruction of Iraq, the restoration and maintenance of peace and security in the country, and the development of political, administrative, and economic institutions in Iraq."

At the August 15 meeting of the Political and Diplomatic JCC, the U.S. and Iraqi delegations discussed President Obama's decision to extend protections for the DFI. The Iraqi side affirmed its commitment to resolve outstanding claims over the coming months to set the conditions for those protections to expire in 2014.[18]

Human Rights

Latest UN Assessment

The resurgent violence that started in 2012 is a central concern in the latest UN semiannual report on human rights in Iraq. In releasing the report on June 27, Martin Kobler, the former Special Representative of the Secretary-General for Iraq, said: "We have consistently urged Iraqi leaders to engage in dialogue and develop policies that address the root causes of the problem. Too many innocent lives have been lost."

The report, which focused on the second half of 2012, included the following observations:

- While improvements were seen in prisons run by the Ministry of Justice (MOJ), many detainees continued to complain of abuse, mistreatment, and torture at the hands of Ministry of Interior personnel following arrest and during the investigation phase, often with the intention of forcing confessions, before transfer to MOJ facilities.
- Courts remain under-resourced, contributing to long delays in processing cases beyond time limits established by law and overcrowding in many prisons and detention centers.
- Weaknesses identified in Iraq's criminal justice system raise serious concerns about Iraq's use of the death penalty.
- Women and children continue to suffer from domestic and other forms of violence, and women face discrimination and other barriers in accessing economic, social, and educational opportunities.
- Persons with disabilities continue to suffer from discrimination in relation to health care, education, employment, and economic opportunity; and the CoR has yet to pass a law to ensure compliance with the Convention on the Rights of Persons with Disabilities, which the GOI signed in January 2012 and ratified in March 2013.
- Iraq's various ethnic and religious groups, especially members of the Turkmen community, are subjected to various acts of violence, including kidnapping, murder, harassment, and other threats.

- Freedom of expression, opinion, and assembly are matters of concern, with journalists continuing to suffer harassment, abuse, and sometimes violence in carrying out their professional duties (five were killed in 2012) and authorities restricting some peaceful demonstrations by citizens for political reasons.

The UN report generally did not lump the Kurdistan Region with the rest of Iraq and noted that the overall human rights situation in the Region continued to improve, though concerns remain over respect for freedoms of assembly and expression, as well as the protection of journalists. During the reporting period, the Kurdistan Region experienced almost no insurgent violence, but civilians living in areas close to the international borders continued to suffer from the effects of cross-border shelling and military operations conducted by foreign forces.[19]

Human Trafficking

On June 19, DoS released its Trafficking in Persons Report for 2013, placing Iraq among the so-called Tier 2 countries—those whose governments do not fully comply with the Trafficking Victims Protection Act's minimum standards but are making significant efforts to bring themselves into compliance. Iraq had been on the Tier 2 Watch List for the previous four years. DoS found that Iraq had made significant progress, justifying an upgrade to Tier 2.

Iraq passed the Anti-Trafficking in Persons Law in April 2012. Under this law, the government established an antitrafficking department within the MOI, which collected law-enforcement data and operated a new antitrafficking hotline. Also under the law, Iraq created the Central Committee to Combat Trafficking in Persons, which actively furthered the government's antitrafficking efforts. It met multiple times, televised a few of the meetings to raise awareness about trafficking, and included participants from international organizations, foreign governments, and nongovernmental organizations (NGOs).

While citing Iraq's improvement, DoS's 2013 report included the following observations:

- Despite its progress, Iraq remains a source and destination country for men, women, and children subjected to sex trafficking and forced labor.

- The GOI conducted some investigations and at least one prosecution under the new law. However, it continued to fail to investigate and punish government officials complicit in trafficking offenses.
- The GOI has done little to help victims of forced labor and sex trafficking, and it continues to prosecute victims and prohibit NGOs from running shelters for them. However, the GOI identified trafficking victims (none had been identified in previous years) and identified some victims who had been imprisoned for prostitution. The Ministry of Human Rights recommended that the Higher Judicial Council reopen their cases under the antitrafficking law. The GOI also has established a temporary shelter, identified a location for a permanent shelter, and drafted shelter guidelines.
- Although the GOI prohibits NGOs from operating shelters for trafficking victims, some government officials cooperate with NGOs and occasionally refer victims to them. A national trafficking victim referral mechanism has been drafted, but has not yet been finalized.
- Iraqi women and girls are often lured into forced prostitution both within Iraq and in neighboring countries.
- Iraq's large population of internally displaced persons and refugees are particularly vulnerable to forced labor and sex trafficking. Refugees from Syria have been subjected to a wide spectrum of activities: women enter into commercially dependent relationships with Iraqi men, men work without contracts, and children are pressured into begging.
- Iraq is a destination for migrants from many countries who are either lured to Iraq under false pretenses or subjected to involuntary servitude or forced prostitution once they arrive.[20]

End Notes

[1] Open-source documents in English and Arabic, 4/2013–8/2013; UNAMI, press releases, various dates, unami.unmissions.org.

[2] Open-source documents in English and Arabic, 7/2013–8/2013; DoS, press release, "U.S. Condemns Terrorist Attacks in Iraq and Pledges To Help Combat al-Qaeda," 8/10/2013, iraq.usembassy.gov/pr08112013.html.

[3] Open-source documents in English and Arabic, 4/2013–8/2013; DoS, press release, "Joint Statement of the U.S.-Iraq Political and Diplomatic Joint Coordination Committee," 8/15/2013, www.state ps/2013/08/213169.htm.

[4] Open-source documents in English and Arabic, 7/2013–8/2013.

[5] UNHCR, Syria Regional Refugee Response Inter-agency Information Sharing Portal, data.unhcr.org/syrianrefugees/country. php?id=103; OCHA, ReliefWeb, Syrian Arab Republic, reliefweb.int/country/syr; GOI, CoM, "Council of Ministers Decisions in Session 36 in 8/20/2013," www.cabinet.iq/ArticleShow. aspx?ID =3504; UNHCR, "Iraq Operation: Monthly Statistical Update on Return," 12/2011, 12/2012, and 4/2013; open-source documents in English and Arabic, 5/2013–8/2013.

[6] GOI, Office of the Prime Minister, press release, "Prime Minister Nuri al-Maliki Meets President of Kurdistan, Massoud Barzani," 7/7/2013; KRG, press releases, "President Barzani Receives Prime Minister Maliki," 6/11/2013, "President Barzani Visits Baghdad," 7/9/2013; open-source documents in English and Arabic, 6/2013–7/2013.

[7] IHEC, Election Results 2013, ihec.iq/en/ index.php/ntaij.html, and Final Results of Provincial Council Elections for Anbar and Nineveh Provinces, www.ihec.iq/en/index.php/ news/3861.html; open-source documents in English and Arabic, 4/2013–8/2013.

[8] Booz & Company, *Integrated National Energy Strategy,* Summary of the Final Report, 6/12/2013.

[9] GOI, Ministry of Oil, Domestic Consumption, www.oil.; MEES, *Weekly Energy, Economic dr Geopolitical Outlook,* Vol. 56 No. 22, 5/31/2013, p. 2, and Vol. 56 No. 30, 7/26/2013, p. 2; Booz & Company, *Integrated National Energy Strategy,* Summary of the Final Report, 6/12/2013; open-source documents in English and Arabic, 5/2013–8/2013.

[10] *The Review: Kurdistan Region of Iraq,* 7/2013, pp. 33–36, www.krg.org/a/d. aspx?s=010000&l=12&a=47763 6/2013; MEES, *Weekly Energy, Economic dr Geopolitical Outlook,* Vol. 56 No. 24, 6/14/2013, p. 2; open-source documents in English and Arabic, 6/2013–8/2013.

[11] Technip, press release, "Technip Awarded Contract for the Karbala Refinery in Iraq," 6/4/2013; GOI, Ministry of Oil, press releases, "Iraq Builds a 300 Thousand Barrel/Day Refinery Which Is the Largest in the Country," 6/26/2013, and "Announcement from the Petroleum Contracts & Licensing Directorate," 8/15/2013, www.oil; Booz & Company, *Integrated National Energy Strategy,* Summary of the Final Report, 6/12/2013; open-source documents in English and Arabic, 5/2013–8/2013.

[12] MEES, *Weekly Energy, Economic dr Geopolitical Outlook,* Vol. 56 No. 29, 7/19/2013, p. 2; Booz & Company, *Integrated National Energy Strategy,* Summary of the Final Report, 6/12/2013; open-source documents in English and Arabic, 8/2013.

[13] GOI, MOE, press releases, "The Productive Capacity of the National Electricity System up to Ten Thousand Megawatts," 6/16/2013, www.moelc.gov.iq/ar/index.php?name=New s&file=article&sid=883, "Low Gas Pressure Caused the Loss of 1,100 Megawatts and Will Add 1,230 MW to the System Soon," 7/1/2013, www.moelc.gov.iq/ar/index.php? name=News& file=article&sid=910, "Ministry Must Rely on its Capabilities in Providing Fuel for Generating Plants," 7/1/2013, www.moelc.gov.iq/ar/ index.php?name=News&file= article&sid=911, "Targeting of Energy Transmission Line and the Fall of the Seven Towers," 5/23/2013, www. moelc.gov.iq/ar/index.php?name= News&file= article&sid=848, "Deputy Prime Minister for Energy and Electricity Minister Inaugurate the First Phase of the Station SPA," 3/10/2013, www.moelc.gov.iq/ar/index.php?name=New s&file=article&sid=736, "Opening of 1,250 MW al-Qaryat Gas Station in the Holy City of Kerbala," 4/22/2013, www.moelc.gov.iq/ar/ index.php?name=News&file=article&sid=792, "Cabinet Allocates Its Twenty-ninth Session To Discuss the Topic of Electric Power," 7/11/2013, www.moelc.gov.iq/ar/index.php?name=Ne ws&file=article&sid=926, "The Ministry of Electricity To Conclude a First of Its Kind Contract with the Iranian Oil Ministry," 7/22/2013, www.moelc.gov.iq/ar/index.php?name=News &file=article&sid=

957, "Minister of Electricity Renewed Pledges That the End of the Year Will Exceed the Energy Crisis," 7/16/2013, www. moelc.gov.iq/ar/index.php?name=News&file=article&sid =947, and "The Ministry Plans Implemented at a Steady Pace To Solve the Power Crisis in the Country," 7/28/2013, www.moelc. gov.iq/ar/index.php?name=News&file =article &sid=966; GOI, General Secretariat for the Council of Ministers, press release, "Supplying Residential Generators with Free Gas and Oil," 5/21/2013, www.cabinet.iq/ArticleShow. aspx?ID =3151; GOI, CoM, "Council of Ministers Decisions in Session 29 in 7/9/2013," www. cabinet.iq/ArticleShow.aspx?ID =3357; Booz & Company, *Integrated National Energy Strategy,* Summary of the Final Report, 6/12/2013.

[14] UN SPIDER, Iraq: UN-SPIDER Network Acquires Satellite Imagery for Floods, www. un-spider.org/about-us/news/en/6647/2013-05-   13t071000/iraq-un-spider-network-acquires-satellite-imagery-floods; IOM-Iraq, Special Report, "Water Scarcity," 6/2012, p. 2; FAO, Aquastat, "Euphrates-Tigris River Basin," www. fao.org/nr/water/aquastat/basins /euphratestigris/index.stm, and "Iraq," www.fao.org/ nr/water/aquastat/countries_regions /IRQ/ index.stm; UN Iraq, "Water in Iraq Factsheet," 3/2013, wwwjapuiraq.org/documents /1866/Water-Factsheet.pdf; World Bank, Data, "Average Precipitation in Depth (mm per year)," data.worldbank.org/indicator/AG.LND.PRCP. MM; USDA Foreign Agricultural Service, "Southeastern Anatolia Project (GAP)," www. fas.usda.gov/remote/mideast_pecad /gap/ introduction.htm; Republic of Turkey, Ministry of Foreign Affairs, "Ilisu Dam," www.mfa.gov. tr/ilisu-dam.en.mfa; Iran Water and Power Resources Development Co., "Bakhtiari Project," en.iwpco.ir/Bakhtiari/BaseInfo.aspx; GOI, Media Advisor Ali al-Mousawi, "PM Nouri al-Maliki Heads a National High Committee Meeting on Water," 7/8/2013, www.facebook. com/ali.almussawi2; open-source documents in English and Arabic, 8/2013.

[15] GOI, COI and CSO, "Corruption and Integrity Challenges in the Public Sector of Iraq: An Evidence-based Study," 1/2013 (released 6/19/2013).

[16] U.S. Embassy-Baghdad, The Strategic Framework Agreement (SFA) and U.S. Iraqi Bilateral Relations, iraq.usembassy. gov/american-iraqi.html; DoS, Office of the Spokesperson, press release, "Joint Statement of the U.S.-Iraq Political and Diplomatic Joint Coordination Committee," 8/15/2013, www. state. U.S. Embassy-Baghdad, Office of the Spokesman, "The United States and Iraq Inaugurate the Trade and Finance Joint Coordination Committee," 3/6/2013, iraq.usembassy.gov/ pr_march_6_2013b.html, "Iraq-U.S. Joint Coordination Committee on Law Enforcement and Judicial Cooperation," 6/4/2013, iraq. usembassy.gov/pr060413.html.

[17] UN Security Council, Department of Public Information, press release, "Unanimously Adopting Resolution 2107 (2013), Security Council Removes Iraq from Chapter VII Ob-ligations Over Return of Kuwaiti Nationals," 6/27/2013, www.un.org/News/Press /docs/2013/ sc11050.doc.htm; U.S. Embassy-Baghdad, press release, "Statement by Secretary Kerry: UN Security Council Decision To Transfer Chapter VII Mandate to the UN Assistance Mission in Iraq," 6/28/2013, iraq.usembassy. gov/pr-062813.html; open-source documents in English and Arabic, 5/2013–8/2013.

[18] White House, Notice, "Continuation of the National Emergency with Respect to the Sta-bilization of Iraq," 5/17/2013, Executive Order 13303, "Protecting the Development Fund for Iraq and Certain Other Property in Which Iraq Has an Interest," 5/22/2003; DoS, Office of the Spokesperson, press release, "Joint Statement of the U.S.-Iraq Political and Diplomatic Joint Coordination Committee," 8/15/2013, www. state

[19] UNAMI Human Rights Office and OHCHR, *Report on Human Rights in Iraq: July–December 2012,* 6/2013; UNAMI, press release, "Iraq's Human Rights Progress in Question as Violence Takes Its Toll: UN Report," 6/27/2013.

[20] DoS, "Briefing on the 2013 Trafficking in Persons Report," 6/19/2013, and *Trafficking in Persons Report,* 6/2013, www.state tiprpt/2013/.

ACRONYMS

Acronym	Definition
AFOSI	U.S. Air Force Office of Special Investigations
AIG	Assistant Inspector General
AUSA	Assistant U.S. Attorney
BPD	barrels per day
BSA	Board of Supreme Audit
CENTCOM	U.S. Central Command
CERP	Commander's Emergency Response Program
CID	U.S. Army Criminal Investigation Command
CID-MPFU	U.S. Army Criminal Investigation Command-Major Procurement Fraud Unit
CIGIE	Council of the Inspectors General on Integrity and Efficiency
COI	Commission of Integrity (previously the Commission on Public Integrity, or CPI)
CoM	Council of Ministers
CoR	Council of Representatives
CPA	Coalition Provisional Authority
CPA-IG	Coalition Provisional Authority Inspector General
CPI	Commission on Public Integrity
CWC	Commission on Wartime Contracting in Iraq and Afghanistan
DCAA	Defense Contract Audit Agency
DCIS	Defense Criminal Investigative Service
DCMA	Defense Contract Management Agency
DFI	Development Fund for Iraq
DoD	Department of Defense
DoJ	Department of Justice
DoS	Department of State
DRL	DoS Bureau of Democracy, Human Rights, and Labor
ESF	Economic Support Fund

(Continued)

Acronym	Definition
FAR	Federal Acquisition Regulation
FBI	Federal Bureau of Investigation
FERRET	Forensic Evaluation Research and Recovery Enforcement Team
FinCEN	Financial Crimes Enforcement Network (Department of the Treasury)
FOB	forward operating base
GAO	Government Accountability Office
GOI	Government of Iraq
H.R.	House Resolution
IAWG	Iraq Accountability Working Group
ICCTF	International Contract Corruption Task Force
ICE	Immigration and Customs Enforcement
IED	improvised explosive device
IHEC	Independent High Electoral Commission
IIGC	Iraq Inspectors General Council
INCLE	International Narcotics Control and Law Enforcement account
INES	Integrated National Energy Strategy
INL	DoS Bureau of International Narcotics and Law Enforcement Affairs
INTERCEPT	International Criminal Enforcement and Prosecution Team
IRI	International Republican Institute
IRMS	Iraq Reconstruction Management System
IRRF	Iraq Relief and Reconstruction Fund
IRS	Internal Revenue Service
IRS-CI	Internal Revenue Service-Criminal Investigation
ISF	Iraqi Security Forces
ISFF	Iraq Security Forces Fund
ISIS	Islamic State of Iraq and Sham (al-Qaeda group)
IT	information technology
JCC	Joint Coordinating Committee
JCC-I/A	Joint Contracting Command-Iraq/ Afghanistan

Acronym	Definition
JTTF	Joint Terrorism Task Force
KBR	Kellogg Brown & Root Inc.
KRG	Kurdistan Regional Government
LCC	Laguna Construction Company, Inc.
MBPD	million barrels per day
MOE	Ministry of Electricity
MOJ	Ministry of Justice
MW	megawatt
NCIS	Naval Criminal Investigative Service
NDI	National Democratic Institute
NGO	non-governmental organization
OSC-I	Office of Security Cooperation-Iraq
PCIE	President's Council on Integrity and Efficiency
PCO	Project and Contracting Office
PDP	Police Development Program
P.L.	Public Law
PMAC	Prime Minister's Advisory Commission
PRT	Provincial Reconstruction Team
PSC	private security contractor
SFA	Strategic Framework Agreement
SFC	sergeant first class
SIGAR	Special Inspector General for Afghanistan Reconstruction
SIGIR	Special Inspector General for Iraq Reconstruction
SIGPRO	SIGIR Prosecutorial Initiative
SIGTARP	Special Inspector General for the Troubled Asset Relief Program
SPITFIRE	Special Investigative Task Force for Iraq Reconstruction
SRO	stabilization and reconstruction operation
UCMJ	Uniform Code of Military Justice
UN	United Nations
UNHCR	United Nations High Commissioner for Refugees
UNSCR	United Nations Security Council Resolution
USA	U.S. Army
USACE	U.S. Army Corps of Engineers
USAID	U.S. Agency for International Development
USAID OIG	U.S. Agency for International Development Office of Inspector General

(Continued)

Acronym	Definition
USAR	U.S. Army Reserve
USG	U.S. government
USIP	U.S. Institute of Peace
USOCO	U.S. Office for Contingency Operations

In: Iraq
Editor: Gustavo D. Ryder
ISBN: 978-1-62948-478-5
© 2013 Nova Science Publishers, Inc.

Chapter 2

IRAQ: POLITICS, GOVERNANCE, AND HUMAN RIGHTS[*]

Kenneth Katzman

SUMMARY

Nearly two years after the 2011 U.S. withdrawal from Iraq, increasingly violent sectarian divisions are undermining the fragile stability left in place. Sunni Arab Muslims, who resent Shiite political domination and perceived discrimination, have escalated their political opposition to the government of Prime Minister Nuri al-Maliki through demonstrations and violence. Iraq's Kurds are embroiled in separate political disputes with the Baghdad government over territorial, political, and economic issues. The rifts impinged on provincial elections during April—June 2013 and could affect the viability of national elections for a new parliament and government expected in March 2014. Maliki is expected to seek to retain his post in that vote.

The violent component of Sunni unrest is spearheaded by the Sunni insurgent group Al Qaeda in Iraq (AQ-I) as well as groups linked to the former regime of Saddam Hussein. These groups, emboldened by the Sunni-led uprising in Syria as well as perceived discrimination against Sunni Iraqis, are conducting attacks against Shiite neighborhoods, Iraqi Security Force (ISF) members, and Sunni supporters of Maliki with increasing frequency and lethality.

---

[*] This is an edited, reformatted and augmented version of Congressional Research Service, Publication No. RS21968, dated August 22, 2013.

The attacks appear intended to reignite all-out sectarian conflict and provoke the fall of the government. To date, the 800,000 person ISF has countered the escalating violence without outside assistance and Iraqi forces have not substantially fractured along sectarian lines. However, a July 2013 major prison break near Baghdad cast doubt on the ISF ability to counter the violence longer term.

U.S. forces left in December 2011 in line with a November 2008 bilateral U.S.-Iraq Security Agreement. Iraq refused to extend the presence of U.S. troops in Iraq, seeking to put behind it the period of U.S. political and military control. Some outside experts and some in Congress have asserted that U.S. influence over Iraq has ebbed significantly since, tarnishing the legacy of U.S. combat deaths and funds spent on the intervention. Program components of what were to be enduring, close security relations—extensive U.S. training for Iraq's security forces through an Office of Security Cooperation—Iraq (OSC-I) and a State Department police development program—have languished or are ending in part because Iraqi officials perceive the programs as indicators of residual U.S. tutelage. The U.S. civilian presence in Iraq has declined from about 17,000 to about 10,500 and is expected to fall to 5,500 by the end of 2013. Still, Iraqi efforts to acquire sophisticated U.S. equipment such as F-16 combat aircraft, air defense equipment, and attack helicopters gives the Administration some leverage over Baghdad.

Although recognizing that Iraq wants to rebuild its relations in its immediate neighborhood, the Administration and Congress seek to prevent Iraq from falling under the sway of Iran, with which the Maliki government has built close relations. However, the legacy of the 1908-88 Iran-Iraq war, Arab and Persian differences, Iraq's efforts to reestablish its place in the Arab world, and Maliki's need to work with senior Iraqi Sunnis limit, Iranian influence over the Baghdad government. Still, fearing that a change of regime in Syria will further embolden the Iraqi Sunni opposition, Maliki has not joined U.S. and other Arab state calls for Syrian President Bashar Al Assad to leave office and Iraq has not consistently sought to prevent Iranian overflights of arms deliveries to Syria.

Iraq took a large step toward returning to the Arab fold by hosting an Arab League summit on March 27-29, 2012, and has substantially repaired relations with Kuwait, the state that Saddam Hussein invaded and occupied in 1990. In June 2013, the relationship with Kuwait helped Iraq emerge from some Saddam-era restrictions under Chapter VII of the U.N. Charter.

OVERVIEW OF THE POST-SADDAM POLITICAL TRANSITION

A U.S.-led military coalition, in which about 250,000 U.S. troops participated, crossed the border from Kuwait into Iraq on March 19, 2003. Turkey refused to allow any of the coalition force to move into Iraq from the north. After several weeks of combat, the regime of Saddam Hussein fell on April 9, 2003. During the 2003-2011 presence of U.S. forces, Iraq completed a transition from the dictatorship of Saddam Hussein to a plural political system in which varying sects and ideological and political factions compete in elections. A series of elections began in 2005, after a one-year occupation period and a subsequent seven-month interim period of Iraqi self-governance. There has been a consensus among Iraqi elites since 2005 to give each community a share of power and prestige to promote cooperation and unity. Still, disputes over the relative claim of each community on power and economic resources permeated almost every issue in Iraq and were never fully resolved. These unresolved differences—muted during the last years of the U.S. military presence—have reemerged since mid-2012 and threaten to return Iraq to a period of sectarian conflict.

Initial Transition and Construction of the Political System

After the fall of Saddam's regime, the United States set up an occupation structure, reportedly based on concerns that immediate sovereignty would favor established Islamist and pro-Iranian factions over nascent pro-Western secular parties. In May 2003, President Bush, reportedly seeking strong leadership in Iraq, named Ambassador L. Paul Bremer to head a "Coalition Provisional Authority" (CPA), which was recognized by the United Nations as an occupation authority. Bremer discontinued a tentative political transition process and in July July 2003 appointed a non-sovereign Iraqi advisory body, the 25-member "Iraq Governing Council" (IGC). During that year, U.S. and Iraqi negotiators, advised by a wide range of international officials and experts, drafted a "Transitional Administrative Law" (TAL, interim constitution), which became effective on March 4, 2004.[1]

After about one year of occupation, the United States, following a major debate between the CPA and various Iraqi factions, appointed an Iraqi interim government on June 28, 2004. That date met the TAL-specified deadline of

June 30, 2004, for the end of the occupation period, which also laid out the
elections roadmap discussed below.

Major Factions Dominate Post-Saddam Politics

The interim government appointed by the CPA was headed by a prime
minister, Iyad al-Allawi. He is leader of the Iraq National Accord (INA), a
secular, non-sectarian faction that had long opposed Saddam Hussein. Allawi
is a Shiite Muslim but his supporters are mostly Sunni Arabs, including some
former members of the Baath Party. The president of the interim government
was Sunni tribalist Ghazi al-Yawar.

- *Da'wa Party.* The interim government was heavily influenced by
  parties and factions that had long campaigned to oust Saddam. These
  included long-standing anti-Saddam Shiite Islamist parties, such as
  the Da'wa Party and the Islamic Supreme Council of Iraq (ISCI), both
  of which were Iran-supported underground parties working to
  overthrow Saddam Hussein since the early 1980s. The largest faction
  of the Da'wa Party is led by Nuri al-Maliki, who displaced former
  leader Ibrahim al-Jaafari in 2006.
- *Islamic Supreme Council of Iraq* (ISCI) is led by the Hakim family—
  the sons of the revered late Grand Ayatollah Muhsin Al Hakim, who
  hosted Iran's Ayatollah Ruhollah Khomeini when he was in exile in
  Iraq during 1964-78. In the immediate post-Saddam period, Abd al-
  Aziz al-Hakim led the group after the August 2003 assassination of
  his elder brother, Mohammad Baqr al-Hakim, in a bombing outside a
  Najaf mosque. After Abd al-Aziz al-Hakim's death from lung cancer
  in August 2009, his son Ammar, born in 1971, succeeded him as ISCI
  chief.
- *Sadrists.* Another Shiite Islamist faction, one loyal to radical cleric
  Moqtada Al Sadr, whose family had lived under Saddam's rule, gelled
  as a cohesive party after Saddam's ouster and also formed an armed
  faction called the Mahdi Army. Sadr is the son of revered Ayatollah
  Mohammad Sadiq Al Sadr, who was killed by Saddam's security
  forces in 1999, and a relative of Mohammad Baqr Al Sadr, a Shiite
  theoretician and contemporary and colleague of Ayatollah Khomeini.
- *Kurdish Factions: KDP and PUK.* Also influential in post-Saddam
  politics are the long-established Kurdish parties the Kurdistan
  Democratic Party (KDP) headed by Masoud Barzani, son of the late,

revered Kurdish independence fighter Mullah Mustafa Barzani, and
the Patriotic Union of Kurdistan (PUK) headed by Jalal Talabani.

- *Iraqi National Congress* (INC). Another significant longtime anti-
Saddam faction was the INC of Ahmad Chalabi. The group had
lobbied extensively in Washington D.C. since the early 1990s for the
United States to overthrow Saddam, but did poorly in post-Saddam
Iraqi elections.

- *Iraqi National Alliance* (INA). Another major exile group that became
prominent in post-Saddam Iraq was the Iraqi National Alliance of
Iyad al-Allawi. Allawi is a Shiite but most of the group reportedly is
Sunni. After returning to Iraq, Allawi went on to become prime
minister of the interim government and then leader of the major anti-
Maliki secular bloc now called *"Iraqiyya."* In opposing Maliki,
Iraqiyya has been allied with various Sunni groups such as Al-
Hadba'a—a party of hardline Sunni Arabs mainly in Nineveh
Province and committed to an "Arab and Islamic identity" (anti-
Kurdish) for the province. That faction is led by COR Speaker Osama
al-Nujayfi and his brother Atheel.

Interim Government Formed and New Coalitions Take Shape

Iraqi leaders of all factions agreed that elections should determine the
composition of Iraq's new power structure. The beginning of the elections
process was set for 2005 to produce a transitional parliament that would
supervise writing a new constitution, a public referendum on a new
constitution, and then the election of a full term government under that
constitution.

In accordance with the dates specified in the TAL, the first post-Saddam
election was held on January 30, 2005 for a 275-seat transitional National
Assembly (which would form an executive), four-year-term provincial
councils in all 18 provinces ("provincial elections"), and a Kurdistan regional
assembly (111 seats). The Assembly election was conducted according to the
"proportional representation/closed list" election system, in which voters
chose among "political entities" (a party, a coalition of parties, or people). The
ballot included 111 entities, nine of which were multi-party coalitions. Still
restive over their displacement from power in the 2003 U.S. invasion, Sunni
Arabs (20% of the overall population) boycotted, winning only 17 Assembly
seats, and only 1 seat on the 51-seat Baghdad provincial council. Moqtada Al
Sadr, whose armed faction was then fighting U.S. forces, also boycotted the
election, leaving his faction poorly represented on the provincial councils.

The resulting transitional government placed Shiites and Kurds in the highest positions. PUK leader Jalal Talabani was president and then Da'wa party leader Ibrahim al-Jafari was prime minister. Sunnis were Assembly speaker, deputy president, a deputy prime minister, and six ministers, including defense.

Permanent Constitution[2]

A major task accomplished by the elected transitional Assembly was the drafting of a permanent constitution, adopted in a public referendum of October 15, 2005. A 55-member drafting committee in which Sunnis were underrepresented produced a draft providing for:

- The three Kurdish-controlled provinces of Dohuk, Irbil, and Sulaymaniyah to constitute a legal "region" administered by the Kurdistan Regional Government (KRG), which would have its own elected president and parliament (Article 113).
- a December 31, 2007, deadline to hold a referendum on whether Kirkuk (Tamim province) would join the Kurdish region (Article 140).
- designation of Islam as "a main source" of legislation.
- all orders of the CPA to be applicable until amended (Article 126), and a "Federation Council" (Article 62), a second chamber with size and powers to be determined in future law (not adopted to date).
- a 25% electoral goal for women (Article 47).
- families to choose which courts to use for family issues (Article 41); making only primary education mandatory (Article 34).
- having Islamic law experts and civil law judges on the federal supreme court (Article 89). Many Iraqi women opposed this and the previous provisions as giving too much discretion to male family members.
- two or more provinces to join together to form new autonomous "regions." This provision was reaffirmed and implemented by an October 2006 law on formation of regions.
- "regions" to organize internal security forces, legitimizing the fielding of the Kurds' *peshmerga* militia (Article 117). This continued a TAL provision.
- the central government to distribute oil and gas revenues from "current fields" in proportion to population, and for regions to have a role in allocating revenues from new energy discoveries (Article 109).

These provisions left many disputes unresolved, particularly the balance between central government and regional and local authority. The TAL made approval of the constitution subject to a veto if a two-thirds majority of voters in any three provinces voted it down. With Sunni-Shiite tensions still high, Sunnis registered in large numbers (70%-85%) to try to defeat the constitution, despite a U.S.-mediated agreement of October 11, 2005 to have a future vote on amendments to the constitution. The Sunni provinces of Anbar and Salahuddin had a 97% and 82% "no" vote, respectively, but the constitution was adopted because Nineveh province voted 55% "no"—short of the two-thirds "no" majority needed to vote the constitution down.

December 15, 2005 Elections Establish the First Full-Term Goverment

The December 15, 2005, elections were for a full-term (four-year) national government (also in line with the schedule laid out in the TAL). Each province contributed a set number of seats to a "Council of Representatives" (COR), a formula adopted to attract Sunni participation. There were 361 political "entities," including 19 multi-party coalitions, competing in a "closed list" voting system (in which votes are cast only for parties and coalitions, not individual candidates). Voters chose lists representing their sects and regions, and the Shiites and Kurds again emerged dominant. The COR was inaugurated on March 16, 2006, but political infighting caused the replacement of Jafari with another Da'wa figure, Nuri Kamal al-Maliki, as Prime Minister.

On April 22, 2006, the COR approved Talabani to continue as president. His two deputies were Adel Abd al-Mahdi (incumbent) of ISCI and Tariq al-Hashimi, leader of the Iraqi Islamic Party (IIP). Another Sunni figure, the hardline Mahmoud Mashhadani (National Dialogue Council party), became COR speaker. Maliki won COR approval of a 37-member cabinet (including two deputy prime ministers) on May 20, 2006. Three key slots (Defense, Interior, and National Security) were not filled permanently until June 2006, due to infighting. Of the 37 posts, there were 19 Shiites; 9 Sunnis; 8 Kurds; and 1 Christian. Four were women.

2006-2011: SECTARIAN CONFLICT AND U.S.-ASSISTED RECONCILIATION

The 2005 elections were considered successful by the Bush Administration, but they did not resolve the Sunni-Arab grievances over their diminished positions in the power structure. Subsequent events suggested that the elections in 2005 might have worsened the violence by exposing and reinforcing the political weakness of the Sunni Arabs. With tensions high, the bombing of a major Shiite shrine within the Sunni-dominated province of Salahuddin in February 2006 set off major sectarian unrest, characterized in part by Sunni insurgent activities against government and U.S. troops, high-casualty suicide and other bombings, and the empowerment of Shiite militia factions to counter the Sunni acts. The sectarian violence was so serious that many experts, by the end of 2006, were considering the U.S. mission as failing, an outcome that an "Iraq Study Group" concluded was a significant possibility absent a major change in U.S. policy.[3]

As assessments of possible overall U.S. policy failure multiplied, the Administration and Iraq agreed in August 2006 on a series of "benchmarks" that, if adopted and implemented, might achieve political reconciliation. Under Section 1314 of a FY2007 supplemental appropriation (P.L. 110-28), "progress" on 18 political and security benchmarks—as assessed in Administration reports due by July 15, 2007, and then September 15, 2007—was required for the United States to provide $1.5 billion in Economic Support Funds (ESF) to Iraq. President Bush exercised the waiver provision. The law also mandated an assessment by the Government Accountability Office, by September 1, 2007, of Iraqi performance on the benchmarks, as well as an outside assessment of the Iraqi security forces (ISF).

In early 2007, the United States began a "surge" of about 30,000 additional U.S. forces (bringing U.S. troop levels from their 2004-2006 baseline of about 138,000 to about 170,000) in order to blunt insurgent momentum and take advantage of growing Sunni Arab rejection of extremist groups.

The Administration cited as partial justification for the surge the Iraq Study Group's recommendation of such a step. As 2008 progressed, citing the achievement of many of the major Iraqi legislative benchmarks and a dramatic drop in sectarian violence, the Bush Administration asserted that political reconciliation was advancing. However, U.S. officials maintained that the extent and durability of the reconciliation would depend on implementation of adopted laws, on further compromises among ethnic groups, and on continued attenuated levels of violence.

Iraqi Governance Strengthens As Sectarian Conflict Abates

The passage of Iraqi laws in 2008 that were considered crucial to reconciliation, continued reductions in violence accomplished by the U.S. surge, and the continued turn of many Sunni militants away from violence, facilitated political stabilization. A March 2008 offensive ordered by Maliki against the Sadr faction and other militants in Basra and environs ("Operation Charge of the Knights") pacified the city and caused many Sunnis and Kurds to see Maliki as willing to take on radical groups even if they were Shiite. This contributed to a decision in July 2008 by several Sunni ministers to end a one-year boycott of the cabinet, bringing relative stability back to the central government.

Local Governance: Provincial Powers Law and Provincial Elections

In 2008, a "provincial powers law" (Law 21) was adopted to decentralize governance by delineating substantial powers for provincial (governorate) councils. The provincial councils enact provincial legislation, regulations, and procedures, and choose the province's governor and two deputy governors. The provincial administrations draft provincial budgets and implement federal policies. Some central government funds are given as grants directly to provincial administrations for their use, although most of Iraq's budget is controlled centrally. There were efforts in 2012 in some provinces to consult with district and municipal level officials to assure a fair distribution of provincial resources. The term of the provincial councils is four years from the date of their first convention. (This law was substantially revised by a law adopted in late June 2013 to give the provincial governments substantially more power, as discussed further below.)

The provincial elections had been planned for October 1, 2008, but were delayed when Kurdish restiveness over integrating Kirkuk into the KRG caused a presidential council veto of the July 22, 2008, draft of the required election law. That draft provided for equal division of power in Kirkuk (among Kurds, Arabs, and Turkomans) until its status is finally resolved, a proposal strongly opposed by the Kurds because it would dilute their political dominance there. On September 24, 2008, the COR passed another election law, providing for the provincial elections by January 31, 2009, but putting off provincial elections in Kirkuk and the three KRG provinces. That draft was enacted and applied to the January 31, 2009 election: it provided for six reserved seats for minorities: Christian seats in Baghdad, Nineveh, and Basra; one seat for Yazidis in Nineveh; one seat for Shabaks in Nineveh; and one seat for the Sabean sect in Baghdad. The number of reserved seats for minorities was increased for the April 20, 2013, provincial elections.)

In the 2009 elections, about 14,500 candidates vied for the 440 provincial council seats in the 14 Arab-dominated provinces of Iraq. About 4,000 of the candidates were women. The average number of council seats per province was about 30,[4] down from a set number of 41 seats per province (except Baghdad) in the 2005-2009 councils. The Baghdad provincial council had 57 seats. The reduction in number of seats also meant that many incumbents were not reelected. The elections were conducted on an "open list" basis—voters were able to vote for a party slate, or for an individual candidate (although they also had to vote for that candidate's slate). This procedure strengthened the ability of political parties to choose who on their slate will occupy seats allotted for that party, thereby favoring well-organized parties.[5] About 17 million Iraqis (any Iraqi 18 years of age or older) were eligible for the vote, which was run by the Iraqi Higher Election Commission (IHEC). Pre-election violence was minimal. Turnout was about 51%, somewhat lower than some expected.

The vote totals were certified on March 29, 2009. Maliki's "State of Law Coalition" (a coalition composed of his Da'wa Party plus other mostly Shiite allies) was the clear winner, taking 126 out of the 440 seats available. ISCI went from 200 council seats before the election to only 50, which observers attributed to its perceived close ties to Iran and its corruption. Iyad al-Allawi's faction won 26 seats, a gain of 8 seats, and a competing Sunni faction loyal to Tariq al-Hashimi won 32 seats, a loss of about 15 seats. Sunni tribal leaders who were widely credited for turning Iraqi Sunnis against Al Qaeda-linked extremists in Iraq, had boycotted the 2005 elections but participated in the 2009 elections. Their slate came in first in Anbar Province.

Within 15 days of that (by April 13, 2009) the provincial councils began to convene to elect a provincial council chairperson and deputy chairperson. Within another 30 days after that (by May 12, 2009) the provincial councils selected (by absolute majority) a provincial governor and deputy governors. Although Maliki's State of Law coalition fared well, his party still needed to strike bargains with rival factions to form provincial administrations. The next provincial elections in Arab-dominated provinces were held during April - June 2013, as discussed below.

The March 7, 2010, Elections: Shiites Fracture and Sunnis Cohere

After a strong showing for his list in the provincial elections, Maliki was favored to retain his position in the March 7, 2010, COR elections that would choose the next government. Maliki derived further political benefit from the U.S. implementation of the U.S.-Iraq "Security Agreement" (SA), discussed below. Yet, as 2009 progressed, Maliki's image as protector of law and order was tarnished by several high-profile attacks, including major bombings in Baghdad on August 20, 2009, in which almost 100 Iraqis were killed and the buildings housing the Ministry of Finance and of Foreign Affairs were heavily damaged. As Maliki's image of strong leadership faded that year, Shiite unity broke down and a strong rival Shiite slate took shape—the "Iraqi National Alliance (INA)" consisting of ISCI, the Sadrists, and other Shiite figures. The INA coalition believed that each of its component factions would draw support from their individual constituencies to produce an election victory.

To Sunni Arabs, the outwardly cross-sectarian Iraq National Movement ("Iraqiyya") of former transitional Prime Minister Iyad al-Allawi (a broader coalition than his INA faction) rhad strong appeal. There was an openly Sunni slate, leaning Islamist, called the Accordance, and some Sunni figures joined Shiite slates in order to improve their chances of winning a seat.

Table 1. Major Coalitions for 2010 National Elections

State of Law Coalition (slate no. 337)	Led by Maliki and his Da'wa Party. Included Anbar Salvation Front of Shaykh Hatim al-Dulaymi, which is Sunni, and the Independent Arab Movement of Abd al-Mutlaq al-Jabbouri. Appealed to Shiite sectarianism during the campaign by backing the exclusion of candidates with links to outlawed Baath Party.
Iraqi National Alliance (slate no. 316)	Formed in August 2009, considered the most formidable challenger to Maliki's slate. Consisted mainly of his Shiite opponents and was perceived as somewhat more Islamist than the other slates. Included ISCI, the Sadrist movement, the Fadilah Party, the Iraqi National Congress of Ahmad Chalabi, and the National Reform Movement (Da'wa faction) of former Prime Minister Ibrahim al-Jafari. This slate was considered close to Ayatollah Sistani.

Table 1. (Continued)

Iraqi National Movement ("Iraqiyya"—slate no. 333)	Formed in October 2009 by former Prime Minister Iyad al-Allawi who is Shiite but his faction appeals to Sunnis, and Sunni leader Saleh al-Mutlaq (ex-Baathist who leads the National Dialogue Front). The coalition included the IIP and several powerful Sunni individuals, including Usama al-Nujaifi and Rafi al-Issawi.
Kurdistan Alliance (slate no. 372)	Competed again as a joint KDP-PUK Kurdish list. However, Kurdish solidarity was shaken by July 25, 2009, Kurdistan elections in which a breakaway PUK faction called Change (Gorran) did unexpectedly well. Gorran ran its own separate list for the March 2010 elections.
Unity Alliance of Iraq (slate no. 348)	Led by Interior Minister Jawad Bolani, a moderate Shiite who has a reputation for political independence, but included the Sunni tribal faction led by Shaykh Ahmad Abu Risha, brother of slain leader of the Sunni Awakening movement in Anbar. The list also included first post-Saddam defense minister Sadun al-Dulaymi.
Iraqi Accordance (slate no. 338)	A coalition of Sunni parties, including some breakaway leaders of the IIP. Led by Ayad al-Samarrai, then-speaker of the COR. Was viewed as a weak competitor for Sunni votes against Allawi's Iraqiyya.

Sources: Carnegie Endowment for International Peace; various press.

Election Law and "De-Baathification" Controversies

While coalitions formed to challenge Maliki, disputes emerged over the ground rules for the election. Under the Iraqi constitution, the elections were to be held by January 31, 2010, in order to allow 45 days before the March 15, 2010, expiry of the COR's term. Because the provisions of the election laws shape the election outcome, (covering such issues as voter eligibility, whether to allot quota seats to certain constituencies, and the size of the next COR), the major Iraqi communities were divided and the COR repeatedly missed self-imposed deadlines to pass it. Many COR members leaned toward a closed list system, but those who wanted an open list vote (allowing voters to vote for candidates as well as coalition slates) prevailed. The Kurds prevailed in insisting that current food ration lists be used to register voters, but there was a compromise that eased Sunni and Shiite Arab fears about an excessive Kurdish vote in Kirkuk. Sunnis ultimately lost their struggle to have "reserved seats" for Iraqis in exile; many Sunnis had gone into exile after the fall of

Saddam Hussein. Each province served as a single constituency (see **Table 2**, for the number of seats per province).

The version of the election law passed by the COR on November 8, 2009 (141 out of 195 COR deputies voting) expanded the size of the COR to 325 total seats. Of these, 310 were allocated by province, with the constituency sizes ranging from Baghdad's 68 seats to Muthanna's seven. The COR size, in the absence of a recent census, was based on taking 2005 population figures and adding 2.8% per year growth.[6] The remaining 15 seats to be minority reserved seats (8) and "compensatory seats" (7)—seats allocated from "leftover" votes—votes for parties and slates that did not meet a minimum threshold to win any seat.

The electoral process was at least partly intended to bring Sunni Arabs further into the political structure. This goal was jeopardized by a major dispute over candidate eligibility for the March 2010 elections. In January 2010, the Justice and Accountability Commission (JAC, the successor to the "De-Baathification Commission" that worked since the fall of Saddam to purge former Baathists from government) invalidated the candidacies of 499 individuals (out of 6,500 candidates running) on many different slates. The JAC was headed by Ali al-Lami, a Shiite who had been in U.S. military custody during 2005-2006 for alleged assistance to Iranian agents active in Iraq. He was perceived as answerable to or heavily influenced by Ahmad Chalabi, who had headed the De-Baathification Commission. Both were part of the Iraqi National Alliance slate and both are Shiites, leading many to believe that the disqualifications represented an attempt to exclude prominent Sunnis from the vote. Appeals reinstated many of them, although about 300 had already been replaced by other candidates on their respective slates. Among those disqualified and later reinstated were two senior Iraqiyya slate members: National Dialogue Front party leader Saleh al-Mutlaq and Dhafir al-Ani. Lami was assassinated on May 26, 2011, presumably by Sunnis who viewed him as an architect of the perceived discrimination.) Chalabi, a member of parliament as of the 2010 elections, initially replaced Lami, but Maliki dismissed him in favor of the Minister for Human Rights to serve in that role concurrently. The JAC continues to vet candidates, and did so for the 2013 provincial elections.

Election and Results

There were about 6,170 total candidates spanning 85 coalitions, that ran in the elections. The major blocs are depicted in Table 1. Total turnout was about 62%, according to the IHEC. The final count was announced on March 26,

2010. As noted in Table 2, Iraqiyya won a narrow plurality of seats (two-seat margin over Maliki's State of Law slate). The Iraqi constitution (Article 73) mandates that the COR "bloc with the largest number" of members gets the first opportunity to form a government and Allawi demanded the first opportunity to form a government. However, on March 28, 2010, Iraq's Supreme Court ruled that a coalition that forms after the election could be deemed to meet that requirement, denying Allawi the first opportunity to form a government.

The vote was to have been certified by April 22, 2010, but factional disputes delayed the certification. Several international observers, including then-U.N. Special Representative for Iraq Ad Melkert (and head of the U.N. Assistance Mission—Iraq, UNAMI), indicated that there was no cause to suggest widespread fraud. (Melkert was replaced in September 2011 by Martin Kobler, who is in turn being replaced by Bulgarian diplomat Nickolay Mladenov as of September 2013.) After appeals of some of the results, Iraq's Supreme Court certified the results on June 1, 2010, triggering the following timelines:

- Fifteen days after certification (by June 15, 2010), the new COR was to be seated and to elect a COR speaker and deputy speaker. (The deadline to convene was met, although, as noted, the COR did not elect a leadership team and did not meet again until November 11, 2010.)
- After electing a speaker, but with no deadline, the COR was to choose a president (by a two-thirds vote). (According to Article 138 of the Iraqi constitution, after this election, Iraq is to have a president and at least one vice president—the "presidency council" concept was an interim measure that expired at the end of the first full-term government.)
- Within another 15 days, the largest COR bloc is tapped by the president to form a government.
- Within another 30 days (by December 25, 2010), the prime minister-designate is to present a cabinet to the COR for confirmation (by majority vote).

Post-Election Government

Part of the difficulty forming a government after the election was the close result, coupled with the perception that Iraqi politics is a "winner take all" proposition. In accordance with timelines established in the Constitution, the newly elected COR convened on June 15, 2010, but the session ended after less than a half hour without electing a COR leadership team. The various factions made little progress through August 2010, as Maliki insisted he remain prime minister for another term and remained in a caretaker role. The United States stepped up its involvement in political talks, but it was Iraqi politics that led the factions out of an impasse. On October 1, 2010, Maliki received the backing of most of the 40 COR Sadrist deputies. Despite Maliki's reliance on Sadrist support, the Obama Administration backed a second Maliki term while demand that Maliki form a government inclusive of Sunni leaders. Illustrating the degree to which the Kurds reclaimed their former role of "kingmakers," Maliki, Allawi, and ISCI leader Hakim met in the capital of the Kurdistan Regional Government-administered region in Irbil on November 8, 2010, to continue to negotiate on a new government.

On November 10, 2010, with reported direct intervention by President Obama, the "Irbil Agreement" was finalized in which (1) Allawi agreed to support Maliki and Talabani to remain in their offices for another term; (2) Iraqiyya would be extensively represented in government—one of its figures would become COR Speaker, another would be defense minister, and another (presumably Allawi himself) would chair an oversight body called the "National Council for Strategic Policies;"[7] and (3) easing the de-Baathification laws. Observers praised the agreement because it included all major factions and was signed with KRG President Masoud Barzani and then U.S. Ambassador to Iraq James Jeffrey in attendance.

Second Full-Term Government (2010-2014) Formed[8]

At the November 11, 2010, COR session to implement the agreement, Iraqiyya figure Usama alNujaifi (brother of Nineveh Governor Atheel Nujaifi) was elected COR speaker. Several days later, Talabani was reelected president and Talabani tapped Maliki as prime minister-designate, giving him until December 25, 2010 to achieve COR confirmation of a cabinet. That requirement as accomplished on December 21, 2010. Among major outcomes were the following:

- As for the State of Law list, Maliki remained prime minister, and retained for himself the Defense, Interior, and National Security (minister of state) posts pending permanent nominees for those positions. The faction took seven other cabinet posts, in addition to the post of first vice president (Khudair al Khuzai of the Da'wa Party) and deputy prime minister for energy issues (Hussein Shahristani, previously the oil minister).

- For Iraqiyya, Saleh al-Mutlaq was appointed a deputy Prime Minister; Tariq alHashimi remained a vice president (second of three). The bloc also obtained nine ministerial posts, including Finance Minister Rafi al-Issawi (previously a deputy prime minister).

- For the Iraqi National Alliance, Adel Abdul Mahdi kept his vice president post (third of three) until he resigned in 2011, and the coalition obtained 13 cabinet positions, parceled out among its various factions. The Sadrists got eight ministries, including Housing, Labor and Social Affairs, Ministry of Planning, and Tourism and Antiquities, as well as one of two deputy COR speakerships. An INA technocrat, Abd al Karim Luaibi, was appointed oil minister. A Fadilah party member, Bushra Saleh, became minister of state without portfolio and the only woman in the cabinet at that time. Another Fadila activist was named minister of justice. The Sadrists later gained additional influence when a Sadrist became governor of Maysan Province.

- The Kurdistan Alliance received major posts aside from Talabani. The third deputy prime minister is Kurdish/PUK figure Rows Shaways, who has served in various central and KRG positions since the fall of Saddam. Arif Tayfour is second deputy COR speaker. Alliance members had six other cabinet seats, including longtime Kurdish (KDP) stalwart Hoshyar Zebari remaining as foreign minister (a position he's held throughout the post-Saddam periods). Khairallah Hassan Babakir, was named trade minister in a February 13, 2011 bloc of ministerial appointments.

POST-U.S. WITHDRAWAL POLITICAL UNRAVELING

The power-sharing agreement only temporarily muted, but did not resolve, the underlying differences among the major communities. Maliki's opponents have accused him of undermining the Irbil Agreement and seeking to concentrate power in his and his faction's hands. The critics assert that he has monopolized control of the Defenses, Interior, and National Security (intelligence) posts by refusing to split those ministries among the major political factions. Maliki has appointed allies and associates as acting ministers of those ministries: Sadun Dulaymi—a Sunni Arab member of the Iraq Unity

Alliance is acting Defense Minister; Falih al-Fayad, a Shiite, is acting Minister of State for National Security; and Adnan al-Asadi, another Shiite, is acting Interior Minister.

Maliki's critics also assert that he has sought to directly control the security forces and to use them for political purposes. Through his Office of the Commander-in-Chief, he directly commands the 10,000 person Counter-Terrorism Service, of which about 4,100 are Iraqi Special Operations Forces (ISOF). These forces are tasked with countering militant groups, although Maliki's critics assert that he uses them to intimidate his senior Sunni critics and Iraq's Sunnis more broadly. His critics further assert that Maliki has put under his executive control several supposedly independent bodies. In late 2010, he successfully requested that Iraq's Supreme Court rule that several independent commissions—including the Independent Higher Election Commission (IHEC) that runs Iraq's elections and the Commission of Integrity, the key anticorruption body—be supervised by the cabinet. [9] In March 2012, Maliki also asserted governmental control over the Central Bank, which is constitutionally to be independent. In October 2012, Maliki reportedly directed investigative agencies to arrest the the Central Bank governor and his top staff for allegedly allowing unauthorized bulk transfers of foreign currency out of the country.

Political Crisis Begins Immediately after U.S. Withdrawal Completion

Political disputes among the major factions intensified as U.S. forces left Iraq. In November 2011, security forces arrested 600 Sunnis for involvement in an alleged coup plot. On December 19, 2011, the day after the final U.S. withdrawal (December 18, 2011)—and one week after Maliki met with President Obama in Washington, D.C., on December 12, 201—the government announced an arrest warrant against Vice President Tariq al-Hashimi, another major Iraqiyya figure. He was accused of ordering his security staff to commit acts of assassination, and three such guards were shown on Iraqi television "confessing" to assassinating rival politicians at Hashimi's behest. Hashimi fled to the KRG region and refused to return to face trial in Baghdad unless his conditions for a fair trial there were met. A trial in absentia in Baghdad convicted him and sentenced him to death on September 9, 2012, for the alleged killing of two Iraqis. There was not an international outcry over the sentence, corroborating the view of some U.S.

diplomats that there might have been some truth to the allegations. Hashimi remains in Turkey, where he eventually fled, meaning the death sentence will likely never be implemented.

The Hashimi arrest cast doubt on President Obama's assertion, marking the U.S. withdrawal, that Iraq is now "sovereign, stable, and self-reliant." U.S. officials attempted to contain the crisis by intervening with the various political factions. The effort produced some results when Maliki arranged the release of some of the Baathists arrested in early 2012 and agreed to legal amendments to give provinces more autonomy over their budgets and the right of consent when national security forces are deployed.[10] (These concessions were included in a revised provincial powers law adopted by the COR in June 2013.) The Maliki concessions prompted Iraqiyya COR deputies and ministers to resume their duties by early February 2012.

In March 2012, the factions tentatively agreed to hold a "national conference," to be chaired by President Talabani, respected as an even-handed mediator, to try to reach durable solutions to the outstanding fundamental Sunni-Shiite-Kurdish issues. A "preparatory committee" was named to establish an agenda and format, but it repeatedly failed to meet. March 20, 2012 comments by KRG President Barzani, accusing Maliki of a "power grab" by harnessing control of the security forces dimmed prospects for holding the conference, although Maliki formally tried to convene it on April 5, 2012. The conference was not held.

With attempts to repair the rifts failing, Maliki critics met in late April 2012 in the KRG region, at the invitation of Barzani. Attending were Iraqiyya leader Allawi, Iraqiyya member and COR speaker Osama Nujaifi, and Moqtada Al Sadr, in what reportedly was his first visit to the Kurdish north. At the conclusion of the meetings, the four threatened a vote of no-confidence unless Maliki adhered to the "principles and framework" of a democratic approach to governance. By mid-June 2012, these critics had collected signatures from 176 COR deputies to request a no-confidence vote. Under Article 61 of the constitution, signatures of only 20% of the 325 COR deputies (65 signatures) are needed to trigger a vote, but President Talabani (who is required to present a valid request to the COR to hold the vote) stated on June 10, 2012, that there were an insufficient number of valid signatures to proceed with that vote.[11] One key factor in thwarting the no-confidence effort was Maliki's convincing the Sadrists to back out of the no-confidence campaign. Maliki also reached out to Sunni leaders to calm tensions with them and deputy Prime Minister Saleh al-Mutlaq resumed his duties. On the other hand,

Minister of Communications Mohammad al-Allawi, an Iraqiyya member, resigned in late August 2012.

Political Crisis Evolves into Major Sectarian Rift in 2013

Political disputes flared again after the widely respected political mediator President Talabani suffered a stroke on December 18, 2012. The day he was flown out of Iraq for treatment on December 20, 2012, Maliki moved against another perceived Sunni adversary, Finance Minister Rafi al-Issawi, by arresting ten of his bodyguards. That action touched off anti-Maliki demonstrations in the Sunnis cities of Anbar, Salahuddin, and Nineveh provinces, as well as in Sunni districts of Baghdad.

As demonstrations continued, what had been primarily disputes among elites was transformed into mass unrest that threatened to return Iraq to the major Sunni-Shiite sectarian conflict that occurred during 2006-2008. The thrust of the Sunni unrest is based on perceived discrimination by the Shiite-dominated Maliki government. Some Sunni demonstrators were reacting not only to the moves against Issawi and other Sunni leaders, but also to the fact that the overwhelming number of prisoners in Iraq's jails are Sunnis, according to Human Rights Watch researchers. Sunni demonstrators have demanded the release of prisoners, particularly women; a repeal of "Article 4" anti-terrorism laws under which many Sunnis are incarcerated; reform or end to the de-Baathification laws that has been used against Sunnis; and improved government services.[12]

During January—March 2013, the use of small amounts of force against demonstrators caused the unrest to worsen. On January 25, 2013, the ISF killed nine protesters on a day when oppositionists killed two ISF police officers. Sunni demonstrators protested every Friday during that period, on some occasions blocked the roads leading from Iraq to Jordan and to Syria, and began to set up encampments in some cities. Some observers believe that the protest movement was emboldened by the Sunni-led rebellion in neighboring Syria. Some protesters began to carry pictures of Saddam Hussein, enraging Maliki and other Shiite officials.

Politically, the escalating Sunni unrest caused further rifts at the leadership level. Allawi and Saleh al-Mutlaq called on Maliki to resign and Moqtada Al Sadr widened cracks in Shiite solidarity by supporting the demonstrators. The COR passed a law limiting Maliki to two terms (meaning he could not serve again after 2014 elections), although Iraqi courts did not uphold that law. Issawi resigned as Finance Minister and took refuge in Anbar province with Sunni tribal leaders, some of whom Maliki ordered arrested, including Shaykh Ahmad Abu Risha and Shaykh Hussein al-Jabburi. In March 2013, Kurdish ministers suspended their participation in the central government and returned to the Kurdistan region and no Kurdish leader went to Baghdad to meet with Secretary of State John Kerry during his March 24, 2013, visit to Iraq. COR Speaker Nujaifi met with Secretary Kerry during that visit.

During January—March 2013, Maliki tried, without success to date, to mollify the Sunni leaders and protesters. He formed a committee, headed by deputy Prime Minister Shahristani, to examine protester grieveances and suggest reforms. He released some imprisoned Sunnis, including 300 released on January 14, 2013. On the other hand, he signaled that he might restructure the government into a "majority government"—abandoning the power-sharing arrangement and presumably further reducing Sunni participation in the central government.

Escalation after April 2013 Hawijah Incident

The protests affected - and were affected by - the April 20, 2013, provincial elections. On March 19, 2013, the government postponed the elections in two Sunni provinces, Anbar and Nineveh, until June 20, 2013. The government refused Secretary of State Kerry's requests, made during his March 24, 2013 visit, to reverse that postponement. On April 23, 2013, three days after the first group of provinces voted, the ISF stormed a Sunni protest camp in the town of Hawijah, near the mostly Kurdish city of Kirkuk. About 40 civilians and 3 ISF were killed in the battle that ensued. In the following days, many Sunni demonstrators and tribal leaders took up arms and called on followers to arm themselves. Sunni gunmen took over government buildings in the town of Suleiman Pak for a few days. ISF checkpoints in many Sunni areas were attacked by gunmen, and Anbar tribal leaders gave the government an ultimatum to pull all ISF forces out of the province. At the political level, Iraqiyya pulled out of the COR entirely, and three Sunni ministers resigned, following one (Agriculture Minister Izzedin Al Dowlah) who had resigned one month earlier. In a speech to the nation on April 24, 2013, Maliki urged dialogue to calm the unrest but also leaned toward those advisers urging a military solution by stating that the ISF "must impose security in Iraq."

U.S. officials reportedly pressed Maliki not to use the military to suppress Sunni protests, arguing that such a strategy has led to all-out civil war in neighboring Syria, and also worked with Sunni tribal leaders to appeal for calm. On April 29—30, 2013, Kurdish leaders began a dialogue with the central government and, as a first step, reached agreement for Kurdish ministers to return to their positions in Baghdad. In May 2013 Maliki shuffled his top security forces command, probably in part to sideline figures that Sunnis blame for ordering attacks on protesters. Several faction leaders met at the home of Ammar al-Hakim to try to discuss ways out of the political impasse, although without a clear outcome. Maliki himself was not invited because of his formal governmental position, and Iyad al-Allawi and Moqtada Al Sadr did not attend either, according to Iraqi observers.

April 2013 Provincial Elections Occur Amid the Tensions

Some experts argue that the provincial election results demonstrate that most Iraqis want to avoid sectarian conflict and want to work to rebuild political power-sharing. The elections were held on April 20, 2013 in twelve provinces, and on June 20, 2013 in Anbar and Nineveh Province. The mandate of the current nine-member IHEC, which runs the election, expired at the end of April 2012, and the COR confirmed a new panel in September 2012. The IHEC set the April 20, 2013 election date on October 30, 2012, while deciding that the elections would not be held in the three KRG-controlled provinces or in the province of Kirkuk. As noted, in May 2013, the cabinet announced the vote in Anbar and Nineveh would be held on June 20, 2013, somewhat earlier than an initial postponement to July 4, 2013. The KRG provinces will vote on September 21, 2013, but the election there will be broader than just provincial elections, as discussed below.

The deadline for party registration was on November 25, 2012, and the IHEC subsequently published a list of 261 political entities that registered to run. The COR's law to govern the election passed in December 2012, providing for an open list vote, as was the case in the previous provincial election. The deadline to register coalitions of political entities was December 20, 2012, and 50 coalitions registered. Individual candidate registration was completed by December 25, 2012, and about 8,150 candidates registered to run 'for the 447 seats up for election (including those in Anbar and Nineveh that voted on June 20, 2013). The JAC excluded about 200 candidates for alleged Baathist ties, but that figure was lower than the number many Sunnis expected. The campaign period started on schedule on March 1, 2013.

With the April 20, 2013 vote being held mostly in Shiite areas, the election shaped up as a test of Maliki's popularity. Maliki's State of Law coalition remained relatively intact, consisting mostly of Shiite parties, including Fadilah (Virtue) and the ISCI-offshoot the Badr Organization. ISCI registered its own "Citizen Coalition" (the name of its bloc in the COR), and Sadr registered a separate "Coalition of Liberals." Among the mostly Sunni groupings, Allawi's Iraqiyya and 18 smaller entities ran as the "Iraqi National United Coalition." A separate "United Coalition" consisted of supporters of the Nujaifis (COR speaker and Nineveh governor), Vice President Tariq al-Hashimi, and Rafi al-Issawi. A third Sunni coalition is loyal to Saleh al-Mutlaq. The two main Kurdish parties ran under the Co-Existence and Fraternity Alliance.

Voting and Results. Turnout on April 20, 2013 was estimated at about 50%. Election day violence was minimal, although a reported 16 Sunni candidates were assassinated prior to the election. According to results finalized on May 19, 2013, Maliki's State of Law won a total of about 112 seats, and it won a plurality in seven of the twelve provinces that voted. Maliki's list did particularly well in the major urban centers of Baghdad and Basra, but, even in those provinces, it has had to ally with other groups to form provincial administrations. ISCI's Citizen Coalition won back some of the losses it suffered in the 2009 elections, winning a total of about 75 seats. Sadr's slate won a reported total of about 59 seats, including a plurality in Maysan province. Among Sunnis, the United Coalition bested the Iraqiyya-led coalition—an outcome most relevant in the two majority Sunni provinces that voted that day—Diyala and Salahuddin. However, in Salahuddin, a local coalition headed by the governor of the province won a plurality.

The June 20, 2013 election in Anbar and Nineveh was primarily a contest among the Sunni blocs. In heavily Sunni Anbar, the Nujaifi bloc won a slight plurality. In Nineveh, where the Nujaifis previously held an outright majority of provincial council seats (19 or 37), their slate suffered a significant setback. The Kurds won 11 out of the province's 39 seats, and the Nujaifi grouping came in second with eight seats. Sunnis willing to work with Maliki rather than implacably oppose him won an almost equal number of seats as the harder line Nujaifi grouping[13] - a result that some experts interpret as reflecting the inclination of all Iraqis, regardless of sect, to avoid returning to a period of sectarian conflict.

Post-Election and Current Situation

Even as the factions attempt to negotiate a political solution, attacks on government forces, Shiite communities and even against Sunnis cooperating are continuing and, by some measures, escalating. However, most of these attacks are carried out by Al Qaeda in Iraq and affiliated militant groups, which appear to be deriving some measure of popular support from Sunnis resentful of Maliki's perceived efforts to marginalize the Sunni community politically and economically. The vast majority of the violence is not being committed by Iraqi Sunnis unaffiliated with these groups, by all accounts. According to the U.N. Assistance Mission-Iraq (UNAMI), about 2,500 Iraqis were killed in political violence during April—June 2013. Of those, over 1,050 were killed in May 2013 alone. UNAMI stated that over 1,000 Iraqis died in political violence during July 2013, of which about 90% were civilians. These are the highest death tolls in Iraq since 2008 and has led observers to assess that Iraq might be returning to the 2006-8 period of sectarian conflict.

Some developments in June and July 2013 offered the potential for compromise and a reduction in the violence in the near future. In June 2013 the COR revised the 2008 provincial powers law to give the provinces substantially more authority relative to the central government, including some control over security forces (Article 31-10). The revisions also specify a share of revenue to be given to the provinces and mandate that within two years, control of the province-based operations of central government ministries be transferred to the provincial governments.[14] In July 2013, the cabinet approved a package of reforms easing the de-Baathification laws—a key demand of the Sunni protesters. The reforms, if they become law, would allow many former Baathists to hold government positions. In addition, Maliki reportedly has sought to engage some of the Sunni leaders he formally sought to marginalize, including deputy Prime Minister Mutlaq and some members of Allawi's Iraqiyya faction.

KRG Elections

Provincial elections in the KRG-controlled provinces were not held during the January 2009 provincial elections or during the March 7, 2010, COR vote. These elections had previously been scheduled for September 27, 2012, but in June 2012 the KRG announced a postponement because the IHEC ruled that Christian voters could only vote for Christian candidates—a ruling the Kurds said restricted the rights of minorities. In April 2013, the KRG announced that on September 21, 2013, the three KRG provinces will hold provincial elections, as well as elections for the Kurdistan National Assembly (KNA) and the KRG presidency. However, on July 1, 2013, the KNA voted to extend Barzani's term two years, meaning there will not be a KRG presidential vote on September 21, 2013. The State Department said on July 2, 2013 that it is confident that the KNA elected in September will finalize a KRG constitution and set presidential elections possibly earlier than 2015.

2014 COR Elections

The term of the existing COR expires no later than early 2014, and the elections are tentatively planned for some time in March 2014. That schedule could change if the political crisis or escalating violence leads causes a postponement. Maliki reportedly has given indications to his allies and other senior Iraqis that he will seek to retain his prime ministership, although it is possible that an agreement that he not run again could form part of a settlement to the sectarian unrest roiling Iraq.

Kirkuk Referendum

There is also to be a vote on a Kirkuk referendum at some point, if a negotiated settlement is reached. However, a settlement does not appear within easy reach as of early 2012 and no referendum is scheduled.

District and Sub-District Elections

District and sub-district elections throughout Iraq were previously slated for July 31, 2009. However, those have been delayed as well, and no date has been announced.

Constitutional Amendments

There could also be a vote on amendments to Iraq's 2005 constitution if and when the major factions agree to finalize the recommendations of the constitutional review commission (CRC). There has been no movement on this issue for at least three years, and no indication such a referendum will be held in the near future.

Sunni Insurgents: Al Qaeda in Iraq and Others

The 2012-2013 Sunni unrest is providing "political space" for longstanding violent Sunni elements to escalate attacks on the political system. The primary targets of the Sunni insurgent groups have been pilgrims to the various Shiite shrines and holy sites in Iraq; Shiite neighborhoods and businesses; ISF personnel; government installations; and some Sunnis who are cooperating with the government. The violent elements might be seeking to reinforce the effectiveness of the peaceful protest to undermine the confidence of the ISF; to force Shiite ISF personnel out of Sunni areas; or to reignite the sectarian war that prevailed during 2006-2008. All of these motivations, in the view of the militants, could have the effect of destabilizing Maliki and his

Shiite-led rule. The insurgent attacks have not accomplished these objectives, but the expansion of the unrest since April 2013 could lead to these outcomes.

The primary Sunni militant group is Al Qaeda in Iraq (AQ-I), which operates under the name of the Islamic State of Iraq (ISI). The leader of AQ-I leader is Abu Bakr Al Baghdadi. U.S. officials estimated in November 2011 that there might be 800-1,000 people in Al Qaeda-Iraq's network, of which many are involved in media or finance of operations.[15] An antecedent of AQ-I was named by the United States as a Foreign Terrorist Organization (FTO) in March 2004 and the designation applies to AQ-I. AQ-I appears primarily focused on influencing the future of Iraq - and possibly also Syria, as discussed below - although attacks and attempted attacks in neighboring Jordan have been attributed to the group. In October 2012, Jordanian authorities disrupted an alleged plot by AQ-I to bomb multiple targets in Amman, Jordan, possibly including the U.S. Embassy there. AQ-I is extensively involved in the Syria conflict, as discussed later, but it does not appear to have close links to remaining senior Al Qaeda leaders believed mostly still in Pakistan or to Al Qaeda in the Arabian Peninsula (AQAP) in Yemen.

As examples of escalating AQ-I violence in Iraq since the U.S. withdrawal, from February 2012 until the end of that year, there were about a dozen days on which AQ-I conducted multi-city attacks that killed twenty-five or more Iraqis each of those days. On at least four of these days, multiple attacks killed more than 100 Iraqis. In July 2012, AQ-I downed a government helicopter and compelled 15 Diyala Province "*mukhtars*"—chosen community liaisons with the central government—to resign. In August 2012, AQ-I insurgents briefly captured a local government building in Haditha (Anbar Province) and raised an Al Qaeda battle flag over it.

Attacks attributed to AQ-I have become more frequent since Sunni demonstrations began in late December 2012, and have escalated further in frequency and intensity since the Hawija incident of April 23, 2013. The State Department report on international terrorism for 2012, released May 30, 2013, credits the Iraqi government with focusing its counter-terrorism efforts on AQ-I.[16] Yet, according to some experts, AQ-I is now able to carry out about 40 mass casualty attacks per month, much more than the ten per month of 2010, and that many AQ-I attacks now span multiple cities.[17] A stark indication of AQ-I's increased freedom of action came on July 21, 2013 when the group attacked prisons at Abu Ghraib and Taji; the Taji attack failed but the attacks on Abu Ghraib freed about 800 prisoners, including several hundred purported AQ-I members. Iraq recaptured or killed about 20% of those who escaped, but the attack on the heavily fortified Abu Ghraib - involving the use of suicide attackers and conventional tactics – shook confidence in the ISF.

It is not known the extent to which Sunni oppositionists who have taken up arms against the government in April 2013 are working with AQ-I, if at all. Doing so could tarnish the image of the demonstrators. Some experts say that AQ-I is increasingly building alliances with Sunni tribal leaders and has adjusted its message in 2013 to try to win more Sunni political support. Other experts say that many Iraqi Sunni tribal leaders continue to shun AQ-I and senior Sunni Iraqi political leaders, even those most opposed to Maliki, tend to forcefully denounce AQ-I attacks.

Naqshabandi Order (JRTN)

Some groups that were prominent during the insurgency against U.S. forces remain allied with AQ-I or active independently as part of the Sunni unrest. One such Sunni group, linked to ex-Baathists, is the Naqshabandi Order, known by its Arabic acronym "JRTN."[18] It is based primarily in Nineveh province. Prior to the escalation of Sunni violence in 2013, the JRTN was responsible primarily for attacks on U.S. facilities in northern Iraq, which might have contributed to the State Department decision in mid-2012 to close the Kirkuk consulate. The faction has supported the Sunni demonstrations, and in February 2013 Sunnis linked to the JRTN circulated praise for the protests from the highest ranking Saddam regime figure still at large, Izzat Ibrahim al Duri. Other rebels are said to be linked to longstanding insurgent groups such as the 1920 Revolution Brigades or the Islamic Army of Iraq.

Other Armed Sunni Groups: Sons of Iraq Fighters

One Sunni grievance aside from those discussed above has been the slow pace with which the Maliki government implemented its pledge to fully integrate the approximately 100,000 "Sons of Iraq" fighters. Also known as "Awakening" fighters, these are former insurgents who in 2006 began cooperating with U.S. forces against AQ-I. The Iraqi government later promised them integration into the Iraqi Security Forces (ISF) or government jobs. As of early 2013, about 70,000 had been integrated into the ISF or given civilian government jobs, while 30,000-40,000 continue to man checkpoints in Sunni areas and are paid about $300 per month by the government. In part to salve Sunni grievances and prevent the Sons of Iraq fighters from joining Sunni opposition activities, in early 2013 the government increased their salaries by about 66% to $500 per month. There are no indications that a significant number of Sons of Iraq fighters has joined AQ-I or other Sunni insurgent groups since Sunni anti-government activities escalated.

KRG-Central Government Disputes[19]

Since the end of the U.S.-led war to liberate Kuwait in early 1991, the United States has played a role in protecting Iraq's Kurds from the central government. Iraq's Kurds have tried to preserve this "special relationship" with the United States and use it to their advantage. Iraq's Kurdish leaders have long said they do not seek outright independence or affiliation with Kurds in neighboring countries, but rather to secure and expand the autonomy they have achieved. The issues dividing the KRG and Baghdad include not only KRG autonomy but also disputes over territory and resources, particularly the ability of the KRG to export its oil.

The Iraqi Kurds themselves are not cohesive, divided principally between two main factions—the Patriotic Union of Kurdistan, PUK, and the Kurdistan Democratic Party, KDP. The two have strengthened their bargaining position with Baghdad by abiding by a power sharing arrangement formalized in 2007. The KRG has a President, Masoud Barzani, directly elected in July 2009, an elected Kurdistan National Assembly, and an appointed Prime Minister. Since January 2012, the KRG Prime Minister has been Nechirvan Barzani (Masoud's nephew), who returned to that post after three years in which the post was held by PUK senior figure Barham Salih. PUK leader Jalal Talabani, as noted above, serves as president of Iraq. Masoud Barzani's son, Suroor, heads a KRG "national security council."

The Kurds also—as permitted in the Iraqi constitution—field their own force of *peshmerga* (Kurdish militiamen) numbering perhaps 75,000 fighters. They are generally lightly armed. Kurdish leaders continue to criticize Maliki for paying out of the national budget only about half of the total peshmerga force—those who are incorporated into "regional guard brigades" under the control of the KRG's Ministry of Peshmerga Affairs. However, about half are not incorporated into this structure and therefore are funded out of the KRG budget. KRG President Barzani, during his U.S. visit in April 2012, discussed the reform of the *peshmerga* into a smaller but more professional and well trained force.

The increasing disillusionment of Kurdish leaders with Maliki could produce lasting political realignment. During 2012, Kurdish leaders echoed the Sunni Arab criticisms of Maliki. KRG President Barzani began to break with

Maliki in March 2012, accusing him of monopolizing power. Following a visit to Washington, DC, in early April 2012, Barzani indirectly threatened to allow a vote on Kurdish independence unless Maliki resolves the major issues with the KRG.[20] In June 2012, the Kurds in the COR joined the Iraqiyya-led effort to vote no confidence against Maliki. The animosity has continued in 2013 but the Kurdish leadership and Maliki have continued to engage and exchange views and visits, calming tensions to some extent.

Still, forces of the two political entities face each other. In late 2012, KRG-Baghdad animosity nearly produced all-out conflict between the KRG and Baghdad. In mid-November 2012, a commercial dispute between an Arab and Kurd in Tuz Khurmatu, a town in Salahuddin Province straddling the Baghdad-KRG territorial border, caused a clash and a buildup of ISF and Kurdish troops facing off. Several weeks of U.S. and intra-Iraq mediation resulted in a tentative agreement on December 6, 2012, for both sides to pull back their forces and for local ethnic groups to form units to replace ISF and *peshmerga* units along the Baghdad-KRG frontier. The agreement was only partially implemented. In May 2013, it was reported that peshmerga forces had advanced their positions in Kirkuk province, taking advantage of the withdrawal of the ISF from areas of Sunni demonstrations. In June 2013, a mixed Arab-Kurdish unit of the ISF—"Brigade 16"—split and the KRG assumed de-facto control of the territory controlled by the Kurdish half of the brigade.

The continued clashes and frontier tensions could be attributed, in part, to the end of the "combined security mechanism" (CSM) set up by the United States when its troops were in Iraq. The CSM began in January 2010, consisting of joint (ISF-U.S-Kurdish) patrols, maintenance of 22 checkpoints, and U.S. training of participating ISF and *peshmerga* forces. The mechanism was administered through provincial level Combined Coordination Centers, and disagreements were referred to a Senior Working Group and a High Level Ministerial Committee.[21]

The KRG-peshmerga clashes have been spurred in part by the lack of any progress in recent years in resolving the various territorial disputes between the Kurds and Iraq's Arabs. The most emotional of which is the Kurdish insistence that Tamim Province (which includes oil-rich Kirkuk) is "Kurdish land" and must be formally affiliated to the KRG. There was to be a census and referendum on the affiliation of the province by December 31, 2007, in accordance with Article 140 of the Constitution, but the Kurds have agreed to repeated delays in order to avoid jeopardizing overall progress in Iraq. Nor has the national census that is pivotal to any such referendum been conducted; it was scheduled for October 24, 2010, but then postponed. It still has not begun, in part because of the broader political crisis as well as differences over how to account for movements of populations into or out of the Kurdish controlled provinces.

On the other hand, some KRG-Baghdad disputes have moved forward. The Property Claims Commission that is adjudicating claims from the Saddam regime's forced resettlement of Arabs into the KRG region is functioning. Of the 178,000 claims received, nearly 26,000 were approved and 90,000 rejected or ruled invalid, as of the end of 2011, according to the State Department. Since 2003, more than 28,000 Iraqi Arabs settled in the KRG area by Saddam have relocated from Kirkuk back to their original provinces.

Attempting to resolve these disputes has been part of the work of UNAMI, which has been consultations with all parties for several years.[22] The mandate of UNAMI—which is also to facilitate national reconciliation and civil society, and assisting vulnerable populations—was established in 2003 and has been renewed every year since. U.N. Security Council Resolution 2061 of July 25, 2012, renewed the mandate for another year (until July 24, 2013).

KRG Oil Exports

The KRG and Baghdad are still at odds over the Kurds' insistence that it export oil that is discovered and extracted in the KRG region. Baghdad reportedly fears that Kurdish oil exports can potentially enable the Kurds to set up an economically viable independent state and has called the KRG's separate energy development deals with international firms "illegal." It nonetheless has allowed KRG oil exports to proceed under a long-standing agreement in which revenues from KRG oil exports go into central government accounts. The central government distributes proceeds to the KRG and pays the international oil companies working in the KRG.

Oil exports from the KRG have been repeatedly suspended, for varying periods of time, over central government withholding of payments to the international energy firms. A suspension of oil exports through the national oil grid began in April 2012 after the KRG accused Baghdad of falling $1.5 billion in arrears to the companies extracting oil in the KRG region. The dispute escalated in July 2012 when the KRG began exporting crude oil by road to Turkey but was defused temporarily and KRG exports through the national grid resumed on August 9, 2012. The KRG threatened another halt by September 15, 2012 if the international companies were not paid, but this was calmed by a September 14, 2012 agreement providing for the Kurds to raise exports to 250,000 barrels per day for 2013 (from the 2012 level of less than

200,000 barrels per day) and for Baghdad to pay about $900 million in arrears due the international firms. The agreement held for several months, but the KRG reduced its oil exports in late November 2012 because of slow Baghdad payments to the oil firms involved. KRG oil exports ceased again entirely on December 26, 2012. The national budget adopted by the COR on March 7, 2013 allocated only $650 million to the companies exporting KRG oil; the Kurds had sought $3.5 billion for that purpose. Because of this provision, Kurdish members reportedly boycotted the budget vote and Kurdish ministers temporarily ceased working in Baghdad. KRG oil flow resumed in 2013 but remains vulnerable to a cutoff if political tensions flare again. If these issues were to be permanently resolved, the KRG has the potential to increase exports to 1 million barrels per day by 2019.[23]

Related to the disputes over KRG oil exports is a broader disagreement over foreign firm involvement in the KRG energy sector. The October 2011 KRG signing of an energy development deal with U.S. energy giant Exxon-Mobil represents a further dimension of the energy row with Baghdad. The central government denounced the deal as illegal, in part because the oil fields involved are in or very close to disputed territories. The KRG has sought to defuse this consideration by saying that if the territory of the oil fields is subsequently judged to be part of central government-administered territory, then the revenues would be reallocated accordingly. The central government threatened to cancel the firm's existing contract to develop the West Qurna oil field near Basra, but decided instead on February 13, 2012 to prevent Exxon Mobil from bidding for new work in Baghdad-controlled Iraq. On March 17, 2012, Baghdad claimed that Exxon-Mobil had frozen the KRG contract, but the KRG denies the company has stopped work in the KRG region, and Exxon began production in the KRG in late 2012.[24] Further disputes occurred over a July 2012 KRG deal with Total SA of France; in August 2012 the central government told Total SA to either terminate its arrangement with the KRG or give up work on the central government Halfaya field.

Turkish Involvement

The growing relationship between Turkey and the KRG energy sector adds tension to the KRGBaghdad relationship, and causes strains between Turkey and Baghdad. The KRG and Turkey are reportedly discussing a broad energy deal that would include Turkish investment in drilling for oil and gas in the KRG-controlled territory, and they are constructing a separate oil pipeline linking KRG-controlled fields to a pumping station on the Turkish side of the border.[25] That latter pipeline, said by energy experts to be near completion, would reduce the KRG dependence on the national oil export grid—the key source of Baghdad's leverage over the KRG. Calling the potential deal an infringement of Iraqi sovereignty, the Iraqi government has blacklisted Turkey's state energy pipeline firm (TPAO) from some work in southern Iraq. In December 2012, Iraq turned back a plane carrying Turkey's energy minister to a conference in the KRG capital of Irbil. However, Turkey and the KRG continue to negotiate to finalize the large deal.

The Obama Administration opposes the separate KRG-Turkey pipeline deal, as currently structured, on the grounds that all major international energy projects involving Iraq should be negotiated and implemented through a unified central government in Baghdad. A high-level KRG delegation visited Washington D.C. in April 2013 urging the Administration not to side with the Maliki government in opposing the Turkey-KRG pipeline.

Intra-Kurdish Divisions

Further complicating the political landscape are divisions within the Kurdish community. The KRG National Assembly elections, conducted concurrently with the March 2010 national elections throughout Iraq, to some extent, shuffled the political landscape. A breakaway faction of President Talabani's PUK, called "Change" ("Gorran"), headed by Neshirvan Mustafa, won an unexpectedly high 25 seats (out of 111) in the Kurdistan national assembly, embarrassing the PUK and weakening it relative to the KDP. Gorran ran its own list in the March 2010 national elections to the COR and constituted a significant challenge to the Kurdistan Alliance in Sulaymaniyah Province, according to election results. As a result, of the 57 COR seats held by Kurds, 14 are held by parties other than the Kurdistan Alliance. Gorran has 8, the Kurdistan Islamic Union has 4, and the Islamic Group of Kurdistan has 2.

These divisions may also have played a role in the popular demonstrations that occurred in Sulaymaniyah in early 2011. The demonstrations reflected frustration over jobs and services but possibly also over the monopolization of power in the KRG by the Barzani and Talabani clans. Some of these were suppressed by *peshmerga.*

More recently, the infirmity of Iraq's President and PUK leader Jalal Talabani has affected Kurdish politics. Barham Salih, mentioned above, is said to be pressing to replace Talabani as president, in part because the Kurds do not want someone of another ethnicity to become president. Another PUK stalwart, Kosrat Rasoul, who serves as KRG Vice President, is said to be lining up support to succeed Talabani as PUK leader should Talabani leave the scene. Talabani's son, Qubad, had headed the KRG representative office in Washington, DC, until July 2012, when he returned home to become more involved in Kurdish and PUK politics as his father's health fades. Talabani's wife, Hero Ibrahim Ahmad Talabani, is also a major figure in PUK politics and is said to be an opponent of Kosrat Rasoul—possibly to the point where she is willing to work with Gorran against him.

The Sadr Faction's Continuing Ambition and Agitation

Within the broader Shiite community, the faction of Shiite cleric, Moqtada Al Sadr, sees itself as the main representative for Iraq's Shiites, particularly those who are on the lower economic echelons. The large Sadrist constituency has caused an inherent rivalry with Maliki and other Shiite leaders in Iraq. Sadr was part of an anti-Maliki Shiite coalition for the March 2010 elections, then supported Maliki for a second term, and later joined the unsuccessful effort to vote no-confidence against Maliki, only to bow to Iranian pressure to abandon that effort. Sadr has supported Sunni protests against Maliki in the late 2012-early 2013 Sunni unrest, although he has criticized protesters for using symbols of Saddam's regime.

Sadr's shifts against Maliki represent a continuation of a high level of activity he has exhibited since he returned to Iraq, from his studies in Iran, in January 2011. After his return, he gave numerous speeches that, among other themes, insisted on full implementation of a planned U.S. withdrawal by the end of 2011. Sadr's position on the U.S. withdrawal appeared so firm that, in an April 9, 2011, statement, he threatened to reactivate his Mahdi Army militia if U.S. forces remained in Iraq beyond the December 31, 2011, deadline. His followers conducted a large march in Baghdad on May 26, 2011, demanding a full U.S. military exit. The threats were pivotal to the Iraqi decision not to retain U.S. troops in Iraq beyond 2011.

Sadrist Offshoots and Other Shiite Militias

Although Sadr formed what was the largest Shiite militia in post-Saddam Iraq, his efforts apparently unleashed Shiite militant forces that now compete with his movement. Several Shiite militias operate in Iraq, all of which are breakaway factions of the Mahdi Army. They operate under names including Asa'ib Ahl al-Haq (AAH, League of the Righteous), Khata'ib Hezbollah (Hezbollah Battalions), and Promised Day Brigade. (In June 2009, Khata'ib Hezbollah was named by the United States as a Foreign Terrorist Organization

(FTO).) In 2009, Sadr's Mahdi Army integrated into the political process in the form of a charity and employment network called *Mumahidoon*, or "those who pave the way."

The U.S. exit removed the militias' justification for armed activity and, like Sadr's movement, the offshoot Shiite militias are increasingly moving into the political process in Iraq. The State Department report on terrorism for 2012, referenced above, says the Shiite militias are adhering to a ceasefire that went into effect upon the U.S. withdrawal in December 2011. Experts maintain that the militias have not become embroiled in sectarian conflict with Iraq's Sunnis during 2013 despite the escalation of AQ-I and other attacks on Iraqi Shiites, although some militiamen are said to be rearming. On the other hand, Iraqi Shiite militiamen are reportedly increasingly involved in Syria fighting and protecting Shiite shrines in support of the government of Bashar Al Assad.[26]

The Sadrist offshoot militias were purportedly part of an effort by Iran to ensure that the United States completely withdrew from Iraq. U.S. officials accused Shiite militias of causing an elevated level of U.S. troop deaths in June 2011 (14 killed, the highest in any month in over one year). During 2011, U.S. officials accused Iran of arming these militias with upgraded rocket-propelled munitions, such as Improvised Rocket Assisted Munitions (IRAMs). U.S. officials reportedly requested that the Iraqi government prevail on Iran to stop aiding the militias, actions that subsequently, but temporarily, quieted the Shiite attacks on U.S. forces in Iraq. Until the U.S. withdrawal in December 2011, some rocket attacks continued against the U.S. consulate in Basra, which has nearly 1,000 U.S. personnel (including contractors). Reflecting a view that some in these militias might still be capable of and intend to carry out terrorist activity, on November 8, 2012, the Treasury Department designated several Khata'ib Hezbollah operatives, and their Iranian Revolutionary Guard—Qods Force mentors as terrorism supporting entities under Executive Order 13224.

AAH's leaders have returned from Iran and opened political offices, trying to recruit loyalists, and setting up social service programs. The group, reportedly supported by Iran, did not compete in the April 20, 2013, provincial elections but does plan to run candidates in the 2014 national elections. Maliki reportedly is backing the group as a counterweight to the Sadrists.[27] AAH's leader Qais al-Khazali, took refuge in Iran in 2010 after three years in U.S. custody for his alleged role in a 2005 raid that killed five American soldiers.

GOVERNANCE AND HUMAN RIGHTS ISSUES

The continuing political crises discussed above have dashed most hopes that Iraq will become a fully functioning democracy with well-established institutions and rule of law. On the other hand, some experts assert that most Iraqis remain committed to the success of the existing governing structure and that all the outstanding disputes are soluble. Some believe that slow action on laws governing investment, taxation, and property ownership account for the slow pace of building a modern, dynamic economy, although others say the success of Iraq's energy sector is overriding these adverse factors. On the other hand, on April 30, 2012, the COR enacted a law to facilitate elimination of trafficking in persons, both sexual and labor-related.

As far as one major indicator of effective governance, the State Department human rights report for 2012, released April 19, 2013, contains substantial detail on the continuing lack of progress in curbing governmental corruption. The State Department report assesses that political interference and other factors such as tribal and family relationships regularly thwart the efforts of anticorruption institutions, such as the Commission on Integrity (COI). A Joint Anti-Corruption Council, which reports to the cabinet, is tasked with implementing the government's 2010-2014 Anti-Corruption Strategy. Another body is the Supreme Board of Audits, which monitors the use of government funds. The COR has its own Integrity Committee that oversees the executive branch and the governmental anti-corruption bodies. And, the KRG has its own separate anticorruption institutions, including an Office of Governance and Integrity in the KRG council of ministers. Even though anti-corruption efforts have often been derailed, the State Department report stated that, during the first ten months of 2012, over 1,100 government officials had been found guilty of misappropriation of public funds.

National Oil Laws and Other Pending Laws

Adopting national oil laws has been considered key to establishing rule of law and transparency in a key sector. Substantial progress appeared near in August 2011 when both the COR and the cabinet drafted the oil laws long in the works to rationalize the energy sector and clarify the rules for foreign investors. However, there were differences in their individual versions: the version drafted by the Oil and Natural Resources Committee was presented to the full COR on August 17, 2011. The cabinet adopted its separate version on

August 28, 2011; there was some expectation that the COR would take up the issue when it reconvened on September 6, 2011, after the Eid alFitr celebration marking the end of Ramadan. However, it was unclear which version would form the basis of final legislation and the COR postponed further COR action until at least 2012.

The September 2012 KRG-Baghdad agreement, discussed above temporarily boosted hopes for adopting the national oil laws. The KRG adopted its own oil laws in 2007 and had opposed the version adopted by the Iraqi cabinet as favoring too much centralization in the energy sector—centralization that would impinge on KRG control of its energy resources. In connection with the visit to the United States of then KRG Prime Minister Barham Salih, Kurdish representatives said on November 8, 2011, that it is likely that the oil laws would be taken up by the COR by the end of 2011.[28] The September 2012 KRG-Baghdad agreement included a provision to set up a six member committee to review the different versions of the oil laws under consideration and decide which version to submit to the COR for formal consideration. However, no definitive movement on this issue has been announced since.

Energy Sector/Economic Development

The continuing deadlock on oil laws has not, however, prevented progress in the crucial energy sector, which provides 90% of Iraq's budget. Iraq possesses a proven 143 billion barrels of oil, and increasing exports enabled Iraq's GDP to grow by about 12% in 2012, according to the World Bank. Iraqi officials estimated in February 2013 that growth would be about 9% for 2013. After long remaining below the levels achieved prior to the ouster of Saddam Hussein, Iraq's oil exports recovered to Saddam-era levels of about 2.1 million barrels per day by March 2012. Production reached the milestone 3 million barrels per day mark in February 2012, which Iraqi leaders trumpeted as a key milestone in Iraq's recovery, and expanded further to about 3.3 million barrels per day by September 2012. It has remained at about that level since.

Iraqi leaders say they want to increase production to over 10 million barrels per day by 2017. The International Energy Agency estimates more modest but still significant gains: it sees Iraq reaching 6 mbd of production by 2020 if it attracts $25 billion in investment per year, and potentially 8 mbd by 2035.

What is helping the Iraqi production is the involvement of foreign firms, including BP, Exxon-Mobil, Occidental, and Chinese firms. China now buys about half of Iraq's oil exports. Chinese firms such as China National Petroleum Corp. (CNPC) are major investors in several Iraq fields. U.S. firms assisted Iraq's export capacity by developing single-point mooring oil loading terminals to compensate for deterioration in Iraq's existing oil export infrastructure in Basra and Umm Qasr.

The growth of oil exports appears to be fueling a rapid expansion of the consumer sector. Press reports in 2012 have noted the development of several upscale malls and other consequences of positive economic progress. The more stable areas of Iraq, such as the Shiite south, are said to be experiencing an economic boom as they accommodate increasing numbers of Shiite pilgrims to Najaf and Karbala. Iraqi officials said in mid-February 2013 that the country now has about $105 billion in foreign exchange reserves, and that GDP will reach $150 billion by the end of 2013.

General Human Rights Issues

The State Department human rights report for 2012, released April 19, 2013, largely repeated the previous years' criticisms of Iraq's human rights record and the attribution of deficiencies in human rights practices to the overall security situation and sectarian and factional divisions.[29] The State Department report cited a wide range of human rights problems committed by Iraqi government security and law enforcement personnel—as well as by KRG security institutions[30]— including some unlawful killings; torture and other cruel punishments; poor conditions in prison facilities; denial of fair public trials; arbitrary arrest; arbitrary interference with privacy and home; limits on freedoms of speech, assembly, and association due to sectarianism and extremist threats; lack of protection of stateless persons; wide scale governmental corruption; human trafficking; and limited exercise of labor rights. Many of these same abuses and deficiencies are alleged in reports by outside groups such as Human Rights Watch.

On the other hand, U.S. officials assert that civil society organizations are expanding in size and authority to perform formal and informal oversight of human rights in Iraq. During a visit to Iraq on June 28-30, 2013, Deputy Secretary of State William Burns awarded the 2012 "Human Rights Defender Award" to an Iraqi human rights organization, the Hammurabi Human Rights Organization.

Use of Coercive Force

Iraq's government is the product of democratic choices. Therefore, Iraq's government has come under criticism when it has used force against peaceful demonstrators. Such criticism was leveled when 20 Iraqis were killed by security forces in the large February 25, 2011, "Day of Rage" demonstrations called by Iraqi activists. Maliki has also been criticized for the April 2013 Hawijah assault, discussed above, and for occasional subsequent use of force against demonstrators. On the other hand, visiting Foreign Minister Hoshyar Zebari said in August 2013 that the ISF has used substantial restraint, and that incidents such as the Hawijah assault have been few. Other experts say that the ISF's actions in the Hawijah and the earlier Day of Rage events have been investigated by the COR and within the government, suggesting efforts to establish accountability and instill restraint.

Trafficking in Persons

The State Department's Trafficking in Persons report for 2013, released on June 19, 2013, places Iraq in "Tier 2." That was an upgrade from the Tier 2 Watch List rating for Iraq for four previous years. The upgrade was a product of the U.S. assessment that Iraq is making "significant efforts" to comply with the minimum standards for the elimination of trafficking. Previously, Iraq received a waiver from automatic downgrading to Tier 3 (which happens if a country is "watchlisted" for three straight years) because it had developed a plan to make significant efforts to meet minimum standards for the elimination of trafficking and was devoting significant resources to that plan.

Media and Free Expression

While State Department and other reports attribute most of Iraq's human rights difficulties to the security situation and factional infighting, apparent curbs on free expression appear independent of such factors. One issue that troubles human rights activists is a law, passed by the COR in August 2011, called the "Journalist Rights Law." The law purports to protect journalists but left many of the provisions of Saddam-era libel and defamation laws in place. For example, the new law leaves in place imprisonment for publicly insulting the government. The State Department human rights reports have noted continuing instances of harassment and intimidation of journalists who write about corruption and the lack of government services. Much of the private media that operate is controlled by individual factions or powerful personalities. There are no overt government restrictions on access to the Internet.

In March 2012, some observers reported a setback to free expression, although instigated by militias or non-governmental groups, not the government. There were reports of 14 youths having been stoned to death by militiamen for wearing Western-style clothes and haircuts collectively known as "Emo" style. In late June 2012, the government ordered the closing of 44 new organizations that it said were operating without a license. Included in the closure list were the BBC, Voice of America, and the U.S.-funded Radio Sawa. In early 2013, the COR adopted an "Information Crimes Law" to regulate the use of information networks, computers, and other electronic devices and systems. Human Rights Watch and other human rights groups criticized that law as "violat[ing] international standards protecting due process, freedom of speech, and freedom of association,"[31] and the COR revoked it February 2013.

Labor Rights

A 1987 (Saddam era) labor code remains in effect, restricting many labor rights, particularly in the public sector. Although the 2005 constitution provides for the right to strike and form unions, the labor code virtually rules out independent union activity. Unions have no legal power to negotiate with employers or protect workers' rights through collective bargaining.

Religious Freedom/Situation of Religious Minorities

The Iraqi constitution provides for religious freedom and the government generally respected religious freedom, according to the State Department's report on International Religious Freedom for 2012, released May 20, 2013.[32] However, reflecting the conservative Islamic attitudes of many Iraqis, Shiite and Sunni clerics seek to enforce aspects of Islamic law and customs, sometimes coming into conflict with Iraq's generally secular traditions as well as constitutional protections. On September 13, 2012, hundreds—presumably Shiites—took to the streets in predominantly Shiite Sadr City to protest the "Innocence of Muslims" video that was produced in the United States and set off protests throughout the Middle East in September 2012.

Concerns about religious freedom in Iraq tends to center on government treatment of religious minorities—an issue discussed extensively in the State Department International Religious Freedom report. A major concern is the safety and security of Iraq's Christian and other religious minority populations which are concentrated in northern Iraq as well as in Baghdad. These other groups include most notably the Yazidis, which number about 500,000-700,000; the Shabaks, which number about 200,000-500,000; the Sabeans, who number about 4,000; the Baha'i's that number about 2,000; and the Kakai's of Kirkuk, which number about 24,000. Since the 2003 U.S. intervention, more than half of the 1 million-1.5 million Christian population that was there during Saddam's time have left. Recent estimates indicate that the Christian population of Iraq is between 400,000 and 850,000.

Violent attacks on members of the Christian community have tended to occur in waves. About 10,000 Christians in northern Iraq, fearing bombings and intimidation, fled the areas near Kirkuk during October-December 2009. On October 31, 2010, a major attack on Christians occurred when a church in Baghdad (Sayidat al-Najat Church) was besieged by militants and as many as 60 worshippers were killed. Partly as a result, Christian celebrations of Christmas 2010 were said to be subdued—following three years in which Christians had felt confident enough to celebrate that holiday openly. Several other attacks appearing to target Iraqi Christians have taken place since. Some Iraqi Christians blame the various attacks on them on Al Qaeda in Iraq, which is still somewhat strong in Nineveh Province and which associates Christians with the United States. Some human rights groups allege that it is the Kurds who are committing abuses against Christians and other minorities in the Nineveh Plains, close to the KRG-controlled region. Kurdish leaders deny the allegations.

Some Iraqi Christian groups advocate a "Nineveh Plains Province Solution," in which the Nineveh Plains would be turned into a self-administering region, possibly its own province but affiliated or under KRG control. Supporters of the idea claim such a zone would pose no threat to the integrity of Iraq, but others say the plan's inclusion of a separate Christian security force could set the scene for violence and confrontation. Even at the height of the U.S. military presence in Iraq, U.S. forces did not specifically protect Christian sites at all times, partly because Christian leaders do not want to appear closely allied with the United States. The State Dept. religious freedom report for 2011 said that during 2011, U.S. Embassy Baghdad designated a "special coordinator" to oversee U.S. funding, program implementation, and advocacy to address minority concerns.

Funding Issues

The FY2008 consolidated appropriation earmarked $10 million in ESF from previous appropriations to assist the Nineveh Plain Christians. A supplemental appropriation for 2008 and 2009 (P.L. 110-252) earmarked another $10 million for this purpose. The Consolidated Appropriations Act of 2010 (P.L. 111-117) made a similar provision for FY2010, although focused

on Middle East minorities generally and without a specific dollar figure
mandated for Iraqi Christians. The State Dept. International Religious
Freedom report for 2012 said that the United States has funded more than $73
million for projects to support minority communities in Iraq.

Women's Rights

Iraq has a tradition of secularism and liberalism, and women's rights
issues have not been as large a concern for international observers and rights
groups as they have in Afghanistan or the Persian Gulf states, for example.
Women serve at many levels of government, as discussed above, and are well
integrated into the work force in all types of jobs and professions. By tradition,
many Iraqi women wear traditional coverings but many adopt Western dress.
On October 6, 2011, the COR passed legislation to lift Iraq's reservation to
Article 9 of the Convention on the Elimination of All Forms of Discrimination
Against Women.

Executions

The death penalty is legal in Iraq. In June 2012, Amnesty International
condemned the "alarming" increase in executions, which had by then put 70
persons to death. U.N. High Commissioner for Human Rights Navi Pillay also
expressed shock in 2012 over the high number of executions in Iraq. On
August 28, 2012, the government executed 21 people, including three women,
convicted of terrorism-related charges.

Mass Graves

As is noted in the State Department report on human rights for 2012, the
Iraqi government continues to uncover mass graves of Iraqi victims of the
Saddam regime. This effort is under the authority of the Human Rights
Ministry.

The largest to date was a mass grave in Mahawil, near Hilla, that
contained 3,000 bodies; the grave was discovered in 2003, shortly after the fall
of the regime. In July 2012, a mass grave was discovered near Najaf,
containing the bodies of about 500 Iraqi Shiites killed during the 1991 uprising
against Saddam Hussein. Excavations of mass graves in Wasit and Dhi Qar
provinces began in April and May 2013, respectively.

REGIONAL DIMENSION

Iraq's neighbors, as well as the United States, have high interest in Iraq's stability and its friendship. Iraq's post-Saddam Shiite leadership has affinity for Iran, which supported them in years of struggle against Saddam. Yet, Iraq also seeks to reintegrate into the Arab fold—of which Iran is not a part—after more than 20 years of ostracism following Iraq's invasion of Kuwait in August 1990. That motive mitigates, to some extent, Iranian influence in Iraq because the Arab world is primarily composed of Sunni Muslims and much of the Arab world is at odds with Iran.

Iraq's reintegration into the Arab fold took a large step forward with the holding of an Arab League summit in Baghdad during March 27-29, 2012. Iraq hailed the gathering as a success primarily because of the absence of major security incidents during the gathering. However, only nine heads of state out of the 22 Arab League members attended, of which only one was a Persian Gulf leader (Amir Sabah al-Ahmad Al Sabah of Kuwait). Building on that success, and on its relations with both the United States and Iran, on May 23-24, 2012, Iraq hosted nuclear talks between Iran and six negotiating powers (United States, Britain, France, Germany, Russia, and China).

Iraq is also sufficiently confident to begin offering assistance to other emerging Arab democracies. Utilizing its base of expertise in chemical weaponry during the Saddam Hussein regime, Iraq has provided some technical assistance to the post-Qadhafi authorities in Libya to help them clean up chemical weapons stockpiles built up by the Qadhafi regime. It donated $100,000 and provided advisers to support elections in Tunisia after its 2011 revolution.[33]

Iran

The United States remains at odds with Iran and seeks to limit Iran's influence over Iraq, even though many assert that it was U.S. policy that brought to power Iraqi Shiites long linked to Iran. Some argue that the withdrawal of all U.S. troops from Iraq represented a success for Iranian strategy and that Iranian influence in Iraq is preponderant. Some assess that evidence of Iranian influence can be seen in Iraq's refusal to join U.S. and allied efforts to achieve a transition from the rule of President Bashar Al Assad in Syria.

Prime Minister Maliki has tried to calm fears that Iran exercises undue influence over Iraq, stressing that Iraqi nationalism resists Iranian influence. On Syria, Iraqi leaders stress that Iraq is neutral in the Syrian conflict – differing clearly from Iran's position which is to openly support the Assad regime. During his visit to the United States in mid-August 2013, Foreign Minister Zebari repeated assertions by other Iraqi leaders that Iraq could serve as a bridge to help the United States and Iran rebuild relations, following the accession of relatively moderate Iranian president Hassan Rouhani in early August 2013. Experts also note lingering distrust of Iran from the 1980-1988 Iran-Iraq war, in which an estimated 300,000 Iraqi military personnel (Shiite and Sunni) died. In a December 5, 2011, op-ed in the *Washington Post*, entitled "Building a Stable Iraq," Maliki wrote:

> Iraq is a sovereign country. Our foreign policy is rooted in the fact that we do not interfere in the affairs of other countries; accordingly, we oppose foreign interference in Iraqi affairs.

Defense and security ties between Iran and Iraq have been discussed but little has materialized. In an interview with CNN broadcast on October 23, 2011, Iran's then President Mahmoud Ahmadinejad said Iran planned a closer security relationship with Iraqi forces after U.S. troops depart. After the U.S. withdrawal was completed December 18, 2011, Iran welcomed closer defense ties to Iraq, including training Iraqi forces, although no such training has been reported.

Iraq's Shiite clerics also resist Iranian interference and take pride in Najaf as a more prominent center of Shiite theology and history than is the Iranian holy city of Qom. In late 2011, representatives of Ayatollah Mahmud Shahrudi, an Iraqi cleric long resident in Iraq, opened offices in Najaf, Iraq. This was widely seen as an effort to promote Shahrudi as a possible successor as *marja taqlid* ("source of inspiration,"—the most senior Shiite cleric) to the increasingly frail Grand Ayatollah Ali al-Sistani. During an April 22-23, 2012, visit to Iran, Maliki met with Shahrudi, in addition to meeting senior Iranian figures. Outgoing president Ahmadinejad made his second visit as president to Iraq during July 17-18, 2013, reportedly visiting Shiite holy sites in addition to meeting with Iraqi leaders.

There are indications the Shiite-led government of Iraq has sought to shield pro-Iranian militants who committed past acts of violence against U.S. forces. In May 2012, Iraqi courts acquitted and Iraq released from prison a purported Hezbollah commander, Ali Musa Daqduq, although he subsequently remained under house arrest. He had been in U.S. custody for alleged activities against U.S. forces but, under the U.S.-Iraq Security Agreement (discussed below) he was transferred to Iraqi custody in December 2011. In July 2012, U.S. officials asked Iraqi leaders to review the Daqduq case or extradite him to the United States, but Iraq released him in November 2012 and he returned to Lebanon, despite U.S. efforts to persuade Iraq to keep him there.

Still others see Iranian influence as less political than economic, raising questions about whether Iran is using Iraq to try to avoid the effects of international sanctions. Some reports say Iraq is enabling Iran's efforts by allowing it to interact with Iraq's energy sector and its banking system. In July 2012, the Treasury Department imposed sanctions on the Elaf Islamic Bank of Iraq for allegedly conducting financial transactions with the Iranian banking system that violated the Comprehensive Iran Sanctions, Accountability, and Divestment Act of 2010 (CISADA, P.L. 111- 195). Those sanctions were lifted in May 2013 when Elaf reduced its involvement in Iran's financial sector. Iraq also is at least indirectly assisting U.S. policy toward Iran by supplying oil customers who, in cooperation with U.S. sanctions against Iran, are cutting back buys of oil from Iran. Iran's exports to Iraq reached about $10 billion from March 2012-March 2013, a large increase from the $7 billion in exports in the prior one year.

Iranian Opposition: People's Mojahedin/Camp Ashraf and PJAK

The Iraqi government treatment of the population of Camp Ashraf, a camp in which over 3,500 Iranian oppositionists (People's Mojahedin Organization of Iran, PMOI) have resided, is an indicator of the government's close ties to Iran. The residents of the camp accuse the government of repression and of scheming to expel the residents or extradite them to Iran, where they might face prosecution or death. An Iraqi military redeployment at the camp on April 8, 2011, resulted in major violence against camp residents in which 36 of them were killed.

In November 2011, Maliki insisted that camp will close at the end of 2011, and the U.N. High Commissioner for Refugees, the European Union, and other organizations worked to broker a solution that avoids violence or forcible expulsion. In late December 2011 Maliki signed an agreement with the United Nations on December 26, 2011, to relocate the population to former U.S. military base Camp Liberty. The PMOI eventually accepted the agreement and completed the relocation. The relocation was a major factor in the U.S. decision, formalized on September 28, 2012, to take the PMOI off the U.S. list of Foreign Terrorist Organizations. Still, the PMOI alleges that Iraq is denying some services to the residents of Camp Liberty and that these residents are suffering in the conditions there. The group blamed pro-Iranian militias, particularly Khata'ib Hezbollah, discussed above, for a mortar attack on Camp Liberty on February 16, 2013, that killed six PMOI residents of the camp. Each resident is being evaluated by the U.N. High Commissioner for Refugees for the potential for relocation outside Iraq, and a tentative plan to relocate a sizeable number of Liberty residents to Albania remains under discussion.

Iran has periodically acted against other Iranian opposition groups based in Iraq. The Free Life Party (PJAK) consists of Iranian Kurds, and it is allied with the Kurdistan Workers' Party that opposes the government of Turkey. Iran has shelled purported camps of the group on several occasions. Iran is also reportedly attempting to pressure the bases and offices in Iraq of such Iranian Kurdish parties as the Kurdistan Democratic Party of Iran (KDP-I) and Komaleh.

Syria

One of the major disagreements between the United States and Iraq is on the issue of Syria. U.S. policy is to achieve the ouster of President Bashar Al Assad. Maliki's government, as noted above, stresses official "neutrality," but it is said to perceive that a post-Assad Syria would be dominated by Sunni Arabs who will align with other Sunni powers. Maliki and his close associates reportedly see the armed rebellion in Syria as aggravating the political unrest in Iraq by emboldening Iraqi Sunnis to Assad of Syria to escalate armed activities against the Maliki government.

Iraq has refrained from sharp criticism of Assad for using military force against protests and Iraq abstained on an Arab League vote in November 2011 to suspend Syria's membership. (Yemen and Lebanon were the only two "no" votes.) Perhaps to ensure Arab participation at the March 2012 Arab League summit in Baghdad, Iraq voted for a January 22, 2012, Arab League plan for a transition of power in Syria. As an indication of Iraq's policy of simultaneously engaging with the United States on the Syria issue, Foreign Minister Hoshyar Zebari has attended U.S.-led meetings of countries that are seeking Assad's ouster.

An issue that has divided Iraq and the United States since August 2012 has been Iraq's reported permission for Iranian arms supplies to overfly Iraq en route to Syria.[34] Iraq has searched a few of these flights, particularly after specific high-level U.S. requests to do so, but it has routinely allowed the aircraft to proceed after finding no arms aboard, sometimes because the Iranian aircraft had already dropped off their cargo in Syria. Instituting regular inspections of these flights was a major focus of the March 24, 2013, visit of Secretary of State Kerry to Baghdad, but the Iraqi leadership - perhaps in an effort to speed up U.S. arms deliveries - has argued that Iraq lacks the air defense and aircraft to interdict the Iranian flights. n anything other than humanitarian goods. The March 2013 Secretary Kerry visit reportedly resulted in an agreement for the United States to provide Iraq with information on the likely contents of the Iranian flights in an effort to prompt Iraqi reconsideration of its position.

As further indication of Maliki's support for Assad, on February 20, 2013, the Iraqi cabinet approved construction on a natural gas pipeline that will traverse Iraq and deliver Iranian gas to Syria. The project is potentially sanctionable under the Iran Sanctions Act that provides for U.S. penalties on projects of over $20 million that help Iran develop its energy sector, including natural gas.

Aside from official Iraqi policy, the unrest in Syria has generated a scramble among Iraqi factions to affect the outcome there. In addition to becoming emboldened by the Syria rebellion, AQ-I members—who are active in the Iraqi regions that border Syria—have reportedly entered Syria to help the mostly Sunni opposition to President Assad.[35] On March 4, 2013, suspected AQ-I members killed 48 Syrian military personnel, and their Iraqi military escorts; the Syrians had fled a battle on the border into Iraq and were ambushed while being transported south within Iraq pending repatriation to Syria. On December 11, 2012, the United States designated a Syrian jihadist rebel group, the Al Nusrah Front, as a Foreign Terrorist Organization (FTO), asserting that it is an alias of AQ-I. The leader of AQ-I, Al Baghdadi, largely confirmed the U.S. assertion on April 11, 2013, by issuing a statement that "Al Nusrah Front is but an extension of the Islamic State of Iraq [the name AQ-I operates under in Iraq]." AQ-I's ambitions for a larger role in the Syria rebellion has prompted some tensions with the Syrian affiliates of Al Qaeda; Al Baghdadi reportedly has relocated to Syria to support a more active AQ-I role there. In part because of the Iraq-Syria Al Qaeda tensions, in mid-2013 AQ-I adopted yet another name, Al Qaeda for Iraq and the Levant, to assert its role in the Syria conflict.

At the same time, as noted above, there have been numerous reports that Iraqi Shiite militiamen—who generally operate far from the border with Syria—have gone to Syria to fight on behalf of the Assad regime. The Iraqi government has sought, with minimal success - or perhaps lack of effort - to prevent these fighters from going there.

The KRG appears to be assisting the Syrian Kurds, who joined the revolt against Assad in July 2012. KRG President Barzani has hosted several meetings of Syrian Kurds to promote unity and a common strategy among them, and the KRG reportedly has been training Syrian Kurdish militia forces to prepare them to secure an autonomous Kurdish area if and when Assad falls. On November 6, 2012, Barzani warned the two major Syrian Kurdish factions—the Democratic Union Party (PYD) and the Kurdish National Council—to avoid discord after the two had been clashing inside Syria. In August 2013, in response to fighting between the Syrian Kurds and Syrian Islamist rebel factions, Barzani threatened to deploy KRG peshmerga to help the Syrian Kurds. The threat was later tempered to the sending of KRG envoys to Syria to investigate the fighting, and no Iraqi pershmerga have been sent to Syria, to date.

Turkey

Turkey's concerns have historically focused mostly on the Kurdish north of Iraq, which borders Turkey, and some of those issues have been discussed in the section on the KRG/Kurds. Turkey has historically been viewed as concerned about the Iraqi Kurdish insistence on autonomy and Iraqi Kurds' ethnically based sympathies for Kurdish oppositionists in Turkey. The anti-Turkey Kurdistan Workers' Party (PKK) has long maintained camps inside Iraq, along the border with Turkey. Turkey continues to conduct periodic bombardments and other military operations against the PKK encampments in Iraq. For example, in October 2011, Turkey sent ground troops into northern Iraq to attack PKK bases following the killing of 24 Turkish soldiers by the PKK. However, suggesting that it has built a pragmatic relationship with the KRG, Turkey has emerged as the largest outside investor in northern Iraq and is building an increasingly close political relationship with the KRG as well, as discussed above.

As Turkey's relations with the KRG have deepened, relations between Turkey and the Iraqi government have worsened. Turkey's provision of refuge for Vice President Tariq al-Hashimi has been a source of tension; Maliki unsuccessfully sought his extradition for trial. On August 2, 2012, Turkish Foreign Minister Ahmet Davotoglu visited the disputed city of Kirkuk, prompting a rebuke from Iraq's Foreign Ministry that the visit constituted inappropriate interference in Iraqi affairs. And, tensions have been aggravated by their differing positions on Syria: Turkey is a prime backer of the mostly Sunni rebels there whereas Baghdad is leaning toward the pro-Assad position. And, as noted, Baghdad has sought to block an expansion of Turkey's energy relations with the KRG.

Gulf States

Iraq has reduced tensions with several of the Sunni-led Persian Gulf states who have not fully accommodated themselves to the fact that Iraq is now dominated by Shiite factions. All of the Gulf states were represented at the March 27-29, 2012 Arab League summit in Baghdad summit but Amir Sabah of Kuwait was the only Gulf head of state to attend. Qatar sent a very low-level delegation which it said openly was meant as a protest against the Iraqi government's treatment of Sunni Arab factions.

Saudi Arabia had been widely criticized by Iraqi leaders because it has not opened an embassy in Baghdad, a move Saudi Arabia pledged in 2008 and which the United States has long urged. This issue was mitigated on February 20, 2012, when Saudi Arabia announced that it had named its ambassador to Jordan, Fahd al-Zaid, to serve as a non-resident ambassador to Iraq concurrently. However, it did not announce the opening of an embassy in Baghdad. The Saudi move came after a visit by Iraqi national security officials to Saudi Arabia to discuss greater cooperation on counterterrorism and the fate of about 400 Arab prisoners in Iraqi jails. The other Gulf countries have opened embassies and all except the UAE have appointed full ambassadors to Iraq.

The government of Bahrain, which is mostly Sunni, also fears that Iraq might work to empower Shiite oppositionists who have demonstrated for a constitutional monarchy during 2011. Ayatollah Sistani is revered by many Bahraini Shiites, and Iraqi Shiites have demonstrated in solidarity with the Bahraini opposition, but there is no evidence that Iraq has had any direct role in the Bahrain unrest.

Kuwait
The relationship with Kuwait has always been considered difficult to resolve because of the legacy of the 1990 Iraqi invasion. However, greater acceptance of the Iraqi government was demonstrated by the visit of Kuwait's then prime minister to Iraq on January 12, 2011. Maliki subsequently visited

Kuwait on February 16, 2011, and, as noted above, the Amir of Kuwait attended the Arab League summit in Baghdad in March 2012. The Prime Minister of Kuwait visited in mid-June 2013,which led to an agreement to remove the outstanding issues of Kuwaiti persons and property missing from the Iraqi invasion from U.N. Security Council (Chapter VII) supervision to oversight by UNAMI under Chapter VI of the U.N. Charter. This transition was implemented by U.N. Security Council Resolution 2107 of June 27, 2013. The two countries have also resolved the outstanding issues of maintenance of border demarcation.

The resolution of these issues follows the U.N. Security Council passage on December 15, 2010 of Resolutions 1956, 1957, and 1958. These resolutions had the net effect of lifting most Saddamera sanctions on Iraq, although the U.N.-run reparations payments process remains intact (and deducts 5% from Iraq's total oil revenues). As of the end of December 2012, a U.N. Compensation Commission set up under Security Council Resolution 687 has paid $38.8 billion to claimants from the 1990-91 Iraqi occupation of Kuwait, with an outstanding balance of $13.6 billion to be paid by April 2015.

U.S. MILITARY WITHDRAWAL AND POST-2011 POLICY

A complete U.S. military withdrawal from Iraq by the end of 2011 was a stipulation of the November 2008 U.S.-Iraq Security Agreement (SA), which took effect on January 1, 2009. Following the SA's entry into force, President Obama, on February 27, 2009, outlined a U.S. troop drawdown plan that provided for a drawdown of U.S. combat brigades by the end of August 2010, with a residual force of 50,000 primarily for training the Iraq Security Forces, to remain until the end of 2011. An interim benchmark in the SA was the June 30, 2009, withdrawal of U.S. combat troops from Iraq's cities. These withdrawal deadlines were strictly adhered to.

Question of Whether U.S. Forces Would Remain Beyond 2011

During 2011, with the deadline for a complete U.S. withdrawal approaching, continuing high-profile attacks, fears of expanded Iranian influence, and perceived deficiencies in Iraq's nearly 800,000 member security forces caused U.S. officials to seek to revise the SA to keep some U.S. troops in Iraq after 2011. Some U.S. experts feared the rifts among major ethnic and sectarian communities were still wide enough that Iraq could still become a "failed state" unless some U.S. troops remained. U.S. officials emphasized that the ongoing ISF weaknesses centered on lack of ability to defend Iraq's airspace and borders. Iraqi comments, such as an October 30, 2011, statement by Iraqi Army Chief of Staff Lieutenant General Babaker Zebari that Iraq would be unable to execute full external defense until 2020-2024, reinforced those who asserted that a U.S. force presence was still needed.[36] Renegotiating the SA to allow for a continued U.S. troop presence required discussions with the Iraqi government and a ratification vote of the Iraqi COR.

Several high-level U.S. visits and statements urged the Iraqis to consider extending the U.S. troop presence. Maliki told visiting Speaker of the House John Boehner, during an April 16, 2011, visit to Baghdad that Iraq would welcome U.S. training and arms after that time.[37] Subsequent to Boehner's visit, Maliki, anticipating that a vote of the COR would be needed for any extension, stated that a request for U.S. troops might be made if there were a "consensus" among political blocs (which he later defined as at least 70% concurrence).[38] This appeared to be an effort to isolate the Sadr faction, the most vocal opponent of a continuing U.S. presence.

On July 11, 2011, then Secretary of Defense Leon Panetta urged Iraqi leaders to make an affirmative decision, and quickly. On August 3, 2011, major factions gave Maliki their backing to negotiate an SA extension. In September 2011, a figure of about 15,000 remaining U.S. troops, reflecting recommendations of the U.S. military, was being widely discussed.[39] The *New York Times* reported on September 7, 2011, that the Administration was considering proposing to Iraq to retain only about 3,000-4,000 forces, mostly in a training role.[40] Many experts criticized that figure as too low to carry out intended missions.

President Obama Announces Decision on Full Withdrawal

The difficulty in the negotiations—primarily a function of strident Sadrist opposition to a continued U.S. presence—became clearer on October 5, 2011, when Iraq issued a statement that some U.S. military personnel should remain in Iraq as trainers but that Iraq would not extend the legal protections contained in the existing SA. That stipulation failed to meet the requirements of the Defense Department, which feared that trying any American soldier under the Iraqi constitution could lead to serious crises at some stage. On October 21, 2011, President Obama announced that the United States and Iraq had agreed that, in accordance with the November 2008 Security Agreement (SA) with Iraq, all U.S. troops would leave Iraq at the end of 2011. With the formal end of the U.S. combat mission on August 31, 2010, U.S. forces dropped to 47,000, and force levels dropped steadily from August to December 2011. The last U.S. troop contingent crossed into Kuwait on December 18, 2011.

The continuing Sunni unrest and violence has caused some to argue that U.S. gains were jeopardized and that the Administration should have pressed Iraqi leaders harder to allow a U.S. contingent to remain. Those who support the Administration view say that political crisis was likely no matter when the United States withdrew and that it is the responsibility of the Iraqis to resolve their differences.

Structure of the Post-Troop Relationship

After the withdrawal announcement, senior U.S. officials stated that the United States would be able to continue to help Iraq secure itself using programs commonly provided for other countries. Administration officials stressed that the U.S. political and residual security-related presence would be sufficient to exert influence and leverage to ensure that Iraq remained stable, allied to the United States, continuing to move toward full democracy, and economically growing and vibrant. At the time of the withdrawal, there were about 16,000 total U.S. personnel in Iraq, about half of which were contractors. Of the contractors, most were on missions to protect the U.S. Embassy and consulates, and other State Department and Office of Security Cooperation-Iraq facilities throughout Iraq.

Office of Security Cooperation-Iraq (OSC-I) and Major Arms Sales

The Office of Security Cooperation—Iraq (OSC-I), operating under the authority of the U.S. Ambassador to Iraq, is the primary Iraq-based U.S. institution that interacts with the Iraqi military—primarily by administering the Foreign Military Sales (FMS) programs (U.S. arms sales to Iraq). OSC-I, funded with the Foreign Military Financing (FMF) funds discussed in the aid table below, is the largest U.S. security cooperation office in the world. It works out of the U.S. Embassy in Baghdad and five other locations around Iraq (Kirkuk Regional Airport Base, Tikrit, Besmaya, Umm Qasr, and Taji). OSC-I plans to transfer its facilities to the Iraqi government by the end of 2013.

The total OCS-I personnel numbers over 3,500, but the vast majority are security and support personnel, most of which are contractors. Of the staff, about 175 are U.S. military personnel and an additional 45 are Defense Department civilians. About 46 members of the staff administers the Foreign Military Sales (FMS) program and other security assistance programs such as the International Military Education and Training (IMET) program. Since 2005, DOD has administered 231 U.S.-funded FMS cases totaling $2.5 billion, and 201 Iraq-funded cases totaling $7.9 billion. There are a number of other purchase requests initiated by Iraq that, if they all move forward, would add bring the estimated value of all Iraq FMS cases to nearly $25 billion.[41]

The largest FMS case is the sale of 36 U.S.-made F-16 combat aircraft to Iraq, notified to Congress in two equal tranches, the latest of which was made on December 12, 2011 (Transmittal No. 11-46). The total value of the sale of 36 F-16s is up to $6.5 billion when all parts, training, and weaponry are included. Iraq has paid $2.5 billion of that amount, to date. The first deliveries of the aircraft are scheduled for September 2014, although Iraqi officials say that accelerating the deliveries would facilitate Iraqi efforts to inspect Iranian overflights to Syria. Some experts and Iraqi politicians, particularly the Kurds, are calling for withholding the F-16 deliveries unless Maliki recommits to power-sharing with Sunni and Kurdish leaders, loosens ties to Iran, and fully cooperates with U.S. policy on Syria. Iraq's Kurdish leaders have long argued that Maliki could use the F-16's against domestic opponents.

Another large part of the arms sale program to Iraq is for 140 M1A1 Abrams tanks. Deliveries began in August 2010 and the last of them were delivered in late August 2012. The tanks cost about $860 million, of which $800 million was paid out of Iraq's national funds. Iraq reportedly is also seeking to buy up to 30 Stryker armored vehicles equipped with gear to detect chemical or biological agents—a purchase that, if notified to Congress and approved and finally agreed with Iraq, would be valued at about $25 million. On December 23, 2012, the U.S. Navy delivered two support ships to Iraq, which will assist Iraq's fast-attack and patrol boats that secure its offshore oil platforms and other coastal and offshore locations. The United States also plans to sell Iraq equipment that its security forces can use to restrict the ability of insurgent and terrorist groups to move contaband across Iraq's borders and checkpoints (RAPISCAN system vehicles), at cost of about $600 million. Some refurbished air defense guns are being provided gratis as excess defense articles (EDA), but Iraq reportedly resented that the guns did not arrive until June 2013.

To help secure its air space and military capabilities, Iraq has requested to purchase from the United States the Integrated Air Defense System and Apache attack helicopters, with a total sale value of about $10 billion.[42] Iraq argues it cannot, for example, stop Iranian overflights to Syria without the equipment. The sale of the Air Defense system was notified to Congress on August 5, 2013, with a value of $2.4 billion, and includes 681 Stinger shoulder held units, 3 Hawk antiaircraft batteries, and other equipment. On that day, and in the preceding week, DSCA notified about $2.3 billion worth of other sales to Iraq of Stryker nuclear, chemical and biological equipment reconnaissance vehicles, 12 Bell helicopters, the Mobile Troposcatter Radio System, and maintenance support. However, the United States has reportedly not decided on the Apache sale to date, in part because the Apache helicopter could be used against demonstrators or Sunni or Kurdish opponents of the government.

Perhaps to hedge against a potential U.S. cutoff, Iraq seeks to diversify its arms supplies. Maliki visited Russia on October 8, 2012, and signed deals for Russian arms worth about $4.2 billion. The arms are said to include 30 MI-28 helicopter gunships and air defense missiles, including the Pantsir. Iraq might also buy MiG fighter jets in the future, according to press reports. In mid-October 2012, Iraq agreed to buy 28 Czech-made military aircraft, a deal valued at about $1 billion.[43]

Police Development Program

A separate program is the Police Development Program, the largest program that transitioned from DOD to State Department lead, using International Narcotics and Law Enforcement (INCLE) funds. However, Iraq's drive to emerge from U.S. tutelage produced apparent Iraqi disinterest in the PDP. By late 2012, it consisted of only 36 advisers, about 10% of what was envisioned as an advisory force of 350 and it is being phased out entirely during 2013. Two facilities built with over $200 million in U.S. funds (Baghdad Police College Annex and part of the U.S. consulate in Basra) are to be turned over the Iraqi government by December 2012. Some press reports say there is Administration consideration of discontinuing the program entirely.[44]

2013: Iraq Rededicating to U.S. Security Programs?

In addition to administering arms sales to Iraq, OSC-I's conducts train and assist programs for the Iraq military. Because the United States and Iraq have not agreed on a Status of Forces Agreement (SOFA) document (which would grant legal immunities to U.S. military personnel), the 160 OSC-I personnel involved in these programs are mostly contractors. They train Iraq's forces on counterterrorism and naval and air defense. Some are "embedded" with Iraqi forces as trainers not only tactically, but at the institutional level by advising

Iraqi security ministries and its command structure. If a SOFA is agreed, some of these missions could be performed by U.S. military personnel, presumably augmenting the effectiveness of the programs.

The Sunni-led violence that began in late 2012 and has since accelerated has apparently prompted the Iraqi government to reemphasize security cooperation with the United States. On August 19, 2012, en route to a visit to Iraq, Chairman of the Joint Chiefs of Staff General Martin Dempsey said that "I think [Iraqi leaders] recognize their capabilities may require yet more additional development and I think they're reaching out to us to see if we can help them with that."[45] Aside from accelerated delivery of U.S. arms to be sold, [46]Iraq reportedly has expressed interest in expanded U.S. training of the ISF and joint exercises.

After the Dempsey visit, reflecting the Iraqi decision to reengage intensively with the United States on security, it was reported that, at the request of Iraq, a unit of Army Special Operations forces had deployed to Iraq to advise on counterterrorism and help with intelligence, presumably against AQ-I.[47] (These forces presumably are operating under a limited SOFA or related understanding crafted for this purpose.) Other reports suggest that Central Intelligence Agency (CIA) paramilitary forces have, as of late 2012, largely taken over some of the DOD mission of helping Iraqi counter-terrorism forces (Counter-Terrorism Service, CTS) against AQ-I in western Iraq.[48] Part of the reported CIA mission is to also work against the AQ-I affiliate in Syria, the Al Nusrah Front, discussed above.

Reflecting an acceleration of the Iraqi move to reengage militarily with the United States, during December 5-6, 2012, Under Secretary of Defense for Policy James Miller and acting Under Secretary of State for International Security Rose Gottemoeller visited Iraq and a Memorandum of Understanding (MOU) was signed with acting Defense Minister Sadoun Dulaymi. The five year MOU provides for:

- high level U.S.-Iraq military exchanges
- professional military education cooperation
- counter-terrorism cooperation
- the development of defense intelligence capabilities
- joint exercises

The MOU appeared to address many of the issues that have hampered OSC-I from performing the its mission to its full potential. The MOU also reflects some of the more recent ideas put forward, such as joint exercises.

The concept of enhanced U.S.-Iraq cooperation gained further consideration in mid-2013 as the United States sought to prevent the violence in Syria from affecting neighboring states, including Iraq. In late June 2013, General Dempsey said that the United States is looking for ways to improve the military capabilities of Iraq and Lebanon, two countries extensively affected by the Syria conflict. According to Gen. Dempsey, enhanced assistance could involve dispatching training teams and accelerating sales of weapons and equipment. During his August 2013 visit to Washington D.C, conducted primarily to attend meetings of the U.S.-Iraq Political and Diplomatic Joint Coordination Committee (JCC), Foreign Minister Zebari indicated that Iraq wants to expand security cooperation with the United States to enhance ISF capability. His visit came several weeks after the July 21, 2013 Abu Ghraib prison break, discussed above, that caused many experts to say that the lapsing of U.S.-Iraq security cooperation had caused ISF proficiency to deteriorate. Some experts believe the U.S. departure and lapsing of security programs has caused the ISF to lose focus on counter-insurgency strategy, for example.

Regional Reinforcement Capability

In conjunction with the withdrawal, then Defense Secretary Panetta stressed that the United States would retain a large capability in the Persian Gulf region, presumably to be in position to assist the ISF were it to falter, and to demonstrate continuing U.S. interest in Iraq's security as well as to deter Iran. However, experts and U.S. officials have made clear that the reintroduction of U.S. combat troops into Iraq is not under consideration in response to the deteriorating security situation there.

The United States has about 50,000 military personnel in the region, including about 15,000 mostly U.S. Army forces in Kuwait, a portion of which are, as of mid-2012, combat ready rather than purely support forces. There are also about 7,500 mostly Air Force personnel in Qatar; 5,000 mostly Navy personnel in Bahrain; and about 3,000 mostly Air Force and Navy in the UAE, with very small numbers in Saudi Arabia and Oman. The remainder are part of at least one aircraft carrier task force in or near the Gulf at any given time. The forces are in the Gulf under bilateral defense cooperation agreements with all six Gulf Cooperation Council (GCC) states that give the United States access to their military facilities and, in several cases, to station forces and preposition even heavy armor.

The Diplomatic and Economic Relationship

In his withdrawal announcement, President Obama stated that, through U.S. assistance programs, the United States would be able to continue to develop all facets of the bilateral relationship with Iraq and help strengthen its institutions."[49] The bilateral civilian relationship was the focus of a visit to Iraq by Vice President Biden in early December 2011, just prior to the December 12, 2011, Maliki visit to the United States.

The cornerstone of the bilateral relationship is the Strategic Framework Agreement (SFA). The SFA, signed and entered into effect at the same time as the SA, presents a framework for longterm U.S.-Iraqi relations, and is intended to help orient Iraq's politics and its economy toward the West and the developed nations, and reduce its reliance on Iran or other regional states. The SFA provides for the following (among other provisions):

- U.S.-Iraq cooperation "based on mutual respect," and that the United States will not use Iraqi facilities to launch any attacks against third countries, and will not seek permanent bases.
- U.S support for Iraqi democracy and support for Iraq in regional and international organizations.
- U.S.-Iraqi dialogue to increase Iraq's economic development, including through the Dialogue on Economic Cooperation and a Trade and Investment Framework Agreement.
- Promotion of Iraq's development of its electricity, oil, and gas sector.
- U.S.-Iraq dialogue on agricultural issues and promotion of Iraqi participation in agricultural programs run by the U.S. Department of Agriculture and USAID.
- Cultural cooperation through several exchange programs, such as the Youth Exchange and Study Program and the International Visitor Leadership Program.

State Department-run aid programs are intended to fulfill the objectives of the SFA, according to State Department budget documents. These programs are implemented mainly through the Economic Support Fund, and the State Department budget justification for foreign operations for FY2014 indicates that most U.S. economic aid to Iraq for FY2014 will go to programs to promote democracy; adherence to international standards of human rights; rule of law, and conflict resolution. Programs funded by the State Department Bureau of International Narcotics and Law Enforcement (INL) will focus on rule of law, moving away from previous use of INL funds for police training.

Funding will continue for counterterrorism operations (NADR funds), and for anti-corruption initiatives.

U.S. officials stress that the United States does not bear the only burden for implementing the programs above, in light of the fact that Iraq is now a major oil exporter. For programs run by USAID in Iraq, Iraq matches dollar for dollar the U.S. funding contribution.

The State Department as Lead Agency

Virtually all of the responsibility for conducting the bilateral relationship falls on the State Department, which became the lead U.S. agency in Iraq as of October 1, 2011. With the transition completed, the State Department announced on March 9, 2012, that its "Office of the Iraq Transition Coordinator" had closed. In concert with that closure, the former coordinator, Ambassador Pat Haslach, assumed a senior post in another State Department bureau.

In July 2011, as part of the transition to State leadership in Iraq, the United States formally opened consulates in Basra, Irbil, and Kirkuk. An embassy branch office was considered for Mosul but cost and security issues kept the U.S. facility there limited to a diplomatic office. The Kirkuk consulate close at the end of July 2012 in part due to security concerns and to save costs. As reflected in its FY2014 budget request, the State Department is planning to replace the U.S. consulate in Irbil with a New Consulate Compound in Irbil.

Not only have U.S. plans for some consulates been altered, but the size and cost of the U.S. civilian presence in Iraq is undergoing reduction. In part this is because Iraqi leaders chafed at continued U.S. tutelage and have been less welcoming of frequent U.S. diplomatic exchanges. U.S. diplomats have had trouble going outside the Zone for official appointments because of security concerns. U.S. officials said in mid-2012 that the U.S. Embassy in Baghdad, built at a cost of about $750 million, carries too much staff relative to the needed mission. From nearly 17,000 personnel at the time of the completion of the U.S. withdrawal at the end of 2011, the number of U.S. personnel in Iraq has fallen to about 10,000 as of mid-2013, and is expected to fall to about 5,500 by the end of 2013.[50] Of the total U.S. personnel in Iraq, about 1,000 are U.S. diplomats or other civilian employees of the U.S. government.[51] The Ambassador in Iraq is Robert Stephen Beecroft, who was confirmed by the Senate in September 2012. The size of the U.S. presence is related to the debate over whether the State Department, using security contractors, can fully secure its personnel in Iraq. No U.S. civilian personnel in Iraq have been killed or injured since the troop withdrawal.

Some believe that the reduction in personnel reflects waning U.S. influence in Iraq. The March 24, 2013, visit by Secretary Kerry might have been intended to try to reverse the apparent decline in the U.S. profile in Iraq. His visit was the first by a Secretary of State since 2009.

Others say that U.S. influence in private remains substantial. Still others have called for enhanced use of the meetings established by the SFA, to promote peaceful resolution of the rifts in the Iraqi political system and enhance U.S. influence.[52] No meeting of the leadership-level Higher Coordinating Committee was held in 2012, but some argue that an HCC meeting should be held in 2013, potentially attended by President Obama and Prime Minister Maliki. Foreign Minister Zebari's August 2013 visit was in conjunction with one of the JCCs established by the SFA, as noted above. How the Maliki government decides to handle the Sunni uprising could provide indications of the degree of U.S. influence; as noted above, the U.S. is counseling restraint and dialogue and opposes a "military solution" to the uprising. As shown in Table 3 below (in the note), the State Department request for operations (which includes costs for the Embassy as well as other facilities and all personnel in Iraq) is about $1.18 billion for FY2014—less than half the $2.7 billion requested for FY2013, and down 66% from the $3.6 billion provided in FY2012. FY2012 was considered a "transition year" to State Department leadership, and requiring high start-up costs.

No Sanctions Impediments

As the U.S.-Iraq relationship matures, some might focus increasingly on U.S.-Iraq trade and U.S. investment in Iraq. After the fall of Saddam Hussein, all U.S. economic sanctions against Iraq were lifted. Iraq was removed from the "terrorism list," and the Iraq Sanctions Act (Sections 586- 586J of P.L. 101-513), which codified a U.S. trade embargo imposed after Iraq's invasion of Kuwait, was terminated. As noted above in the section on the Gulf states, in December 2010, a series of U.N. Security Council resolutions removed most remaining "Chapter VII" U.N. sanctions against Iraq, with the exception of the reparations payments to Kuwait. The lifting of U.N. sanctions allows any country to sell arms to Iraq. However, Iraq still is required to comply with international proliferation regimes—meaning that it is generally barred from reconstituting Saddam era weapons of mass destruction programs. On October 24, 2012, Iraq demonstrated its commitment to compliance with these restrictions by signing the "Additional Protocol" of the Nuclear Non-Proliferation Treaty. Because sanctions have been lifted, there are no impediments to U.S. business dealings with Iraq.

Table 2. March 2010 COR Election: Final, Certified Results by Province

Province	Elected Seats in COR	Results
Baghdad	68	Maliki: 26 seats; Iraqiyya: 24 seats; INA: 17 seats; minority reserved: 2 seats
Nineveh (Mosul)	31	Iraqiiya: 20; Kurdistan Alliance: 8; INA: 1; Accordance: 1; Unity (Bolani): 1; minority reserved: 3
Qadisiyah	11	Maliki: 4; INA: 5; Iraqiyya: 2
Muthanna	7	Maliki: 4; INA: 3
Dohuk	10	Kurdistan Alliance: 9; other Kurdish lists: 1; minority reserved: 1
Basra	24	Maliki: 14; INA: 7; Iraqiyya: 3
Anbar	14	Iraqiyya: 11; Unity (Bolani): 1; Accordance: 2
Karbala	10	Maliki: 6; INA: 3; Iraqiyya: 1
Wasit	11	Maliki: 5; INA: 4; Iraqiyya: 2
Dhi Qar	18	Maliki: 8; INA: 9; Iraqiyya: 1
Sulaymaniyah	17	Kurdistan Alliance: 8; other Kurds: 9
Kirkuk (Tamim)	12	Iraqiyya: 6; Kurdistan Alliance: 6
Babil	16	Maliki: 8; INA: 5; Iraqiyya: 3
Irbil	14	Kurdistan Alliance: 10; other Kurds: 4
Najaf	12	Maliki: 7; INA: 5
Diyala	13	Iraqiyya: 8; INA: 3; Maliki: 1; Kurdistan Alliance: 1
Salahuddin	12	Iraqiyya: 8; Unity (Bolani): 2; Accordance: 2
Maysan	10	Maliki: 4; INA: 6
Total Seats	325	Iraqiyya: 89 + 2 compensatory = 91
	(310 elected + 8 minority reserved + 7 compensatory)	Maliki: 87 + 2 compensatory = 89 INA: 68 + 2 compensatory = 70 (of which about 40 are Sadrist) Kurdistan Alliance: 42 +1 compensatory = 43
		Unity (Bolani): 4
		Accordance: 6
		other Kurdish: 14
		minority reserved: 8

Source: Iraqi Higher Election Commission, March 26, 2010.

Notes: Seat totals are approximate and their exact allocation may be subject to varying interpretations of Iraqi law. Total seat numbers include likely allocations of compensatory seats. Total seats do not add to 325 total seats in the COR due to some uncertainties in allocations.

Table 3. U.S.Assistance to Iraq: FY2003-FY2013 (appropriations/allocations in millions of $)

	FY '03	04	05	06	07	08	09	10	11	12	Total 03-12	FY13 Est.	FY14 Request
IRRF	2,475	18,389	—	10	—	—	—	—	—	—	**20,874**	—	—
ESF	—	—	—	1,535.4	1,677	429	541.5	382.5	325.7	250	**5,140**	262.9	22.5
Democracy Fund	—	—	—	—	250	75	—	—	—	—	**325**		
IFTA (Treasury Dept. Asst.)	—	—	—	13.0	2.8	—	—	—	—	—	**15.8**		
NADR	—	—	3.6	—	18.4	20.4	35.5	30.3	29.8	32	**170**	30.3	25.6
Refugee Accounts (MRA and ERMA)	39.6	.1	—	—	78.3	278	260	316	280	—	**1,100**		
IDA	22	—	7.1	.3	45	85	51	42	17	—	**269**		
Other USAID Funds	470	—	—	—	—	23.8	—	—	—	—	**494**		
INCLE	—	—	—	91.4	170	85	20	702	114.6	137	**1,320**	850	23.1
FMF	—	—	—	—	—	—	—	—	—	850	**850**	900	500
IMET	—	1.2	—	—	1.1	—	2	2	1.7	2	**10**	2	2
DOD—ISF Funding	—	—	5,391	3,007	5,542	3,000	1,000	1,000	1,155	—	**20,095**		
DOD—													

Table 3. (Continued)

	FY '03	04	05	06	07	08	09	10	11	12	Total 03-12	FY13 Est.	FY14 Request
Iraq Army DOD—	51.2	—	210	—	—	—	—	—	—	—	261		
CERP DOD—Oil	—	140	718	708	750	996	339	263	44.0	—	3,958		
Repair DOD—Business	802	—	—	—	—	—	—	—	—	—	802		
Support	—	—	—	—	50.0	50.0	74.0	—	—	—	174		
Total	3,859	18,548	6,329	5,365	8,584	5,042	2,323	2,738	1,968	1,519	56,259	2,045.2	573.2

Sources: State Department FY2014 Executive Budget Summary; SIGIR Report to Congress, October 30, 2012; and CRS calculations.

Notes: Table prepared by Curt Tarnoff, Specialist in Foreign Affairs, May 2013. This table does not contain agency operational costs, except where these are embedded in the larger reconstruction accounts. About $3.6 billion was spent for those functions in FY2012, and another $2.7 billion was requested by State Department for these costs in FY2013. The FY2014 request is for $1.18 billion in such costs. IG oversight costs estimated at $417 million. IMET=International Military Education and Training; IRRF=Iraq Relief and Reconstruction Fund; INCLE=International Narcotics and Law Enforcement Fund; ISF=Iraq Security Force; NADR=Nonproliferation, Anti-Terrorism, Demining and Related: ESF=Economic Support Fund; IDA=International Disaster Assistance; FMF=Foreign Military Financing; ISF= Iraqi Security Forces.

Table 4. Recent Democracy Assistance to Iraq
(in millions of current $)

	FY2009	FY2010 (act.)	FY2011	FY2012
Rule of Law and Human Rights	32.45	33.3	16.5	29.75
Good Governance	143.64	117.40	90.33	100.5
Political Competition/Consensus-Building	41.00	52.60	30.00	16.25
Civil Society	87.53	83.6	32.5	55.5
Totals	**304.62**	**286.9**	**169.33**	**202.0**

Source: Congressional Budget Justification, March 2011. Figures for these accounts are included in the overall assistance figures presented in the table above. FY2013 and FY2014 ESF and INCLE-funded programs focus extensively on democracy and governance, rule of law, and anti-corruption.

Table 5.Election Results (January and December 2005)

Bloc/Party	Seats (Jan. 05)	Seats (Dec. 05)
United Iraqi Alliance (UIA, Shiite Islamist). 85 seats after departure of Fadilah (15 seats) and Sadr faction (28 seats) in 2007. Islamic Supreme Council of Iraq of Abd al-Aziz al-	140	128
Hakim has 30; Da'wa Party (25 total: Maliki faction, 12, and Anizi faction, 13); independents (30).		
Kurdistan Alliance—KDP (24); PUK (22); independents (7)	75	53
Iraqis List (secular, Allawi); added Communist and other mostly Sunni parties for Dec. vote.	40	25
Iraq Accord Front. Main Sunni bloc; not in Jan. vote. Consists of Iraqi Islamic Party (IIP,	—	44
Tariq al-Hashimi, 26 seats); National Dialogue Council of Khalaf Ulayyan (7); General		
People's Congress of Adnan al-Dulaymi (7); independents (4).		
National Iraqi Dialogue Front (Sunni, led by former Baathist Saleh al-Mutlak) Not in Jan.	—	11
2005 vote.		
Kurdistan Islamic Group (Islamist Kurd) (votes with Kurdistan Alliance)	2	5
Iraqi National Congress (Chalabi). Was part of UIA list in Jan. 05 vote	—	0
Iraqis Party (Yawar, Sunni); Part of Allawi list in Dec. vote	5	—

Table 5. (Continued)

Bloc/Party	Seats (Jan. 05)	Seats (Dec. 05)
Iraqi Turkomen Front (Turkomen, Kirkuk-based, pro-Turkey)	3	1
National Independent and Elites (Jan)/Risalyun (Message, Dec.) pro-Sadr	3	2
People's Union (Communist, non-sectarian); on Allawi list in Dec. vote	2	—
Islamic Action (Shiite Islamist, Karbala)	2	0
National Democratic Alliance (non-sectarian, secular)	1	—
Rafidain National List (Assyrian Christian)	1	1
Liberation and Reconciliation Gathering (Umar al-Jabburi, Sunni, secular)	1	3
Ummah (Nation) Party. (Secular, Mithal al-Alusi, former INC activist)	0	1
Yazidi list (small Kurdish, heterodox religious minority in northern Iraq)	—	1

Notes: Number of polling places: January: 5,200; December: 6,200; Eligible voters: 14 million in January election; 15 million in October referendum and December; Turnout: January: 58% (8.5 million votes)/ October: 66% (10 million)/December: 75% (12 million).

End Notes

[1] Text, in English, is at http://www.constitution.org/cons/iraq/TAL.html.

[2] Text of the Iraqi constitution is at http://www.washingtonpost.com/wp-dyn/content/article/2005/10/12/AR2005101201450.html.

[3] "The Iraq Study Group Report." Vintage Books, 2006. The Iraq Study Group was funded by the conference report on P.L. 109-234, FY2006 supplemental, which provided $1 million to the U.S. Institute of Peace for operations of an Iraq Study Group. The legislation did not specify the Group's exact mandate or its composition.

[4] Each provincial council has 25 seats plus one seat per each 200,000 residents over 500,000.

[5] The threshold for winning a seat is the total number of valid votes divided by the number of seats up for election.

[6] Analysis of Iraq expert Reidar Visser. "The Hashemi Veto." http://gulfanalysis.wordpress.com/2009/11/18/thehashemi-veto

[7] Fadel, Leila and Karen DeYoung. "Iraqi Leaders Crack Political Deadlock." *Washington Post*, November 11, 2010.

[8] The following information is taken from Iraqi news accounts presented in http://www.opensource.gov.

[9] Parker, Ned and Salar Jaff. "Electoral Ruling Riles Maliki's Rivals." *Los Angeles Times*, January 23, 2011.

[10] Tim Arango. "Iraq's Prime Minister Gains More Power After Political Crisis." *New York Times*, February 28, 2012.

[11] "Embattled Iraqi PM Holding On To Power for Now." Associated Press, June 12, 2012.

[12] Author conversations with Human Rights Watch researchers, March 2013.

[13] Kirk Sowell. "Sunni Voters and Iraq's Provincial Elections." July 12, 2013.

[14] Reidar Vissar. "Provincial Powers Revisions, Elections Results for Anbar and Nineveh: Is Iraq Headed for Complete Disintegration?" June 27, 2013.

[15] Michael Schmidt and Eric Schmitt. "Leaving Iraq, U.S. Fears New Surge of Qaeda Terror." *New York Times*, November 6, 2011.

[16] http://www.state

[17] Michael Knights. "Rebuilding Iraq's Counterterrorism Capabilities." *Washington Institute for Near East Policy*, July 31, 2013.

[18] The acronym stands for Jaysh al-Rijal al-Tariq al-Naqshabandi, which translated means Army of the Men of the Naqshabandi Order.

[19] For more information on Kurd-Baghdad disputes, see CRS Report RS22079, *The Kurds in Post-Saddam Iraq*, by Kenneth Katzman.

[20] Interview with Masoud Barzani by Hayder al-Khoie on Al-Hurra television network. April 6, 2012.

[21] "Managing Arab-Kurd Tensions in Northern Iraq After the Withdrawal of U.S. Troops." Rand Corporation, 2011.

[22] Meeting with congressional staff, February 24, 2011.

[23] Jane Arraf. "Iraq's Unity Tested by Rising Tensions Over Oil-Rich Kurdish Region." *Christian Science Monitor*, May 4, 2012.

[24] Iraq Oil Report. Exxon to Start Drilling in Disputed Kurdish Blocks. October 18, 2012.

[25] International Crisis Group. "Iraq and the Kurds: The High-Stakes Hydrocarbons Gambit." April 19, 2012.

[26] Abigail Hauslohner. "Iraqi Shiites Take Up the Cudgels for Syrian Government." *Washington Post*, May 27, 2013.

[27] Liz Sly. "Iran-Tied Group Is On Rise in Iraq." Washington Post, February 19, 2013.

[28] Author conversation with then KRG Washington, DC, representative Qubad Talabani, November 8, 2011.

[29] http://www.state

[30] One notable example in the State Department report for 2012 cites the death in April 2012 in a KRG intelligence prison of the mayor of the KRG city of Sulaymaniyah; the KRG concluded he committed suicide but the family of the mayor alleged he had been tortured to death.

[31] Human Rights Watch. "Iraq's Information Crimes Law: Badly Written Provisions and Draconian Punishments Violate due Process and Free Speech." July 12, 2012.

[32] http://www.state

[33] Tim Arango. "Iraq Election Official's Arrest Casts Doubt on Prospects for Fair Voting." *New York Times*, April 17, 2012.

[34] Kristina Wong, "Iraq Resists U.S. Prod, Lets Iran Fly Arms to Syria." *Washington Times*, March 16, 2012.

[35] Sahar Issa. "Iraq Violence Dips Amid Rise in Syria." *Philadelphia Inquirer*, February 21, 2012.

[36] "Iraq General Says Forces Not Ready 'Until 2020.'" Agence France Presse, October 30, 2011.

[37] Prashant Rao. "Maliki Tells US' Boehner Iraqi Troops Are Ready." *Agence France Presse*, April 16, 2011.

[38] Aaron Davis. "Maliki Seeking Consensus on Troops." *Washington Post*, May 12, 2011.

[39] Author conversations with Iraq experts in Washington, DC, 2011.

[40] Eric Schmitt and Steven Lee Myers. "Plan Would Keep Military in Iraq Beyond Deadline." September 7, 2011.

[41] Iraq Signs Arms Deals Worth $4.2 Billion. *Washington Post*, October 10, 2012; Tony Capaccio. "Iraq Seeks Up to 30 General Dynamics Stryker Vehicles." Bloomberg News, November 19, 2012.

[42] John Hudson. "Iraqi Ambassador: Give Us bigger Guns, And Then We'll Help on Syria." July 17, 2013.

[43] Adam Schreck. "Iraq Presses US For Faster Arms Deliveries." Yahoo.com, October 18, 2012.

[44] Tim Arango. "U.S. May Scrap Costly Efforts to Train Iraqi Policy." *New York Times*, May 13, 2012.

[45] "U.S. Hopes For Stronger Military Ties With Iraq: General" Agence France-Presse, August 19, 2012.

[46] Dan De Luce. "U.S. 'Significant' in Iraq Despite Troop Exit: Dempsey." Agence France-Presse, August 21, 2012.

[47] Tim Arango. "Syrian Civil War Poses New Peril For Fragile Iraq." New York Times, September 25, 2012.

[48] Adam Entous et al. "CIA Ramps Up Role in Iraq." *Wall Street Journal*, March 12, 2013.

[49] Remarks by the President on Ending the War in Iraq." http://www.whitehouse.gov, October 21, 2011.

[50] Ernesto Londono. "U.S. Clout Wanes in Iraq." *Washington Post*, March 24, 2013.

[51] Tim Arango. "U.S. Plans to Cut Its Staff by Half at Iraq Embassy." *New York Times*, February 8, 2012.

[52] Ryan Crocker. "Iraq on The Brink." *Washington Post*, op-ed. May 1, 2013.

INDEX

C

J

K

L

T

V

W

U

Y